Kinship and Survival

For [illegible] & Roger
With love

Keith.

*Seal of Sir Walter de Middlemast 1296 (Public Record Office)*

# Kinship and Survival
# The Middlemas Name through 600 Years

Keith Middlemas

The Grimsay Press

The Grimsay Press
an imprint of
Zeticula
57 St Vincent Crescent
Glasgow
G3 8NQ
Scotland.

http://www.thegrimsaypress.co.uk
admin@thegrimsaypress.co.uk

First published in 2009


**ISBN-13 978-1-84530-064-7 Paperback**

*To all the kin-group.*

*However the name is spelled:*
*mas, mass, mis, miss, mast, most*

*Seal of Sir William de Middlemas 1436 (Ayrshire Archives)*

# Acknowledgements

**Archive collections and libraries**

Ayrshire Archives Centre
National Archives of Scotland
National Library of Scotland
Northumberland Record Office
Scottish Border Archive Selkirk

**Illustrations**

Biblioteque National, Paris
Biblioteque Royale de Belgique
Bodleian Library, MS collections
British Library, MS collections
Christie's Images
National Museum of Scotland
Public Record Office, London
Royal Commission on Ancient Monuments, Scotland
Victoria and Albert Museum, MS collections

**Research assistance and paleography**

Alison Mowat

# Contents

# List of Illustrations and Maps

# 1.

# Family, History, Identity

Does a family history need a justification? We all have them – if unwritten – and should remember Sir Alec Douglas-Home's reply to Harold Wilson's jibe about the 17th Earl becoming Prime Minister, that the Leader of the Opposition was also "the 17th Mr Wilson." DNA analysis demonstrates our immeasurable antiquity and the mitochondrial staircase can prove exactly where, in the female line, we come from, if the ancient bones still exist.

But if we ask, who are we, in ordinary terms, we tend to mean our family defined by its name – what since the High Middle Ages in Britain has been called *surname* (through a tribal name association was already habitual in Judea at the time of Abraham, and *griots* in West Africa can recite a hundred generations of chiefly lineage over 2½ thousand years.

About the origins of surnames, swirls argument without end, since proof, in the sense of documentation, is rarely adequate for families not of noble birth before the 16th century. If they fought bravely in one notable battle, married well or achieved ballad status as notable robbers, defenders of the poor, or plotters against kings, proof may exist but since many of these clearly ended in death or disappearance of the name within a higher ranking escutcheon, the trail may soon run cold.

For ordinary folk, surnames emerge in the later Middle Ages steadily across the 14th and 15th centuries, some because of dwelling place ("of x") some from craft or trade (Bowyer, Fletcher, Archer to choose only one martial craft) or office, such as Marshall. Preoccupied with status as always, later medieval families emphasised the Latin *de* as meaning "of": the land they owned, at whatever level in the feudal hierarchy, rather than "from", merely the place they lived in or originated from – a distinction made clear in Scottish vernacular by "of" and "in" (a rule not always strictly observed.)

Time passing, the *de* as "in" disappeared, replaced by a real surname; and except as an exercise in heraldry or antiquarianism, the de as in "of" also eventually vanished, leaving like the Cheshire cat only the faint aura of a long-dated snobbery. The problem in tracing the historic family then changes, from establishing whether John of X was related to William of X, to whether John X was or was not the lineal son of William X. As all researchers know, this conundrum can relatively easily be solved (though not in all cases) once parish registers of births, marriages and deaths begin in the 16$^{th}$ century and become more or less accurate by the late 17$^{th}$; and fairly conclusively, aided by the decennial census, after 1841 – not the first, but the first to give all surnames and occupations.

In between, stretch at least three centuries in which (apart from the landed families and nobility with hereditary titles, the *noblesse d'épée*) the surname is not enough, unless very unusual. In any village in England, or toun in Scotland, one may find several families of the same name living – as was the case across all Europe. In the Highlands of Scotland, parts of Wales, much of Ireland, Sicily, Aquitaine, La Mancha, names were also aggregated under a wider identity of agnatic (male-designated) kinship or clan: between whose numbers actual blood relationships were often tenuous or as near to non-existent as eighth or tenth cousinage. To which must be added the complexity of adopted names or clans, a variable strategy adopted by migrants, ranging from Cathar victims of persecution in the 14$^{th}$ century, to fugitives from anti-Semitic pogroms in the late 19$^{th}$ and 20$^{th}$ centuries.[1]

There exist, then, strict documentary limits to the practice of genealogy which impact at some point for everyone as an effective cut-off for family lineage. This simple fact was ignored, habitually, at a time when ancient lineage counted for status, even power. "New men" sought to establish famous parentage at a time of rapid upward mobility from Tudors to the Revolution settlement after 1688, and few were as honest as Queen Elizabeth's first Minister, Robert Cecil, to ask "what is nobility but ancient riches?"

As a result, not all pedigrees in early editions of Burke's Peerage or Landed Gentry are historically impeccable. Some are merely guesswork under another name. Most focus on the branch with the grandest past rather than the strict male (or female mitochondrial) line with the result that many pedigrees still claim descent via collateral branches from French kings or John of Gaunt, Duke of Lancaster, rather than John Smith, blacksmith.

No harm in fairytales and legends, whose purpose was to substantiate status in advance of the advantageous marriage that might provide the easiest way to wealth and power, when a cash market in land barely existed; or where appointments in noble or even royal households depended on respectable birth, before offering access to patronage and prosperity for one's descendants. Much the same preceded entry to professional work such as church, law or army.

To set out in the early 21st century to write the history of a family expanding numerically across time requires rather more: in terms of discipline, the use of insights from archaeology, sociology, economics, as well as straightforward history. It requires luck, first if the subject has an unusual or distinctive name, second, if the documents exist, not only in certain time-clusters, but across the long run of reigns. It takes only one accidental fire, or punitive raid like the Harcourt devastation of the Scottish borders in 1544-5, to eliminate large parts of a monastic or estate archive, creating a breach which may be irreparable.

To point out that Britain has escaped conquest since the Norman invasion, and that the exercise is therefore easier here than in Italy or Germany, may apply to most of England but not to Wales, Ireland or much of Scotland, beset by invasions for 150 years from the 1290s to the 1460s, and by recurrent war with England down to the time of Flodden a half century later; little surprise then, that the exercise is harder there. Fewer documents exist in any case in a smaller, separate kingdom like Scotland or Catalonia, where administration was less centralised in the Middle Ages and records perhaps more widely and insecurely based and therefore more vulnerable than they were in the Tower of London.

Two related problems exist in the context of limited availability of evidence: establishing continuity and maintaining coherence at any point for the whole kin-group. Apart from oral tradition, what reaches written status tends to be legal matters (title to land, transfer of property on death, redress for wrongs, offences criminal or civil, marriage settlements and dowries, legitimation of children's claims or, outside wedlock, illegitimate births), orders from above (demesne, Lord's or King's courts) or agreements, bonds between parties and, increasingly, by the 17th century, personal letters. Little of this other than criminal records before the 16th century reveals surnames at the lower end of the social scale. Even the landowners' younger sons appear rarely. Daughters appear largely in their subjective role as marriageable property or dowry liabilities, emerging with status in their own right mainly as widows possessed of some property.[2]

As the first problem of continuity diminishes with the arrival of better and more securely kept archives, the second increases, as a function of the infant survival rate in what were habitually large families. Indeed, the whole range of subjects of the family, the role of women and the upbringing of children, have until recently been subordinated to questions of Scottish politics and identity.

In the Middlemas case, one single family of the mid-13th century had extended to nearly 200 families in Scotland and south of the Border, mainly in northeast England, by the time of the 1851 census. Clearly it is impossible to chart such a numerical expansion, even if it had not been accompanied by a long, gradual decline in social position from lairds to farmers to tenants and industrial workers, accompanied by widespread migration. Hence the chosen terminal date of the first reliable census, 1841, to which most members of the kin-group alive today can probably relate, with what in the information technology age, is a much-reduced research labour.

***

It used to be said by late 19th century genealogists that it was sufficient once in every generation to update the family history. In this case, to my knowledge, no one has in 700 years tried to write it at all. No one has so far felt that need to record the questions and answers, or to preserve fragile memory, described by Rysant Kapucinski in *Travels with Herodotus*. Hence the need to start from the beginning, from medieval records, in the Scottish case, mercifully mostly now transcribed and printed, to the early modern, many of which in the 17th century such as sasines of land, records of suits and debts, are still in manuscript in "court hand", a vile form of abbreviation devised by literary clerks more for professional lawyers than a still often-illiterate public.

Without labouring the point about difficulties, and after giving thanks to the ever-courteous staff of the National Archives of Scotland, the National Library of Scotland, the Public Record Office, and the Archive of the Border Counties together with those of Northumberland and Durham, the hardest single problem is to relate to the whole family group those kin who only received (merited may be the wrong word) one or two mentions in the records. How to assess from a single phrase, say in 1438, what age was the person and what relation? Deduction and correlation, conjecture and assumption all have their own logic and I have tried to make clear where statements rely on them more than documentary *proof*. This is, of course, the historian's normal activity, to accept the role of accidental survival.

Thus the 15th to 17th century history of the (junior) Grieston branch of the Middlemas kin-group is far better documented than that of Lilliesleaf and Eildon, which was originally, and again after the 1620s, the senior branch. Simply, Middlemas of Grieston became more important, played on a wider stage. Even more, records of them in that period were of importance to central government and were kept centrally, in Stirling or Edinburgh, where they may have been less subject to mice, mould or initial clerical error. On the other hand, since nearly all earlier records are available in printed form, it is in the 17th and 18th century and afterwards, that most remains to be discovered, especially about the specifics of rural life and conditions, among manuscript sources in the NAS, county record offices or private collections of the great 19th century estates.

Since Alex Haley's "Roots," published in 1976, cut through the barrier of slave experience in the Southern States to an actual middle passage in the slave trade era, through the adept use of oral history, to rediscover a West African origin and *griot* recitation of the original captive ancestor, genealogy and the tracing of identity have become massively popular, even televised sports. Librarians of the great public collections reel under the pressure of public demand today, replacing the handful of 19th century scholarly amateurs. Meanwhile, thanks partly to the belief of Mormon churches in a sort of posthumous baptism, and partly to the work of local and national archivists, a complete archive of christenings and marriages, (but not yet burials) is available in Britain under the OPRS label, taken from parish registers, some beginning in the 16th century, some not till the 18th.

Indexed by name, but giving minimal information other than the names of parties to a marriage or parent(s) of a baby, date of event and parish, these provide a basic framework. Huge assumptions must nevertheless be made if kin connections are to be linked up: that in rural or small town society, people married within a narrow geographical range of perhaps five to ten miles, and an even narrower social one; that the majority died at an age which we would consider barely mature, from hard labour, contagious disease and recurrent plague, or in childbirth, so that second marriages were very frequent and infant mortality very high. The average age of first marriages varied in the early modern period in southern Scotland between 22 and 25, depending on whether the partners were urban or rural, and first birth of a legal child occurred predictably within a year. Whether or not the Kirk was more successful than the old church in its exhortations, illegitimacy continued to flourish. Such assumptions helped me to shape the OPRS evidence towards a logical structure but one cannot assume that all events were recorded. Certainly many infants who died before three or four years old do not appear at all and recorded christenings may come long after birth. Conversely, and especially in Scotland under the post-Reformation Presbytery system, a greater degree of accuracy may be assumed than in Anglican northeastern England.

Yet families and branches of families, senior or cadet, often simply disappear. They lose wealth and land, they fail to produce male heirs, they sink down, unable to survive in the fiercely competitive social system; heirs are feckless or barren, crops fail, sheep and cattle die of murrain or scab, plague strikes almost every generation from its first onset as the “English disease” in 1350 to the Civil War, fathers and sons die in battle, like the first great patron of the Middlemases the Fourth Earl of Douglas and his brother James at Verneuil in 1424.

The pyramid sides were far steeper than they are today and the way down, even to extinction, could be more rapid than the way up, even if spurred by noble or royal favour. If there is an underlying theme to this story, therefore, it concerns survival over the *longue durée*, in particular during the transition from middle ages to the early modern world. One has to ask not only *how* and *why*, but what were the choices available at different times which might ensure survival. In addition to its Peerage and Landed Gentry, Burke used to publish a series called "The Vicissitudes of Families" and, as late as 1953, the then Carter King of Arms wrote to the Times:

> The factor of which we most need to know more is the incidence of downward social mobility. Of the immemorial frequency of upward social mobility we have ample evidence and *a priori* considerations suggest that the converse must have been at least as frequent. Concrete evidence, however, is harder to come by because those who go downhill tend to pass out of the genealogist's ken and to lack the wish or opportunity to trace or record their origins, though they may preserve vague traditions.

Vicissitudes certainly point the Middlemas history, as well as an instructive, if always local conformity with many of the trends elucidated in recent Scottish historiography and social geography, making it perhaps a valuable case study, validating wider reinterpretations. In this sense, it may pass beyond "family history" to approach the old ideal of "history in a grain of sand." This is important because with only a few exceptions – the most vivid being the 15th century cleric Sir William de Middlemas – this book has no biographies, in the usual sense, only the transition narrative of an extended kin-group over six hundred years. Quite simply, not enough records exist, even after trawling through many archives, to allow one the sort of personal description of an individual that characterises the modern art of historical biography. Impact on the times, motivation, loyalties, feuds or enlistment in great causes, can indeed be assessed; but not the emotions or personal idiosyncrasies which only letters can convey.

Yet it *is* possible, as Linda Colley puts it, "to tack between the individual and (wider) histories in such a way as to bring them into simultaneous view...to re-evaluate biography as a way of deepening our understanding of the past."[3] There need therefore be no excuse for indulging in what, for me, began as a chance inquiry 35 years ago. As Alice Munro puts it, there is a human need to establish where we came from, and how: "it happens mostly in our old age, when our personal futures close down and we cannot imagine – sometimes cannot believe in – the future of our children's children."[4]

So be it. In my early 70s, I am well aware that, as she put it "we cannot resist the rifling around in the past, sifting the untrustworthy evidence, linking stray names and questionable dates and anecdotes together, hanging on to threads, insistent on being joined to dead people and therefore to life." I offer what a historian can, in what for me has been a fascinating imperative, the best available evidence, the establishment where possible of people in time and place and what they did, and perhaps also, why they acted so.

This book is however primarily written for those who in the broad sense can be called kin, sharing a name spelled in several different ways, even in the same document or on the same tombstone. (Curiously, as the kin-group expanded, so the variations diminished, so that by the later 18th century the final "t" disappears, and three main end-variants emerge: mas, mass, miss.)

***

A second theme, migration, underpins the work. As I argue in Chapter 2, the family's origins were Anglo-Norman, and the first migration took place from northwest France to northern England at some point perhaps a century after the actual Norman Conquest. They travelled to Northumberland and then to the fertile land south of Kelso and up the Tweed Valley. But even to a military elite, welcomed by Scottish kings from David I onwards as exponents of feudal systems of tenure and warrior service apt for his new court and central administration, land was not always or easily made available. Most of the better soils, the Merse, Mearns and Fife had been intensively farmed by Anglian immigrants for three or four hundred years already. Before the import of nitrogen in the form of Chilean guano in the 19th century, the lands the Normans did acquire could only be dressed with the manure of the sheep and cattle that pastured them. Much of Tweeddale and Teviotdale was sour upland soil. Even the valleys were ill-drained, so that agricultural prime land was limited and productivity – even when rural markets and urban traders developed – not much above subsistence level.

Once the best lands had been parcelled out, which for the Scottish Borders meant long before the 12th and 13th century population explosion, survival for family branches other than the eldest son meant either service in the same family household or another, usually noble, one (which required respectable birth) or a move away onto progressively more marginal upland soil and waste. Pressures eased after the Black Death and its successive waves of the plague; but the need for migration as a resort, albeit over small distances or into the small boroughs (burghs), rarely went away. Indeed it increased in the late 17th and early 18th centuries as larger landowners progressively abandoned "kindly tenure" (extending leases for incumbents rather than evicting sons on death or at a lease's end) in favour of the livestock trade and demesne or "mains" agricultural improvement.

Much of this story then concerns migration in five prolonged stages. Migration is the choice of the underdog, the unlucky, the younger son; but also of the enterprising, the farsighted "man o'parts." At heart, the transitions, especially in the 17th century, were from the land to villages or touns, or cities such as Edinburgh and Newcastle, from agricultural ownership and management with attendant skills to urban crafts and professions. By 1841, only a small percentage of Middlemases remained in the countryside of what James VI of Scotland, who was also James I of England, called after 1603 his "middle shires". The rest had been scattered, like hundreds of other names across the north, to an imperial dimension, which included North America and the West Indies, Ireland, Australasia, even southern England.

This adds different dimensions to how the story is told, beyond traditional genealogy (as set out in Appendix A). In so far as survival options can be examined, some of the evidence allows of short biographies, or key episodes where one man (very rarely one woman) could make a decisive choice. Most of Middlemases rank as no more than T.S. Eliot's "attendant Lord." Yet for each generation, as diversification grew, these choices shaped individuals and children's lives, even if not yet quite in the classic 19th century mode of choice for the gentry inheritors: land, church or army.

At least four Middlemases became lawyers after the mid-16$^{th}$ century. But for most younger sons, as in Ireland, it was a matter of subdividing land holdings, "portions" for daughters, while lairds became mere "bonnet lairds" or husbandmen, or declined to cottar status with only a tiny plot to back up a labourer's wage. In the city, it meant apprenticeship, if possible to what were then regarded as gentry choices of lawyer or doctor or merchant; if not, to what the 19$^{th}$ century knew as "trade" that is crafts, often related as metal workers to the agricultural blacksmiths of the early Border toun.

Up to the later Middle Ages, one survival choice was service in a noble household: if literate, a younger son could go far, as did Sir William de Middlemas after becoming chaplain c. 1410 to the Lord who became fifth Earl of Douglas. Failing that, and still very much depending on respectable upbringing, daughters could be manipulated in the complex web of contracted marriages which existed from earliest times until it became the cynosure of 19$^{th}$ century novelists. Vital as these were and sometimes profitable, marriages did not necessarily bring secure alliances, though they were often used in Scotland to mark an end to bitter Border feuds. There were a few unusual widows too, propertied, quasi-independent, who could at least safeguard their children's future: Scotland was not Waziristan, and widows retained some personal dignity.

One cannot "see" any of them. The first portrait of an ancestor in my family is an 1851 studio photograph of a couple born in the 18$^{th}$ century; the first engraving, of my great grandfather in 1863. We can know roughly "what" they were, their working clothes being little different from landless labourers, their smart dress more likely laughed at than admired in the streets of Edinburgh. We can guess what they looked like, what small arms (short sword and flintlock, steel handled pistol) they carried – and how frequently they used them, as late as the mid-17$^{th}$ century.

Occasionally, we can hear them speak, in Sir William's correspondence with Pope Eugenius IV in the 1430s, in William, Constable of Dunbarton Castle's letters regarding his prisoner the Lord of the Isles in 1615. Mostly, the documentation is dry, legalistic, and personal implications need to be teased out. Yet Sir William's long charter founding a Chantry in Peebles Church in 1435 says as much about his estimate of his place in society and the future of his immortal soul as any 19th century dominie's correspondence or corn-factor's diaries.

We can make reasonable assumptions about literacy at any given time, the available range of marriage partner, perhaps even the degree of mutual affection: certainly, what future they strove to achieve for their children, what skills they had, in battle, at work, in society, and (so long as they were still lairds) what leisure they enjoyed. In one celebrated document, of goods stolen from Plora castle in 1491, their wealth and status emerge clearly from the long inventory of loss.

One can estimate their loyalties and priorities, to kin, family, friend, lords, even at times the King; and discover, where these conflicted, what choices existed. All this is a long way from the romantic stereotypes, second-hand reductions of Sir Walter Scott's many novels, or recollections of ancient Border ballads (still sung, but to different lyrics, in the Alleghenies) in which borderers are always lawless reivers, re-fighting the Battle of Otterburn, or freeing Kinmont Willie from Carlisle Prison – a quasi-criminal existence only too often borne out by the March trials and settlements of grievances. Yet the Borders were, as recent historians demonstrate, at least at the eastern end, less lawless and more complex than legend suggests.

But the criminal records inevitably obtrude, heightened by antipathy and revenge, and by raiding from both Scottish and English sides, for at least two decades after the Scottish and English Crowns were united in 1603, conflicts renewed during the Bishops War which mutated into what we call the Civil War. It is in the nature of documentation that the harsh and unusual gets more space than the humdrum details of peace. But for real, continual disorder and violence, one must look to the West March, not Teviot Tweed and the Merse: it is from there that "the thieves of Levin" (a habitual stereotype) came to murder Thomas Middlemas' family in 1491.

What we have to go on then is inevitably fragmentary, biased in favour of dearth, death and disaster. Ranke's dream of history "as it actually was" has always been impossible, even in the 19th century, even now within the bounds of living memory. There are no "great men" here, nor women. Nevertheless, the substance of human life, affinities, emotions, does come through, sometimes vividly and especially in the 17th century, earthily; and we can guess at when and why they adapted to the Reformation, the Civil War, and why a few of them stood out for the extreme Covenanting position in the 1670s, the "killing time," while others conformed to the mainstream Kirk or simply adapted to Anglican practice once they had emigrated south.

To that extent, and in some cases in each generation, the narrative can be made personal, even within the two great collective imperatives of survival and migration; and it is clear, still in the mid-19th century, that the extended kin-group held within itself certain bonds of mutual identity, collective help in the harsh nexus between a declining rural economy and the desperate conditions of urban existence, not essentially different from 20th century mining towns in South Africa or the favelas of Brazil. Collective help might find jobs, give shelter and advice, or provide support. Whether any of them by 1841 had any memory of the long past is an unanswerable question. My great grandfather, as Treasurer of one of the last learned societies to spring from the Scottish Enlightenment, knew more about mosses and palaeolithic runic stones than he did any family history.

When he died, in 1912, it would have been hard to forecast what massive changes the First World War would bring: how the evolution and final fruition of mass society and mass culture in the inter-war years would erase not only the oral transmission of a sense of an ever-present past, but the significance of history itself after the 1960s as a central element in a future national curriculum. Yet that 1914-18 war provided a mordant tailpiece to the kinship substratum of families. Enlistment rolls in regiments, still county or town-based (the Northumberland Fusiliers raised

54 battalions, more than any other in the history of the British Army), demonstrate patterns of local identity and affinity, as do its war memorials, patterns which had largely disappeared before the onset of its successor in 1939-45.

In one sense then, the end of this book might be set in 1914: but that is for someone else, at another time. What I try to do here is to establish the particular: to trace one group, understand the social and economic basis of its family structures, its levels of education, its distinctiveness (name versions, heraldry, architecture of their houses) and to focus where possible on those who deserve some memorial, either because they rose above the rest of their generation, or because they chose an alternative, to compete or merely to survive in a different way. This is optimistic perhaps, certainly not what Mark Twain pessimistically called "nothing but echoes... we are but a compost heap made up of decayed heredities, moral and physical."

There is a Xhosa saying that there are only three things worth fighting for: land, water and women. In a damp cold climate, the Middlemases seem never to have lacked for any of these but land. Yet they acquired it, held it more or less for 400 years, lost it and adapted to modernity. Many became professionals, but the majority in 1841 are recorded simply as AgLab (agricultural labourers, without specifying what their actual skills were). But they did not disappear like many medieval names. Despite attrition, feud, murder (five in 120 years to say nothing of death in battle) infant mortality, and minor dangers like lawsuits, bad debts or religious persecution, they survived.

***

Thomas Hardy portrays old Tom Darbyfield becoming obsessed with a spurious dream of grandeur when he is told of his illustrious forebears in "Tess of the d'Urbervilles". But the real drama, which his vanity only precipitates, is Tess's own struggle against the whims of the President of the Immortals (God's wisdom, Hardy's revenge). When I began this inquiry, I knew nothing beyond the few details set out in an archetypal Victorian family Bible, starting in 1799, so that my father born in 1906, and my grandfather who served as a young officer in the Percy Artillery before 1914 could tell me something only of the previous century, including the fact, inaccurate, as it turned out, that the first known name was son of an illegitimate labourer. My origins appeared entirely Northumbrian, as were my own affinities, family, relations, National Service with the 5th Fusiliers, a background heightened by a Yorkshire preparatory school, Stowe and Cambridge, marriage to a girl from Devon working in London.

True, my mother shopped in Edinburgh, employed a Scottish nanny; most family holidays were spent on the West coast, fishing and climbing the hills of Glencoe. By chance, attending a seminar at Edinburgh University in the early 1970s, I had spare time enough to wander around the National Library of Scotland, then as now one of the most user-friendly libraries in Europe, and discovered a wide range of references, all pointing to a Middlemas history of far greater antiquity.

Other books had to be written, given the university life of a contemporary historian; and the project, though promised to my father, was set aside for over 30 years. In semi-retirement, but still working as a consultant, I realised circa 2004 that if I did not restart it, I probably never would, the promise would be broken, and such work as had been done, be dissipated or forgotten. Now, with it complete, at least to 1841, I can ask a question about identity. What has this search done to me? Not, fortunately, what it did to poor Tom Darbyfield. But the unexpectedness and substantial documentation of Scottish Border origins has had an effect (as it did 25 years ago on Alex Haley in "Roots") on my perception not only of who I am (at 72, that should be clear enough) but where I fit in. This may be appropriate to a year when my dear daughter-in-law has given birth to our 13th grandchild.

Clearly, we all create our own identities, at different stages of our lives, on top of what we inherit, and we all have multiple affinities, family, political, religious, intellectual, regional, or local. But in the light of a newly re-emerging political debate about Britishness, and also migration/settlement/identity, what does it mean to discover that one's ancestors were Scottish?

Little to do with the romantic version, no tartan, no affinity with rugby supporters at Murrayfield, no credibility for myths such as the "Braveheart" version. After all, there is precious little difference in husbandry, landscape or livestock farming between North Northumberland and Berwickshire or Roxburghshire. The hills of Selkirk and Peebles are not that different from the Cheviots, and the sheep on both sides have a strong stock of Cheviot genes. The Tweed, which for much of its course demarcates the Border, remains one of the better salmon rivers of Europe; and for many Northumbrians at least till the revival of Newcastle, Edinburgh remained a more civilised city than far-off London.

This border, fought over for centuries, was never impassable except in very harsh winters and the Roman Dere Street runs straight through it. The climate is almost identical on both sides, topography, crops, trees are all similar, as are rainfall and hours of sunshine. Even in the so-called Dark Ages, the Tweed and Teviot had fords and a few bridges from the early Middle Ages. Until 1296 and the onset of one hundred and fifty years of war (for which Scottish folly and arrogance was as much to blame initially as Edward I's violent empire-building and aggression) the Borders were, as they had been for centuries under the Anglian kingdom of Northumbria, relatively peaceable. It was not the locals who made the early 14$^{th}$ century wars, but the powers above and beyond them. What followed, the horrific reprisals, raids, slaughter, fire and sword or simple reciprocal banditry and blackmail, emerged, as borderers learned to live in what should be seen as "the lands between" like Poland and Lithuania between Teutonic and Russian empires, sandwiched between the political-military axes of Stirling-Edinburgh and London-York.

That perception of a divided order began to change after 1603, and their differentiation between James VI and I's various middle shires had been substantially eroded by 1707 when the Act of Union passed the two Parliaments. But what evidence exists, suggests that, until at least the late 17$^{th}$ century, the ordinary inhabitants of the four Scottish Border counties and North Northumberland, perhaps even Cumberland, Tyneside and Durham, vested their sense of identity in the region, rather than in their national Scottishness or Englishness. Some would argue that national identity came even later, towards the end of the 18th century. Certainly Enlightenment Edinburgh of the 1750s was recognised by the intellectual elite across Europe as ahead of London, being a European city in the same sense as Venice, Prague or Amsterdam.

So to discover identity from a post-Conquest Norman origin, a name taken from a Northumberland village, lands in Kelso and Tweeddale, needs no great readjustment. It lies like a sort of sedimentary deposit over an original Northumbrian base. But it does alter the context of one's world-view. To put it crudely, a sustained submersion in Scottish history from the 14th century onwards is a sharp shock to a Cambridge-trained historian of the 20th century: landmarks seen from a different angle appear subtly different, the chiaroscuro of moral, social, economic, even religious dilemmas mutates into unexpected forms. So it would be from an Irish, Slovak or Galician point of view.

It has been a strenuous but exhilarating exercise to revisit medieval and early modern history after half a century, some of it in Latin, much in vernacular Scots,[5] and it could not all have been done without help, first and most important from that generation of post war historians, economic historians, geographers, and others who have re-based, even revolutionised the approaches to Scottish history, especially during the Middle Ages, asking endlessly provocative questions about identity and causation; to which I was lucky enough to be introduced in the 1960s when I began my first essay in oral history, *The Clydesiders* (1964).

My one regret is that only very recently have I read the excellent collection of essays edited by Elizabeth Ewan and Janay Nugent (2008) *Finding the Family in Medieval and Early Modern Scotland.* But I am heartened by the parallels between their work and mine and I hope that this book may, in its own way, fit in.

Second, I owe a great debt to the staffs of the Scottish and English libraries and County Record Offices, who have been unfailingly courteous and helpful and to Alison Mowat, whose palaeographic skills opened up the early modern scripts, and who very kindly gave advice, after reading the typescript.

One other personal note: having suggested that readers among this kindred can do enough research to connect 1841 with the present day, I have done the same, for the North Northumberland branch begins when Andrew Middlemas left Hownam in the 1650s, possibly to escape the rigours of Cromwell's military rule, possibly to avoid a plague revisitation, more likely, as a younger son, to find a wife, some land, and better himself across the Cheviot border. In three chapters, in a separate edition and for my direct family, I have traced this to the present day.

In writing this book, I have made the acquaintance of many from the past whom I never knew existed, but now feel that, in part, I know. Which leaves me free to dedicate this volume to all those I can call kin, even if I cannot meet them, joined in a common ancestry.

*Parchment with 96 seals (Public Record Office. London)*

# 2.

# 1296 and All That

History and archaeology have no beginnings, only the search for yet earlier patterns of evolution. Bones are of course nameless, even if we christen them – Lucy – a million years after death. But for identifiable people we depend on names and tangible evidence to tie down myth or supposition. There has to be a first mention, a first document, even if no more than a medieval equivalent of "Kilroy was here."

When the last Celtic King of Scotland Alexander III died in 1286, his infant granddaughter Margaret, known as the "Maid of Norway" became Queen. But aged only three, she died in Orkney in 1290 on her way home across the North Sea. A dismal interregnum set in as twelve feuding claimants surged around the empty throne, led by Comyns, Balliols, and Bruces. Civil war appeared inevitable, in lieu of direct trial by combat.

The story is almost too well-known, yet still open to interpretation. In an era before the formal evolution of the "divine right of kings," earthly arbitration provided perhaps the only way out. Edward Plantagenet, King of England, had set down a theoretical claim to be overlord of all Britain, something already partly achieved by his savage military conquest and refortification of Wales; and this was soon backed up by fanciful chroniclers' visions of the past, among his already highly-centralised and loyal court officials.

It provided a way out. If the twelve contestants or "competitors" appealed to him, acknowledging his right of arbitration as feudal overlord, civil war could be avoided. But the consequences should have been clear: Edward laid down prior conditions, first, recognition of his rights and later on, as opposition grew, the establishment of English royal castles in the southern counties, in effect a sort of annexation of the Borders in lands not central to the Scottish Crown. All twelve competitors accepted the first condition and he awarded the prize to John Balliol in 1292. Even before then, Edward I had already substantiated the doctrine of overlordship in parts of the Borders, ordering Simon Fraser, keeper of Selkirk

Forest, the Bishop of St Andrews, and the Seneschal of Scotland with a dozen other leading nobles and heads of monastic houses to hand over stags and oak trees – a real as well as a symbolic tribute, to be delivered to the authorities of what he called already "our Kingdom of Scotland".

When the new King, John Balliol, returned from doing homage to Edward in Newcastle, he found himself thwarted at all levels by angry Scots, and dubbed the "toom tabard," the empty vessel. Such was the unrest, not least among Scottish families who still held great estates in England, that Balliol was moved to deny Edward's additional claim to review decisions made by his own Scottish courts. Edward then prepared to take the three castles by force but delayed, to settle his war in France first, and King John, finally bold, dismissed his imposed English officials and signed Scotland's first epoch-making treaty with the King of France.

Whether Edward I had willed or even expected this is still disputed, but it gave him the chance to annex Scotland, albeit barely more peaceably than in his conquest of Wales. With a vast army variously estimated between 20 and 30,000 men, accompanied by siege engines, the English invaded in Spring 1296, took Berwick, sacked it murderously, and then after a long circular march as far as Elgin spent subduing the Lowlands and Mearns, set about imposing the formal deeds of submission, following the model briefly rejected by Balliol, on all Scottish earls, nobles and lairds, abbots, bishops and the burghers of larger, mainly royal boroughs.

Some submitted in person earlier on. But in Berwick, on 28 August, the main process began. 1750-odd names and seals (the two not always connected) appear on a series of vellum charters collectively known as the Ragman Roll, now held in the Public Record Office in London, with copies in the French state archives.[6] Those who signed had been summoned by their Sheriffs, either individually, or from the boroughs collectively under a single seal. It is not clear how the names were first set down but soon afterwards, the King's notaries compiled them on continuous parchment roles, four variants of which still exist, all dating from before 1298.

In some cases, the wax seals attached not only broke away but became defaced. Many are now very hard to decipher or downright illegible. But as a record of late 13th century Scottish family heraldry, signifying the elite that had ruled under Alexander III, they are unique: the seals have been called the "Ur-armorial of the Scottish gentry." Nothing comparable exists until the Hague Armorial, collated in 1592, just when preoccupation with vestigial heraldry as status symbol finally subsumed its ancient feudal and military meanings.

Originally numbering 1764 seals, 912 survive. Using computer database techniques, McAndrew has raised the level of identification between names and seals from about one-third to two-thirds – a notable achievement, given the manifest errors caused even at the time by English clerks schooled in Latin and Norman French transcribing unfamiliar Scottish/Middle English names. Some of the results are simply bizarre: Sisoris for Le Tailleur (Taylor)!

Membrane no. 811, the homage of Adam de Hepe and others, carries 19 strings of seals amounting to 90 in all, and the third seal on the fourth string (see illustration)[7] of green wax, in good condition, displays a stag's head cabossed (face on) with a double cross between the antlers, and around it, the words "SrVALTERI de MYDEIVA" (according to Bain, followed by McAndrew). But McAndrew was looking for correlations with names in the *text*, not for names that were absent, which had dropped out of historians' conspectus long before Bain's work.

Careful inspection suggests MYDELMA(ST), which also fits the letter space available around the heraldic device, unlike MYDEIVA, which was probably a mistranscription. This is the first mention of the name in any document, and it can be analysed in several ways. But first, the mere fact that he had been summoned by the Sheriff of Roxburghshire shows that he was regarded as important, in the same category as a range of other knights, holding land by feudal-military tenure, which included among many others the families of Douglas and Scott whose rise in the 14th century was to be spectacular. None of these went to Berwick by accident. Status, if not necessarily power or wealth, were self-evident. Taking the elements in order:

- *Knighthood* indicates the basic feudal unit of service to the Crown, to a Lord, or to a land-owning body such as a monastery, necessarily accompanied by military ability or at least, in the late 13th century, the capacity to deliver armed retainers – in short, a knight's fee.

But knighthood does not mean noble status, only that the holder of a knight's fee was important enough to be summoned to Berwick by the sheriff. It was, after all, vital for Edward I that those who had once owed allegiance to Alexander III now recognised his superior rights. We can assume that, since the seal had been made for Walter individually – or his father, if also Walter – that he was mature, possibly middle-aged or elderly. He was unlikely to have been a recent arrival from the South, more probably of second or third generation, to acquire the prestige that necessitated his homage. Clearly, he was also part of the Roxburgh contingent, and we know from later records that the family descended from him held the same lands from Kelso Abbey and bore the same heraldic seal.

- *Valteri.* Walter, Latinised, a Norman name quite distinct from the Anglian/Scottish Christian names; hence probably, a century after the Norman occupation in 1066, a member of the Anglian Norman military elite, still with its separate culture (though no longer separate language) from the earlier Anglian settlements. This is also confirmed by the crest and its device, the stag with the cross of Lorraine, then a more fashionable and European version of the legend of St Eustace (rather than the 15th century association of a similar legend with St Hubert, see below page 68).
- *De Mydelmast.* Given the formal evolution of 13th century heraldry and the circumstances of the document, the de (either Latin or French) can be presumed to mean "of" rather than "in." But of what and where? Mydelmast means land or at least a place; and this becomes quite complicated.

There are two possible approaches: that the family took its name from the land they held or that they came from outside, bringing it with them. One area of the Kelso monastic lands was known, at least from the 1572 rent-roll, as "Li Middlemastis lands," and this designation survives into the 17th century; while Middlemastwalls appears in later documents and on the Ordnance Survey maps as late as 1841, between Easter and Wester Softlaw, a mile or so south of Kelso, in the fertile land beside the Tweed. But there is nothing earlier than 1572 and it does not appear on the 1292 rent-roll (unless records have disappeared); and it is inherently unlikely that there would be a place or farmstead called Middlemastlands, unless it were occupied by a family of that name. The presumption must be that the lands were designated after the family that were to hold them had arrived.

The second possibility lies 30 miles away, south of the small town of Wooler in Coquetdale, near one of the few established roads around the Cheviots from North Northumberland by Yetholm. Three small villages existed in Anglian (Saxon) times, North and South Middleton and in between, Middlemast-Middleton. The latter became a "deserted village" at some time after the medieval period.

Waves of migrants, Anglian, Saxon, Norman had moved into Scotland during the previous centuries. As early as William the Lion's reign, chroniclers noted his habits, "he held only foreigners dear and would never love his own [Celtic] people."[8] These immigrants were reinforced by younger sons seeking land, or by men with some degree of literacy seeking employment as clerks, once King David I began the process, started earlier on the Continent, of developing a Court bureaucracy by drawing in educated laymen as well as clerics. For this reason, the process of monastic foundation, like Kelso and Melrose, can be seen as an administrative reservoir as well as a pious duty. Young men trained to arms, rewarded by land in the form of knights' fees (or a half fee or lesser fractions of these, as recruits continued to arrive in the 12$^{th}$ or 13$^{th}$ centuries) provided the basis for a defensive force, mounted and well-armoured, if not heavy-horse cavalry, with swords to complement the archers and spearmen of the older Scottish "common army" which provided William Wallace's schiltrons, far more cheaply than any standing army. More prosaically, they also escaped the onerous royal taxation levied in England, as Balliol himself well understood.[9]

The first Douglases came this way to Moray in the mid-12$^{th}$ century, in due course to become Earls, of whom Sir William "le Hardi" held lands beside Kelso and who also signed the Ragman Roll, taking his name from one of the "ten touns of Coquetdale" in

Northumberland. This family was well-established in the Lothians by the 1280s, yet still held land in Northumberland, one of at least 24 families, others of whom had property in Yorkshire and Cumberland.[10] The majority of these came with ready-made names even if, as migrants, their identity and loyalties remained flexible, until the major 14th century wars left them little choice but to ally with one side or the other. As GWS Barrow puts it, "Families which had taken roots in England...adopted more or less fixed surnames, often from the village or manor where the family held its property."[11]

It would be two centuries before any Middlemas called himself Middlemas of Middlemas (equivalent to "of that ilk") as head of the kinship group. But that style or habit, whether Lowland or Highland, related to kin or clan needs for security at later times of internal Scottish discord or unrest. A single family or a single adventurer-migrant might carry his name and his rank/identity with him as a portable asset. Identity indeed, at that time, vested primarily in parentage and degree, certified by a shield of arms or other (usually Christian) symbol, together with the place of birth.[12]

Middleton is a common enough place-name, meaning exactly what it says. Even in Northumberland there are others.[13] Mydelmast, however, is unique. In Saxon, Mädel means a place of meeting for speech or discussion – logical enough where three small villages needed to confer or publish news. Mast/Most implies a regular usage, perhaps a benchmark. Mydelmast Middleton, first mentioned in 1242, never held more than half a dozen families and by the 19th century its remains had become known as Middleton Old Town, although for much of the early modern period it was called North Middleton. The latter name shifted back to its original village, with its fine late 19th century house, and this confusion is reflected in some 19th century accounts.[14]

Documentary evidence suggests that the remains are those originally called Midilmest Middleton...In 1296 there were eight taxpayers and in 1580 11 tenants. The settlement is thought to have migrated in the late 18th century with only a few buildings still standing and recorded. The village is divided into three areas by the stream and by a hollow way aligned roughly east west. Two rows of small plots with smaller enclosures and platforms, which represent at least six buildings, face each other across the hollow way. The remains survive as banks of earth and stone on average .3 metres to .7 metres high but in places stand up to 1.2 metres high. The walls of some buildings are exposed and show that they are constructed of stone with clay bonding. The buildings range between 8 metres and 27 metres long and some are divided into 3 or 4 compartments. A well lies on the south side of the hollow way and is covered with a millstone. To the north of the well there are the remains of what is thought to be a kiln; it survives as a turf-covered mound and is roughly keyhole-shaped in plan. Two areas of ridge and furrow cultivation lie at the northeast and west of the village and measure an average four metres wide from ridge to ridge.[15]

Two of the three villages lie at the northern extremity of the Coquet Valley, but Mydelmast Middleton (according to the English patent rolls) lay in Coquetdale Ward, North Middleton in Glendale. Both formed part of the Saxon earldom of Gospatric II (c. 1135) whose grandson Patrick became first Earl of Dunbar. Close links with Roxburghshire developed and this Earl received the last rites in 1232 from the Abbott at Melrose Abbey. The family survived on both sides of the Border till the 5th Earl was forfeited by Edward III in 1334.

Tiny though these villages were, three families took their names from them or nearby Ilderton – of which the Middletons achieved greater success, followed by disaster. They took over from the Ildertons under Gospatric and seemed secure even after the Scottish wars, until the 1330s when Gilbert de Middleton rebelled spectacularly against Edward II – another story altogether, ending in capture and execution, whose moral for this narrative is merely that they also took the Middleton name from their village.[16]

If it is right to link the Middlemas family with Mydelmast/ Middleton, their departure from the village preceded a 1296 survey which records eight taxpayers of different names. The most likely date is around 50 years earlier, at a time of most rapid population increase, as pressure grew on the village with only a few hundred acres of arable land, still widely forested roundabout.

Whoever it was that left, may have responded to Earl Patric's needs after 1210 to implant men loyal to him and brought up within a more developed feudalism suitable to what was happening now on his new lands of Dunbar, in the triangle pointed by Berwick, Haddington and Kelso. Certainly Kelso Abbey, then the largest and wealthiest in Scotland, which had been moved from David I's original 1128 site near Selkirk to the main strategic river crossing of the Tweed, would have had lands to assign as part of any military protection settlement. Its lands, assessed in the 1292 rental, spread east into the Merse including villages which would host Middlemas families for centuries to come: Sprouston, Greenlaw, Nenthorn, to the east, Midlem and Lilliesleaf and Bowden to the south, Selkirk and Peebles to the west.

That Mydelmast was important enough to be assigned a whole knight's fee. He would have spoken in Middle English, already far from the Saxon tongue of 'Beowulf', nearer to Chaucer, and perhaps some vestigial French. He would have known much about farming and land management, and in particular sheep, appropriate to Kelso monks, known as the best sheep farmers on the Border, with nearly 7,500 head in 1292. Most of Southeast Scotland, up to Fife and Edinburgh was in fact farmed as small units, the habitual pattern of land holding being set by single or fractional knights' fees, a system completed by Alexander II in the mid-13th century (though not applied to the forests of Selkirk and Ettrick).[17]

He already understood the infield-outfield system, prevalent from the 12th century in north Northumberland, and the pastoral Cheviot economy, so would have been equally at ease in the lower Tweed or Merse, or its upper reaches. In the mid-13th century he would have taken advantage of the peaceable discourse between the two kings, Henry III and Alexander III, and would have had little awareness of national identity as that grew up later in what became the long War of Independence. Living within a proto-feudal society, already owing allegiance to a Saxon earl, in a hierarchical but still-mobile society, his needs and ambitions would have been those of a colonist, seeking better land.

Unlike dirt farmer immigrants of the 19th century American Midwest, however, he did not expect to start at the bottom of the pile. Since the best lands were already full of peasant farmers, he needed his military elite status, some education, wealth to buy land or livestock, farming expertise; he could then by the mid-13th century become part of the service class, comprising lay clerics, scribes, clerks, merchants, and/or younger sons seeking to become lords, following the Haigs of Bemersyde, the Riddells and the Douglases.[18] The passage would also have been easier if he found a native heiress. Thus it is likely that he brought both farming and military expertise to a very similar agricultural holding, as a new laird, with a Celtic work force under him, established for centuries and still peasants, not serfs or villeins as in Edward I's England. Taking over from the earlier Anglian elites, he merely replicated the process by which his own, presumably, Norman ancestors had originally reached Northumberland.

***

Though Dere Street, the second-century road north from the Roman Wall towards the Lowlands, still existed as a "dry march" across the Cheviots, he would most likely have taken the easier route by which the first Covenanting army came south to besiege Newcastle in 1638, via Kirknewton and Yetholm – past the burned out timbers of the great Dark Age hall/encampment at Yeavering, with its grandstand hill built for public announcements, its massive hall and elliptical rampart, constructed sometime after the synod of Whitby in 664 which adopted the Catholic version rather than Celtic Christianity.

That combined royal palace and meeting place formed the centrepiece of the kingdom of Bernicia, 400 years before the Conquest, of which Middlemast-Middleton had been a tiny replica. Over that time, Gospatric's domain mutated from Bernicia via the Danelaw and Northumbria, freed even before the Norman regime from the Danish and Scotti-Irish attacks, by the Saxon regime. The point here is that the whole area from southeast Scotland to Northumberland and Cumberland, even parts of Durham was not subjected after 1066 immediately to Norman control in the same way, or to the same extent as southern England. King Harold's victory at Stamford Bridge indeed gave the Saxon epoch an extension of life, despite the massive loss at Hastings the same year.

One needs, therefore, to remember that Northumbria was in some ways more like Wales than the rest of England, not entirely colonised even by the early 13th century, overlaid with a Norman elite administration or military class and maintained – as Wales was – by bases in fortress cities such as York, Newcastle, Berwick or Carlisle. Substantive changes in land tenure, customs and society lagged behind the south, despite William the Conqueror's harrying of the north, by a century at least.[19] This may have prolonged the Normans' northward migration and the intermixture on the way may have lessened their habitual contempt for what they found enroute, thus making admission easier when they finally arrived.

If a traveller today wished to see all the villages and valleys where Middlemases had settled since then, he would go a different route, past Otterburn, site of the famous battle between Douglas and Percy raiding bands in 1388, and over the Cheviot pass called Carter Bar. From the top, northwest and northeast stretches a wide country, Jedwater in front, the Eildon hills in the middle distance, ranging from Selkirk, Peebles and the Moorfoot hills on the western horizon to the nearer line of Cheviots on the east, looming over Kale Water with Kelso north northeast in the distance.

But the vista he sees today, from any standpoint, is not what the young migrant saw, mid-13th century. Now the Border counties, revitalised by European subsidies, are only gently wild, their woodlands well-kept, wide fields of grain, pastured uplands – in all, what they were in the mid-19th century before the great Agricultural Depression, some of the best-farmed estates in Britain. Under the Enlightenment title of "improvement," this was achieved in the second half of the 18th century, and the well-built architecturally distinct farmhouses (mains) and occasional palladian mansion, usually built by the Adam family of architects, stand as statements of resulting economic power and wealth.

Those families who survived the Reformation and the Civil War, who profited from the Act of Union, took advantage of the best levels of Scottish education, and retained over generations not only their survival capacity but the entrepreneurial dynamic, to become the possessors: ennobled, heirs to vast acreages, enclosed parks and estates, minerals and coal mines; and in London, ministerial office and patronage. They have seen out subsequent threats, even Lloyd George's taxation, estate duty, two world wars and the arrival of mass society, mass politics and the welfare state.

To a remarkable extent, they created this landscape, as much as any in Europe.

Conversely, few of the great medieval families survive, though their kin names crossed the medieval-modern divide. The landscape *they* knew was far harsher, bleak, deforested, sour soil, ill-drained or scarcely drained at all, its agriculture limited by poor seed and poor returns on rough grains, bere and oats, with a few peas, wrought by hand labour on a desperately inefficient run-rig system of cultivation; livestock scrawny, prone to ineradicable disease, mostly slaughtered in winter to preserve the meagre stock of fodder for next year's ewes and heifers; the population living in mean housing, indeed hovels, of which Froissart noted "If the English do burn our houses, what consequence is it to us? We can rebuild them cheap enough, provided we have five or six poles and boughs to cover them."

There is no easy way to depict it, except to argue backwards from early travellers' accounts, which vary widely depending on the season, quality of food, drink and bedding, and the weather. But the Merse climate is virtually the same as the Northumberland plain and Arthur Young's comments in the 1780s apply to both. Of those who preceded him, a few are worth quoting to set the geographical scene.

First comes Froissart, who spent six months there at the time of David II and reported the Battle of Otterburn in a racy prose which remains highly readable. "I was acquainted with the greater part of the nobility of that country." He spent 15 days as a guest of Sir William Douglas and may well have encountered Sir William Middlemas's father, a Douglas retainer at Dalkeith Castle in 1387. His travels by horse, where few if any roads existed, his baggage seated behind him, accompanied only by a greyhound, were not materially different for any family of that period, except for his added danger of crossing a border in time of war.[20]

> The Scots are bold, hardy, and much inured to war. When they make their invasions into England, they march from 20 to 4 and 20 leagues without halting, as well by night as day for they are all on horseback, except for the camp followers who are on foot. The Knights and the Squires are well-mounted on large bay horses, the common people on little galloways. They bring no

carriages with them, on account of the mountains they have to pass in Northumberland; neither do they carry with them any provisions of bread or wine; for their habits of sobriety are such, in time of war, that they will live for a long time on flesh half sodden, without bread, and drink the river water without wine. They have therefore no occasion for pots or pans; for they dress the flesh of their cattle in the skins, after they have taken them off; and, being sure to find plenty of them in the country which they invade, they carry none with them. Under the flaps of his saddle, each man carries a broad plate of metal; behind the saddle, a little bag of oatmeal: when they have eaten too much of the sodden flesh, and their stomach appears weak and empty, they place this plate over the fire, mix with water their oatmeal, and when the plate is heated, they put a little of the paste upon it, and make a thin cake, like a cracknel or biscuit, which they eat to warm their stomachs: it is therefore no wonder, that they perform a longer day's march than other soldiers.

He described the French army, lodged uncomfortably in Edinburgh, as

> not such a town as Tournai or Valenciennes: for there are not in the whole town 4000 houses, forcing the French Lords to billet themselves in neighbouring villages as far as Dalkeith and Kelso. For these, the only nobles they could recognise were the earls, Douglas and Moray; the rest they found peevish and importunate when not actually poverty-stricken.
>
> In Scotland you will never find a man of worth: they are like savages, who wish not to be acquainted with anyone, and are too envious of the good fortune of others, and suspicious of losing anything themselves, for their country is very poor. When the English make inroads thither, as they have very frequently done, they order their provisions, if they wish to live, to follow close at their backs; for nothing is to be had in that country without great difficulty. There is neither iron to shoe horses, nor leather to make harness, saddles or bridles: all these things come ready made from Flanders by sea; and should these fail, there is none to be had in the country.

Such a dismal prospect appalled his French colleagues who found a long stay in Scotland "neither honourable nor profitable" – to which their commander had to reply, "It is necessary for those who wish to live with honour in this world to endure good and evil."

Fifty years later, in 1435, came the Italian Aeneas Silvius Piccolomini, in due course to become Pope Pius II, then 30 years old and a skilled much-travelled secret agent working for various masters during the aftermath of the Great Schism – a distinguished humanist and diplomat, inciting James I to renew the wars against England. His comments are similar but he noted curiosities such as coal "a sulphurous stone dug from the earth, used by the people for fuel...the roofs of the houses in the country are made of turf and the doors of the humbler dwellings are made of ox hides."[21]

Nothing came up to European standards, least of all Italian ones, except perhaps the oysters, larger than the English, and the river pearls. "The common people are poor and destitute of all refinement. They eat flesh and fish to repletion and bread only as a dainty. The men are small in stature, bold and forward in temper; the women, fair in complexion, comely and pleasing, but not distinguished for their chastity, giving their kisses more readily than Italian women their hands. There is no wine in the country unless what is imported. All the horses are amblers, and are of small size."

Aeneas returned, via Kelso, where he might have encountered Middlemases before getting himself smuggled across the border at Berwick to avoid the storms that had frightened him on his way up by sea. At Newcastle, "for the first time it seemed that I once more beheld civilisation and a country with a habitable aspect, for Scotland and that part of England adjoining it bear no resemblance to Italy, but are nothing but a rugged wilderness, unvisited by the genial sun."

A series of frescoes in Florence in the Piccolomini Library, show some of this journey but in a wholly stylised manner. No actual paintings of medieval Scottish landscapes exist. Much later, in 1618, the "water poet" James Taylor commented on the "plain homespun laird," ill clothed, unostentatious in his own sheep's woollens, who nevertheless "keeps and maintains 30, 40, 50 servants or perhaps more, every day relieving three or more score poor people at his gate: and besides all this, can give noble entertainment for four or five days together, to five or six Earls and Lords, besides Knights, Gentlemen, and their followers, if they be three or four hundred men and horse of them; where they shall not only feed but feast, and not feast but banquet."

No doubt these were fed on what Taylor called "the infinite numbers of fresh salmons in the river of Tweed." Finally, William Camden, writing in *Britannia*, first published in 1610, describing the Middle Shires and the places familiar by then to at least ten generations of Middlemas kin.

> Teifidale, that is to say, the Valley or Dale by the River *Tefy* or *Teviot*, lying next to England, amongst cliffs of craggy hills and rocks, is inhabited by a warlike people, who by reason of so frequent encounters between the Scots and English in former ages, are always very ready for service and sudden invasions. The first place we meet with amongst these, is *Jedburg*, a borough well frequented, standing near the confluence of the *Tefy* and *Jed*, from whence it takes its name; and *Mailros*, a very ancient Monastery, wherein, in the Church's infancy, were Monks of that ancient institution, that gave themselves to prayer, and with the labour of their hands earn'd their living. And more Eastward, where the *Twede* and the *Tefy* joyn in one stream, *Rosburg* called also *Roxburgh*, and in ancient times *Marchidun*, from its being seated in the *Marches*; where stands a Castle, that by its natural situation, and tow'red fortifications, was in times past exceeding strong.
>
> But the adjacent Territory (called from it *the Sheriffdom of Roxborough*) hath an hereditary Sheriff of the family of *Douglass*, who is usually called *the Sheriff of Teviotdale*. And now Roxborough, by the favour of King James 6 is also a Barony, in the person of *Robert Kerr*, of the house of the *Kerrs*, a very noble and numerous family in this tract; from which are descended the *Fernhersts*, and others, who being educated in the school of *Arms*, have render'd themselves very illustrious.
>
> *Twede* aforesaid runs through the middle of a Valley or Dale, that takes its name from it, abounding in sheep, whose wool is very valuable. This is certainly a Noble River; which having its source amongst the hills more inwardly Westward, and running as it were with a straight Channel by *Drimlar Castle*, by *Peeblis* a Market-Town (which hath for its Sheriff *Baron Zester*) as also Selkirk hard by (which hath one out of the family of Murray of Fallo-hill.
>
> Then being increased by the accession of the River *Teviot* beneath Roxburgh, it watereth the Sheriffdom of *Berwick*, which is most of it the Estate of the *Humes*, wherein the Head of that Family exerciseth now the Jurisdiction of a Sheriff: and then running

> under *Berwick*, the best fortified Town of Britain, (whereof I have already spoken) with a prodigious plenty of *Salmon*, it emptieth it self into the Sea.

In one way or another, by service to or marriage with them, Sir Walter de Middlemas' descendents would be connected to these leading families, and by land holding or office in these towns, by the time Camden's first printing reached the public.

# 3.

# Wars, Resistance and Survival: The 14th Century

A myth grew up in the 1300s about the reign of Alexander III, as if it had been a golden age when, as the *Chronicle of the Kings of Scotland* put it, "their King 'was beloved of God and man, and strove to keep the nations and his land always at peace, and none of his predecessors was able to hold the kingdom with so great peace and rejoicing'." After nearly half a century in which war erupted with terrifying regularity, aggravated by the Black Death, an anonymous poet wrote

Quhen Alysandyr oure Kyng was dede,
That Scotland led in luve and lé,
Away wes sons off ale and brede,
Off wyne and wax, off gamyn and glé:
Oure gold was changyd in to lede. –
Cryst, borne in to Vyrgynyté,
Succoure Scotland and remede,
That stad is in perplexyté.

There had indeed been a period of long peace and good relations between Alexander and Henry III of England, his father-in-law, even if the judgement appears less simple today – one modern historian however labels it an "unspectacular reign," despite the appearance of consolidation.[22] But the very survival of an independent Scotland had been at risk for years after 1291 and from the perspective of those caught up in the devastation wrought by Edward I, the poet had it right.

Any account of the 14th century must recognise three levels of events, if it is to make sense of the period from which the Middlemas family emerged as lairds attached to the dominant interest in southern Scotland, the Black Earls of Douglas: first and best-known, the unending national conflict against English-enforced dominion, second the underlying relationship between Scottish borders and northern England, exemplified by the contest between Douglas and Percy retinues at Otterburn in 1388; and lastly the pattern of individual and family allegiances as these fluctuated between the two sides or coalesced according to the exigencies less of loyalty than of simple survival.

The chronology also falls into three parts: Edward I's initial destruction of all resistance, after the Scots' rout at Dunbar and the submissions at Berwick, down through Robert Bruce's revanche, to his epochal victory over Edward II's army at Bannockburn 1314; then the period of mixed fortunes to the 1350s; and the latter half of the century in which it had become clear that, whatever spectacular successes Edward III, Richard II or Henry V might achieve in set piece battles, Scotland could not actually be conquered again.

In the first period, Edward I held Edward Balliol in English exile and, despite the fierce revolt and early successes of William Wallace, returned not only to smash Wallace's army at Falkirk in 1298 and to wrap up the southwest, but came again with *levées en masse* supported by his fleet on the northeast coast, in 1300, 1301 and 1303-4. During the second of these eruptions, the Bruces also submitted – as they had done in 1296. Yet Robert Bruce continued to plot against any final assumption of Scotland as if it had been a land without a king; and although the Scots' resistance divided further into feud and civil war after Bruce's murder of his main rival, John Comyn of Badenoch, Robert I had himself crowned in 1306.

Not many attended the coronation of a technically illegitimate usurper, whose prospects diminished once the Comyns joined Balliol and Edward I; and very soon Bruce had to flee to the far west coast. But the Douglases and Simon Fraser raised the independent-minded levies of Ettrick Forest, who had supported Wallace eight years earlier, evading the occupying English army under Lord Clifford, until the old and ill Edward I died at Lanercost Priory in July 1307.

Edward's massive invasions, backed up by sea power, had not of course been the first English assaults across the border. But from Carham in 1018 to William the Lion's incursion in 1174, war had been the means of defining the borders of what were regional kingdoms evolving into states, rather than conquest and long-term settlement. That process seemed to have ended during the mid-13th century peace, in which Alexander had consistently rejected

Henry III's claim to feudal overlordship. But it ended with the Scottish Kings' perennial curse, failure to produce a male heir of mature age, that put their future in Edward I's hands.

Edward altered the nature of conflict between them, deploying intensive, repeated wars of great slaughter and devastation, first demonstrated at the murderous taking of Berwick, which like those of Henry III and Edward V were designed permanently to cripple the enemy, and to which the only strategic response could be withdrawal and guerrilla resistance. Yet Edward did not, in the modern sense, employ genocide nor Cromwellian-type plantations of English farmers on Scottish soil. [Edward I's grants of feudal lands to English nobles like Aylmer de Valence Earl of Pembroke, who received the castle and manor at Selkirk in 1306, like those promoting the occupation of Ettrick Forest, were rarely held for long or enforced.] He fought to define the nature of his rule, requiring total submission and loyalty – for which homage and the dissolution of a separate Scottish national rule (but not initially its laws or administration) were a precondition.

Whatever the intention, the effects were, as with Rome's dominion over Carthage, *ubi solitudinem faciunt pacem appellant.* Bruce's rebellion in 1307-09 could hardly be a national one, given his support from fewer than half his country's magnates: the allegiance even of these fed on grudges against the English rather than the patriotic support once shown for Wallace. The majority of middling lairds vacillated, threatened as they were continually with Edward's savage repression, arbitrary exile and executions which in 1303 reached far north of the Firth of Forth.

Widespread collaboration and submission occurred, whatever individual families may have felt about Edward's personal rule, and the civil war between Bruce, Comyn and Balliol supporters in fact rumbled on until the 1340s long after Bannockburn and the diplomatic settlement of 1328.[23] Nevertheless, Bruce's skill at guerrilla warfare, his advantage of being able to work on internal lines of communication across middle Scotland and the Southern Uplands, his easier access to forage, food and recruitment, and his own variant of a scorched-earth policy in front of advancing English armies, staved off defeat. Destruction of a great fortress like Castle Douglas in 1308 developed into a long-term strategy to deny dominant points to English armies dependent on horses and supplies, operating nearly one hundred miles from their base in Newcastle and much more from the northern capital of York. A continuous war of conquest by England being impossible, gains from summer campaigns alone could not easily be consolidated one into another.

Meanwhile Bruce, increasingly secure in the southwest, the Douglas's Border heartland, won support from the Scottish bishops, avid for archdioceses and recognition by Rome. Their view of resistance as a crusade against an almost infidel occupation permeated the Declaration of Arbroath 1320. Yet Pope John XXII refused to recognise Robert Bruce as king and promptly excommunicated him. To which the Scottish Bishops, in effect, said "very well, alone;" Arbroath clearly embodied the claim for a distinctively Scottish church as well as a kingdom-nation.

After 1314, Bruce's kingship stood established as far as allegiance was concerned, except in the southeast where the choice of swearing fealty to him remained dangerous. From the late 1300s Bruce had acted like a king and the acts of the Scottish Parliament exposed Balliol as a mere English puppet. But with no artillery to demolish the English-held castles, Bruce's future still at times depended on recourse to guerrilla war and surprise onslaughts.

In all this, James Douglas "the good Sir James," proved himself essential, winning the key fortresses of Edinburgh and Roxburgh, so that, even before Bannockburn, Edward II held only Stirling, Jedburgh, Berwick, Dunbar, and Bothwell. Relations were renewed with France in 1309 (though a full alliance had to wait another 16 years) and with Norway, while the relative absence of an English fleet opened up trade again with Flanders. Bruce could even raid England and bring the remaining fortresses close to starvation, a provocation which forced Edward II to come north to relieve his garrison at Stirling, where he lost in the irreversible disaster of Bannockburn in front of the castle itself.

Although the position of lairds and nobles in the southeast remained equivocal even after Bannockburn, no effective alternative existed to Bruce, now as Robert I absolved by his bishops from

Comyn's murder, and claiming to rule by divine right. The law of November 1314 forfeited the lands of all who had earlier fought against him, but gave them the final chance to submit, and this, by eliminating many dual landholdings and loyalties, helped to convince the majority of families who till then had maintained economic and social links with Northumberland. It is the first of three possible moments when Sir Walter de Middlemas or his son may have swung into the Douglas orbit but, given that Roxburgh Castle, only three miles from Kelso and the Middlemastlands, soon reverted to English rule, this date seems an unlikely choice.

Robert Bruce's golden years culminated with the seizure of Berwick in 1318, but his overreaching began the same year when he launched a war in Ireland intended partly to face Edward II with conflict on two fronts, partly to find an outlet for the grandiose ambitions of his brother Edward. Any dream of a Celtic alliance, however, turned out to be just that, an illusion, exposed by strategic incompetence, Edward Bruce's death, and an understandable Irish reluctance to follow Scottish requirements. There followed in succession, the Soulis conspiracy and attempts on Bruce's life, accompanied by five years' of severe crop failures and murrains. Renewed English attacks failed only because of Douglas' use of scorched earth tactics, aided by Flemish privateers who beset Edward II's supporting fleet.

Scotland was fortunate that the French need of a full treaty (Corbeil 1326) coincided with Edward II's deposition by Mortimer and Isabella and his subsequent hideous death. The north lay open, Bruce invaded and the English sued for peace, signing the Treaty of Edinburgh in 1328 only one year before Bruce himself died – the casket holding his heart being given for safekeeping to Douglas. The next four years when Robert I's son, David II, was still in his minority, is the second occasion on which a Middlemas may have become a Douglas retainer, but again this is unlikely, given what followed.

There came the onslaught of all those disinherited by Robert I, led again by Edward Balliol with surprising success, against a Scottish force bereft of generals (Douglas having been killed on crusade in Spain against the Moors in 1331). Indeed, historians debate how unified the Border lairds were at any time before the 1370s, given their propensity to follow a diversity of independent interests and motivations. Balliol occupied the southeast, Edward III repudiated the Treaty of Edinburgh and won his first great national battle outside Berwick at Halidon Hill – sending David II into an English exile not redeemed until 1341.

Scottish losses in pitched battle thus proved, long before Crécy or Poitiers, the uselessness of nobles mounted on heavy horses facing archers using the longbow and men at arms on foot. Fresh Border laird family submissions to Edward III revived memories of 1296. Yet, as before, the Scottish revived and turned about. George Barrow comments "Victory was a great settler of doubts and scruples."[24] Soon the Scottish army, led by Andrew Murray, acquired cannons, siege engines and the assistance of French knights on land, French warships to harass the English fleet. Best of all, Edward III, bent on conquest, had his ambitions diverted after 1337 to what became in France the Hundred Years War.

So David II returned to a still-independent kingdom and, like far too many Scottish kings, arrogantly and prematurely went on the attack, only to meet a defeat even worse than Halidon Hill, at Neville's Cross. Once more a prisoner, he could only watch the south reoccupied. Yet Edward III, concerned with the continental struggle and logistically sensible, finally ditched Balliol and gave his prisoner some recognition as a subordinate king. Even if the English could not win, however, neither could the Scots; and Balliol's final cession to Edward III c. 1354 of 2000 librates of land in the East March alone, including most of southern Scotland from Berwick to Edinburgh and all Galloway save Glasgow itself,[25] provided a sort of title to renew war whenever it suited him.

Whether Balliol's gift to Edward III could be maintained was another matter. In practice, Douglas held the hinterland of the southwest and the twin forests of Selkirk and Ettrick: while Sir Thomas Randolph with the Earl of Moray defended the Lothians. The English held their fortified centres dominated by the castles, fortified with up to date technology by the engineer-mason John Lewyn; but surrounded by varying degrees of resistance.

That resistance was by the 1340s imbued with a version of Scottish history in which Robert Bruce's wanderings on the west coast in the 1300s served as a new founding myth, like Aeneas after the fall of Troy looking to establish Rome.[26] Douglas's and Randolph's forays into northern England could be compared with early Roman raids on the Etruscans, while their Anglo-Norman knights riding south as far as York, Wales and the Isle of Man became an integral part of the chivalric, Francophone culture of continental Europe, as they took part in crusades and acted as emissaries during the Great Schism to the alternative Papal Court at Avignon.

In the nature of this culture, shot through with the everyday risks of being caught on the wrong side of whichever army currently occupied the Borders, allegiance at least in south Scotland was less to an ideal of Scottish nationalism than to whichever king was currently successful in maintaining peace, or resistance in time of war. It also lay with the Scottish church which had endorsed it. Both were essentially matters of moral and survival practice, and many families, exhausted, fearful or imprisoned, or simply less bound to a lord by the more formal and feudal tenure the Normans had imposed on England,[27] switched sides repeatedly. Yet the process begun by Robert I in distributing forfeited lands to Douglas and Randolph after Bannockburn,[28] extended by their grants to their own retainers and followers, with more secure possession than Balliol could ever enforce, encouraged other families to come in, especially in the most exposed areas Tweed, Teviot and the Merse.

"The Community of the Realm" had served as a moral-political focus for loyalty among the "competitors" of the 1290s. As an ideal it underpinned Arbroath, and appears to have been internalised by the mid-century, as the lack of submissions to Edward III, even after Neville Cross, indicated. Yet Pope John XXII resisted all pleas for recognition and Roxburgh and Berwick stayed in English hands for another century, the latter being confirmed forever in 1482.

During the whole 14th century, the Middlemas family lived in the shadow of Roxburgh castle, only three miles from their homes, circumscribed by a fear of the mailed fist much greater than that threatening the families further up river, where Douglas protection increased the more the uplands provided refuge, which Edward II's implanted English nobles had signally failed to hold. In the valleys and lowlands of the Merse, short-term military service, 40 days at a time, costly to those possessing what were often only fractions of a knight's fee, exposure to raids and risks of reprisals, never wholly went away.

Resistance, then, carried the same penalties – reprisals and death – as did the Résistance to Nazi occupation in central France in World War II. But it was no easier for farmers in Northumberland and Cumberland who were just as wide open to Scottish raids by fearsome schaveldores and to similar depredations even from their own side; hence it is not surprising that some of these landowners, fired by local quarrels and deprived of protection, threw in their lot with the Scots. As Barrow puts it "The problem for the English government was no longer the drying up of Scottish recruitment to English service, but how to prevent English recruitment to Scottish service."[29]

Villages on both sides were actually depopulated in this period, even before the first assault of plague, the Black Death in 1349-50 which the Scots called "the foul English pest." For lack of ability to wage sustained war, Edward III chose to afflict maximum damage and then retire, a policy which he applied also in France; and memories of both survived for a generation, as Petrarch found in the Loire region twenty years later. The pressure eased a little once Edward III's energy turned to France, but the Border lands became steadily more lawless, riven by bands of armed hobbelars and reivers, competing for agricultural resources already depleted by half a century of overpopulation.

Afterwards, during the Hundred Years War, hostilities on the Border settled into a pattern distinguished by brutality and a culture of raiding, the northern equivalent of chevauchée, carried out by schavaldores on a fearful peasantry. Army forays took place in the summer, before harvest needs decimated the levies; the fury of invasion depended partly on the diplomatic pretext, partly on how well the continental war was going. If the Scots had lost in 1341 due to lack of military technology, over-ambitious aims, and bad luck, their confidence grew as the English suffered reverses in France after 1360. David II had returned finally in 1357 and payments on his ransom ceased immediately.

Yet eighteen more years of battles wracked the region 1384-1402, in which the Scots with French assistance seemed to win with increasing regularity, driving the English out of Teviotdale, only to lose it all at Homildon Hill in 1402, the last full-scale battle until Flodden, over a century later. The fourth Earl of Douglas, Archibald, was taken prisoner, a better outcome for him than the second Earl's fate at Otterburn in 1388, the classic chivalric set piece between Douglas and Percy described by Froissart. Douglas won that encounter but was killed, inspiring the poet's mordant epigraph

but I have dreamed a dreary dream,
beyond the Isle of Skye.
I saw a dead man win a fight
and I think that man was I.

By then, however, the integrity of Scottish territory was assured and Otterburn has to be seen as national warfare fought at second-hand by regional warlords, whose personal motivation came from their old dispute over the legal ownership of Jed Forest.

A new legal order was slowly bringing the Borders under greater central overview (control came much later). March Law had been codified in 1249, but from the mid-14th century, Border disputes began to be properly managed with notaries keeping written records, even if the two sides remained enemies. Mixed juries slowly replaced trial by combat. Wardens had military resources to help them keep the peace, or at least slow down the process of raiding leading straight to war – and who better to run this system than the great magnates, Percy and Douglas, until they became "overmighty" in the eyes of their kings.[30] Released, Douglas captured and demolished Jedburgh Castle in 1409, and although his attack on Roxburgh Castle itself in 1417 broke up in disarray in what was called the "foul (foolish) raid," Henry V's renewed war with France and victory at Azincourt, gave further relief whilst strengthening the Scots' alliance with France.

In this precipitous period, many of the old Anglo-Norman families, Umfraville, Clifford, Ross, and in Northumberland itself the de Vescis vanished, to be replaced by what were in effect up and coming warlords, Douglases, Morays, Stewarts, matched by Percies and Nevilles across the Border. Warlords mutated into regional despots, replicating in their counties both the national cross-border hostilities and the practice of fiefdom alliances. Somewhere in the 1340s, then, is the most likely time that the Middlemases, by now sons or grandsons of Sir Walter, joined the Douglas retinue.

***

Among the many ways up the social scale, marriage promotion usually preceded power and wealth, especially if accompanied by clerkly skills to ease the passage. This had been true with "foreigners" long before Alexander III; and legal office, as part of a great man's household, accelerated the process. Friendship and above all kinship facilitated it. But what should be called Scotland's national emergency, and the loneliness of Robert Bruce's fight back from semi-exile, gave a special impetus to those who joined up to fight with him in the early days.

Douglases, Morays and Stewarts were of course well-established in the $13^{th}$ century, with their own lands, sources of baronial patronage. [The Douglases came from Flanders to the upper Clyde c. 1150, acquired lands in England and had long ties with Kelso Abbey: Sir William "le hardi" Douglas signed the Ragman Roll with his seal, but supported Wallace and died in the Tower of London.] That their futures were entwined with Bruce's, gave them first warlord power, then regional dominion as magnates, while at the same time marginalising other noble houses on the "wrong" side of $14^{th}$ century developments. But the fact that "Anglo-Scottish magnates exhibited varying degrees of attachment to the kingdom in which their lands lay, even though they all accepted the commitments which went with land ownership on both sides of the Border,"[31] explains why it took so long for patterns of allegiance to settle around Bruce's "new men." Only when a laird family recognised that English supremacy could never actually be established against Scottish resistance, did the process finally reach a conclusion: for some as late as the war-torn 1380s, such were the uncertainties endemic after 1296.

Douglas loyalty and military support had been so valuable to Robert I that the "good Sir James" came to preside over the largest territorial empire apart from the Stewarts themselves; it is still a matter of debate whether the Douglases should be seen as patriotic heroes or overmighty lords, whom the chronicler Walter Bowers compared to a "company of ravening wolves." Modern historians mostly view them as willing and vital partners of the crown in running the kingdom, maintaining internal peace by bonds with their retinues, resolving disputes before they became feuds, as with the Dukes of Albany, in the first recorded "bond" in 1409.[32]

But this was not a benign regime, for they were also militaristic and coercive and, to a notable extent, exempted from what in any case was a much lighter, restricted royal bureaucracy than obtained in England after Edward I. Local and regional loyalties inspired the circle of allegiance around great families, who also carried out duties, in their king's name, which in England had long been centralised in London.

Douglas' successful leadership and the protection it offered, had its price; and by the 1400s their politics had a European-wide resonance, amply displayed in what can be read as the family public relations: *The Boke of the Howlet*, circa 1445. In addition to Galloway and the former royal forests of Ettrick given them by Robert I, they controlled four great monasteries whose lands stretched almost to Berwick.

For a whole generation, the inaccessible almost trackless Forest of Ettrick served as their military supply bases from which to attack the English fortresses to the east, and as a fertile area for recruitment for raiding bands, often as large as a hundred horsemen and 1500 foot soldiers. By the 1330s, Douglas had won the allegiance not only of all Ettrick but the valleys of Tweed and Teviot, apart from the Roxburgh castle enclave. Guerilla war tactics, scorched earth and attrition changed after Bannockburn to what were in effect counter-invasions reaching as far as York, often with the help of Northumbrian rebels like Gilbert de Middleton. Otterburn, known in the ballads as Chevy Chase, provided only the most memorable example.

Douglas' military capacity depended on the "companies," resembling the marauding mercenaries of 14$^{th}$ century Italy, led by substantial lairds who, like Murray of Falahill then found promotion. Douglas lordship of the March, granted in 1324, became almost a hereditary fief, which in turn encouraged other lesser lords and lairds to come into his protective web. As Michael Brown puts it, "It was the men not the sheep of the forest which were of greatest importance to the Douglases. The support they gave to Douglas lords between 1307 and the 1350s was crucial in the rise of the family. That Douglas may have been helped by the lack of any major landed rivals, which led freeholders like the Middlemasts and Robsons to follow them..."[33]

The support of lesser lairds mattered, after the Douglas deaths in Spain and at Halidon Hill and during the period of weakness under Hugh "the dull" Douglas, till the first Earl William re-founded the noble house in time, first to dispute Balliol's cession of the south and of the Forest to Edward III, and second by 1360 to recover much of the former Douglas lands. During the long truce before 1384, a hardcore of local lairds finally coalesced behind the family, held together by forms of affiliation of lordship, landholding and obligation: Rutherfords, Scotts, Pringles, Turnbulls, Robsons, and Middlemases served the house of Douglas until its destruction by a later king in the 1450s.[34]

Archibald the Grim, illegitimate son of the "good Sir James" had risen through royal service, married a Murray and inherited influence in the southeast, even before becoming warden of the East March in 1364. Despite family rivalry, after the fiery but rash second earl James' death at Otterburn, he used his own connections, kin, tenants, and bonded friends to reestablish the family preeminence. Hereditary sheriff of Roxburghshire after 1389, he commanded a greater network of power and influence, all of which passed to the fourth earl in 1400.

Long before that, in the 1340s, an unrecorded laird, father of Thomas and William Middlemast, had entered the Douglas firmament. Already a neighbour of Earl William in Kelso, he was given minor office in Ettrick Forest as a currour or estate ranger to bind him in, at some point in the second quarter of the $14^{th}$ century. Yet for at least 70 years after 1296, there is no documentary evidence: which is not entirely surprising, given the scarcity of documents about Roxburgh's environs in Scottish archives and the very different function and emphasis of English Patent and other Rolls of the time which relate to the English holdings inside Scotland.

His first name is unknown, and at first he may not even have held knighthood, but his position as a laird can be guessed at. It is easy enough to define what it was to be a substantial lord, although the Scottish parliamentary peerage only came into existence in the 15th century. Both lords and lairds were landowners by feudal tenure or purchase, or were freeholders; all claimed nobility of birth, and heraldic blazons. But the *laird* was no more than *nobilitas minor*, i.e. of good birth but without a title. Among lairds, large or small, or even the so-called "bonnet lairds" whose acreage might be less than a husbandmen's, a sense of status and aspiration to rise in the social order certainly existed, but perhaps less of a collective identity than among contemporary English gentry.

"Knighthood remained the aspiration of the gentil classes, even if they now occasionally deferred the honour to avoid costly and irksome social (and military) duties. Pride was taken in the display of ancient armorial devices;"[35] and it is noticeable that the next extant Middlemas crest is identical to its predecessor of 1296, except for the design of the cross.

The 1296 Ragman Roll offers a testament of Scottish heraldry unique for another 300 years but it is scarcely a guide to late medieval social differentiation. By 1400 those heads of families who had signed it originally might be at the peak among magnates or mere members of the lord's retinue, desperately seeking upward mobility. Among 1500 to 2000 such families in all Scotland, of whom two to three hundred had their lands in the four southeastern counties, less than a tenth would have been rated as large lairds – each with his own small retinue and household officials.

Land was and remained central to status and survival; and in the later Middle Ages this required assertion of lineage, to substantiate rights in land, as well as farming planning and good management to retain it for the family.

To serve with the Earl of Douglas, the minimum requirement for a freeholder would have been noble birth or ancestry, substantiated by land and continuous heraldry. Sir William de Middlemast, appointed to the senior office of chaplain to the Douglas who became Fifth Earl in 1424, would have ranked in the middle or upper range on all three grounds. But since his elder brother Thomas was destined to hold the lands at Kelso, their father naturally opted for a church career for the younger son, as the best option – just as a daughter, failing a good marriage, might be assigned to a nunnery – at lesser cost than the expense of a dowry.

By the time William Middlemast was born c. 1385, fewer heiresses were available in the Border, thanks to the long-term effects of war and plague, consolidation of estates and rate of family extinction. In the 1380s, earls of Douglas were still giving land with knight's fees to their younger or illegitimate sons, but this was a provision not open to William's father, an existing laird who already held the post of currour in Ettrick Forest at the earl's pleasure. But for an educated younger son, the earl's household offered real prospects; and where better than to start that, than at the monastic school next door in Kelso Abbey?

This is, for lack of documents, an assumption, but it explains why William was able to become a priest by 1405 and why he followed his father's duties in Ettrick Forest, some 15 miles from what were already ancestral Middlemastlands. The knighthood came later, from the fifth Earl not the king, as a token of esteem (one of "my knights"), even before his brief military service,[36] though there is no reason to suspect that William as a young man was not trained in the martial arts. [See below p. 55. By 1400 in any case, the knightly heavy cavalry armed with lances had given way to much lighter mounts, ridden by hobbelars, or raiders who could dismount to fight as infantry with spears in the schilton formation developed much earlier by Wallace at Stirling Bridge.] Not to be versatile was a serious handicap to survival in the Borders.

***

After Douglas acquired the once-royal Forest by the Emerald Charter, there was more opportunity to bind his retainers into the regional network that served as recruiting ground for what, in effect, was his private army. But the Forest also provided civil jurisdiction, via offices such as currour (courier) or ranger, and master currours whose role had long been to safeguard stags for the King's hunting, oak trees for his buildings, and to ensure protection for his flocks that grazed the upland pasture.

Ettrick, like the New Forest in England, was no film-stage dense "Sherwood," but a vast open region which Edward III called "a hospitable covert of the wilderness" for his enemies, originally intended for hunting but increasingly farmed and managed for royal revenue. (David II gave leave to the abbot of Kelso to cut wood at Selkirk Forest to rebuild houses burned in one English campaign.) The moorland soil was poor, the grass rank, and even the richer valley soils often badly drained. Over all Tweed and Teviot, the population numbers that agriculture could support had peaked half a century before the Black Death, and although plague in 1349-50, 1362, 1379-80, and 1401 relieved the pressure[37] (and forced lairds to offer slightly better living conditions to their cottars and husbandmen), farming remained barely more than subsistence. Small fields bounded by banks, long run-rig strips, had existed since Celtic times, laid out according to tribal or family patterns. It was perhaps less defertilised than much of England, given the greater capacity for manuring by sheep and cattle, and the east March was certainly better than the west, but any year of crop failure presaged famine.

Returns on grain in the Merse usually came out better than the European average, and the Marches escaped the worst of the dreadful European cycle of 1315-18, a time "without sun for three years." But while crops and livestock remained vulnerable to English reprisals or foraging, and while the land itself, from Berwick to Ettrick, was often handed out to English captains,[38] even survival could not easily be assured.

Diet remained poor and monotonous even at lairds' tables, to the disapproval of foreign visitors. Life was very short indeed, half of all infants dying by six years old, another half of teenage survivors by 18. Markets served only small localities: where even the royal burghs of Edinburgh, Dundee and Aberdeen had perhaps 2000 inhabitants each in 1302 and Berwick as little as 1500, most others like Kelso or Selkirk, much less than a thousand. (The Scottish population then being approximately 400,000, overwhelmingly rural.) Yet Scotland was spared a peasants' revolt, there being less cause for lord hatred than in England, as Barbour noted in *The Bruce* in 1375.

In fact, on both sides of the Border, plague undermined the social structure, and rentals in kind gave way to cash to the detriment of lairds' rents and to the benefit of peasants. The pound Scots steadily depreciated as its silver content was reduced.[39] Some social mobility occurred in the late 14th century and Scots travelling as far as Newcastle to replace coal miners killed by plague, found themselves faced by anti-immigrant riots and a 1398 statute of removal. Other migrants followed the Douglas into the French army as mercenaries. John of Fordun in the 1380s extolled as a contrast to the wild Gaelic Highlands "lowlanders (who) are home-loving, civilized, trustworthy, tolerant and polite, decently clad, affable, and pacific, firm in their worship of God though always ready to resist an injury."[40] He might have added that they spoke a fair middle-English (but with a distinct Scottish accent); Henryson's poetry stands in comparison with the best of Chaucer.

To try to bridge the long gap between 1296 and the 1380s, one can argue continuity of name (spelled with a final *t* for a century or more and still with the prefix *de*) status, location, and armorial bearing; and the fact that the elder brother living at Middlemastwalls was well-enough known to his laird neighbours to help them adjudicate in a later land demarcation dispute near Kelso, [41] [Thomas Middlemas, by then about 58 years old, swore as to the value of lands at Sprouston (north of Kelso) once worth £20 Scots but which after the wars "are become waste and of no value." This retour, done for John Turnbull, bailie of Sprouston, was important enough to be witnessed by 13 other lairds, including Sir Walter Scott and Patrick Riddell.] while the younger moved to become senior officer in the household of the largest non-royal magnate in Scotland. In the first half of the 15th century they reinforced their position, from the Douglas entourage to the court in Edinburgh, and Border families with which they would then marry, such as Scott of Haining or Douglas of Cavers. Above all, they avoided the failure of very many families to maintain their line which afflicted 13 out of 47 Border names between 1350 and 1400.[42]

*Legend of St Hubert, 15th century (Christies' Images)*

## 4.

# Lovyt Chappelain: The Founding Godfather

A career choice as a priest, but not a monk, for a younger son who was likely also to retain some of his father's duties as a magistrate and official in the Yarrow Ward (one-third of Ettrick Forest), needed to be carefully planned. If a cleric was to have a vicarage rather than be a mere locum on £10 a year, if he was to receive a stipend suitable for a laird family, he had to have a minimum of one, perhaps two or three livings, and if he was to join the Douglas household, he needed to be familiar with a written and musical culture that included not only Latin religious texts and some understanding of French, but the work of late medieval poets and chroniclers – or else his lack of conversation would at once expose him to derision. Whatever Froissart had noted about the revulsion of French knights forced to lodge in primitive Scottish houses in the later 14$^{th}$ century, he and Piccolomini did acknowledge that the greatest houses and their courts, Douglas or Albany, matched contemporary French or Italian standards.

The majority of those who served the fourth Earl Archibald Douglas (circa 1372-1424) sometimes called "the tyneman," as officials or counsellors were of course highly literate clerics who had graduated at a time when Scotland still lacked its own university (Glasgow starting only in 1414) from Paris or Bologna, or if relations with England allowed it, Oxford or Cambridge. There is no evidence that William de Middlemas did – his name does not appear on the rolls of any of them – and his later enemies would accuse him of ignorance of canon law as a result.

But the documents setting out his wishes for the chantry he founded in 1436 demonstrate not only his literacy but an educated perception of ecclesiastical music and plain chant; and the fact that he, as chaplain, highest-ranking officer in a noble household, became the advisor and friend of the fifth Earl (also Archibald, c. 1390-1439) indicates good learning; probably from childhood in his father's house at Middlemastwalls, followed by some years at the Kelso Abbey school nearby, already an academic college and a good conduit to future preferment.

William de Middlemas (c. 1380-1449) appears first, writing to Pope Benedict XIII in 1406, during the Great Schism when Scotland's allegiance was to the Pope in Avignon not Rome. He was already a priest, with the living of Durisdeer (a parish near Moffat in Dumfries in the gift of the Douglases) but petitioned for another, which was granted later that year.[43] Whether the first came in answer to his father's nomination is not clear, but his status and education had been endorsed.

Elaborate conventions and rules still surrounded the question of priestly plurality, but 15th century realities dictated that William received the vicarage of Linton (today one of the few 13th century churches to survive the Scottish Reformation intact), which he held till given in 1423-4 the much larger living of Selkirk Regis.

Appointment as chaplain to Archibald, the eldest son and heir to the fourth Earl, came well before 1410; both men were then in their late 20s. The son's household was far less elaborate,[44] and as yet lacked the father's European dimension. But the heir needed to be kept aware of what went on in his father's circle, especially after Homildon Hill, during the latter's imprisonment in England with James I, 1402-8. William designated "Sir" as "one of my knights" rather than by royal investiture (as had happened with Alexander Hume in 1406) had to combine religious counsel with other duties, as senior officer where his experience in forest administration also came in useful.

Douglas supremacy had been largely restored by Archibald the Grim the third Earl by 1390 in the southwest, while the related "Red" Douglas, Earls of Angus, centred much further north. But around Roxburgh and Jedburgh, the Black Douglas hold was often threatened until the 1390s, another reason to bind in the lairds who as currours and master currours managed for them the three forest wards of Ettrick, Tweed, and Yarrow. After Archibald the Grim's death in 1400, the fourth Earl headed a dynasty relatively secure; yet he faced constant military threats in re-establishing his family's hold in the Lothians. It helped that his wife was Margaret Stewart, daughter of King Robert III; it helped even more that in 1409, on his return from English captivity, he set out the first written bond with the Regent, Duke of Albany, to settle the bounds of their joint authority while King James I remained a prisoner.

*Linton Church in the 18th Century, engraving*

Among the shifting loyalties of that period, which saw the Percies under Hotspur first defeat Douglas, then line up with him against Henry IV before the Battle of Shrewsbury, a process continued by which leading laird families such as Scotts, Turnbulls, Kerrs, and Rutherfords affiliated to the Douglas side, there being no other regional power-centre to match his. Douglas controlled the four great monasteries, Kelso, Melrose, Dryburgh, and Jedburgh, as well as those of Coldingham and Lincluden; his castles of Bothwell, Threave and Newark (the "new work" near Selkirk), his base in Edinburgh, and his financial empire, cutting into royal rents and customs,[45] gave him European princely status, equivalent perhaps to the Gonzaga of Mantua.

Some rivalries remained, with the Hays of Yester for example, during James I's 14 years in prison, while the English still held Roxburgh and Berwick with garrisons of hardened German mercenaries, long habituated to Edward III's and Richard II's policy of raiding, burning and hanging indiscriminately. This was not enough to threaten the division of authority in Scotland between him and Albany. But when the fourth Earl moved further onto the European stage, leading from the front as "a mercenary prince with an army for hire,"[46] he prudently devolved some responsibility to his son and created him Earl of Wigton, with powers to make land grants to the increasingly secure local network of lairds, in his own absence in Burgundy and France (as he had, with equal foresight, before Homildon Hill in 1401).

Of these grants, two survive, both to the "lovyt chappelain schyr Wilyam Myddilmast" – both eventually confirmed by King James I in 1426 on his return at last from England.

The first of these, dated 1423, is in Archibald the son's name, Earl of Wigton, signed "at the New Work" and gave Sir William "his beloved chaplain," two forest steads between the master currour's land and the currour's (which latter he seems already to have held, as his father had done, for these posts were becoming hereditary: Pringles in the ward of Tweed, Scotts in Ettrick, Middlemases in Yarrow). The stead was a tract of land, of no precise size, but with hunting, farming and grazing rights, a market, and in this case, the house and hamlet of Glengabire. As Brown comments, "This small-scale and temporary grant to a hereditary official reinforces the impression of deliberate seigneurial control."[47]

Even so, such an appointment would hardly have been made if William had not had estate administrative experience beforehand; just as he already had military experience, having almost certainly accompanied, as chaplain, his own lord Archibald, on the 1416-20 campaigns against English occupation of Touraine that culminated in the Franco-Scottish victory at Baugé in 1421.

Baugé turned out to be a very significant battle, not only because it held back the English for another three years, but because the death of the English commander, the Duke of Clarence, removed the one heir to the two kingdoms, France and England, set out by the Treaty of Troyes 1420. This caused the Duke of Burgundy to shift allegiance from Henry V to the Dauphin (son of the mad Charles II of France). Although he shifted once again three years later, Baugé also showed that the Scots could field a major army, and that if the English archers could be cut off from their men-at-arms, they could be defeated. Despite the results of Verneuil (below) these lessons influenced the strategy of Joan of Arc, after she raised the siege of Orleans eight years later.

The second grant, dated December 1425, after the fourth Earl had been killed with his son and Wigton's younger brother at the battle of Verneuil, and (following Baugé) after Sir William had been appointed vicar of Selkirk, goes much further. His lord, now fifth Earl, gives his chaplain the magistracy and mastership of Yarrow, together with the master stead and the tower house of Schytinglee, not only for his lifetime but thereafter to his nephew George Middlemas, with all the rights and duties, etc., including the magistracy of the Yarrow baronial court.[48]

Given the Douglas trust in lairds like this, to hold the Forest against English counter-attacks, it is not surprising that William de Middlemas like the Earl of Wigton, did not repeat his military foray and sail with the fourth Earl from the Clyde for France in February 1424. That voyage had been long prepared, its relevance underlined by Wigton's important success at Baugé, its mission to defend France shaped by the French Treaty; yet this was above all, a Douglas venture, undertaken in the absence of the Scottish king, albeit with the consent of Regent Albany and the Scottish church.

France had been the cultural and political model to whose standards the fourth Earl aspired, to the extent of using French masons in building the New Work, and employing French knights in his raids on Northumberland in 1401-2. France also offered opportunities far beyond Scottish constraints. Douglas had already provided a significant Scottish force for the French king in 1412-13, but had been outmanoeuvred over a potential alliance with Burgundy by Henry V in the new English war against France that culminated in Azincourt in 1415.

For four years after that, Douglas father and son raided and harassed the English in Normandy with their companies of mercenary followers, 20 to 50 men – each under a laird, mounting short campaigns in a natural military zone where it remained easy to live off the land, untroubled by a subservient French peasantry, yet without much risk – or profit. But by 1419, Paris had been lost, and the Dauphin needed a real army; not just an array of freebooters. The fourth Earl raised numbers to 6500, deployed in small bands, each under a laird's standard; and it was with this force, employing twice as many archers as men at arms, that Wigton defeated the Duke of Clarence at Baugè in 1421. This held the English advance and allowed the Dauphin to regroup.

The Douglases drew a rich reward: lands, cash, plunder and the title Count of Longueville. Yet the fourth Earl also toyed with the other side, offering to support Henry V if he released James I – and, perhaps as a test of Douglas motivation, this did finally occur – but only after he was dead.

Rewards for playing one side against the other could be high. Henry V died in 1422, and the Dauphin, now King Charles VII, made a pre-emptive bid: the fourth Earl was to become Duke of Touraine, endowed with a royal demesne, all its land and revenues, a rank no other foreigner attained in France at any point in the Middle Ages. It horrified the locals who feared, correctly, the arrival of Scots marauders pillaging the lush countryside beside the Loire. Yet Charles VII had no other choice to halt a renewed English advance into the French heartlands. Fordun depicted the French peasantry's complaints:

> Behold us through the frosty air, begging in rags the scanty dole for all is gone. The hungry Scots and haughty Spaniards in

their time have stripped us to the skin, God wot! And left us to lament and mourn.[49]

John Duke of Bedford led the English army, but it was Douglas' decision to engage in the pitched battled at Verneuil, 17 August 1424: a very harsh battle with no prisoners taken. Douglas nearly won, but his Italian mercenaries and French allies ran away at the climax, setting off a general rout, and he and his brother fell, to be buried at Tours. Few Scots escaped afterwards – Bedford knew who his real enemy was.

Scottish occupation of middle France ended abruptly, as did the title of Duke, which Archibald now fifth Earl claimed, but which Charles VII denied. But the campaign gave time for the French to hold the Loire line and saved Orleans, where they regrouped in 1428-29 and from which, led by Joan of Arc, the final expulsion of the English, that "long receding roar" began.

William de Middlemas's military record[50] may have been brief, but it was also fortunate that he escaped Verneuil, where his Ettrick colleague Robert Pringle was killed. He was equally fortunate that his own King, James I, contrary to Piccolimini's assessment of him as "short, passionate and vindictive," handled the fifth Earl's inherited Douglas empire at first with considerable care, reasserting royal authority in Ettrick less stringently than elsewhere and, as far as William de Middlemas was concerned, recognising the two grants, at Edinburgh on 21st September 1426. Elsewhere, in the two years since his freedom from England, however, he had already restricted the fifth Earl's privileges, including his rights as keeper of Edinburgh Castle. Two royal tours of the Forest in 1424 and 1426, also indicated that the Crown retained its former rights, including pasture for the royal flocks; and that the confirmation for Sir William was a political act not a mere bureaucratic delay.

Archibald Douglas was shrewd enough not to challenge these manoeuvres. He had already had to face James I's confirmation of his widowed mother in the lands of Galloway, thus foregoing one-third of his inheritance till the late 1440s. Excluded de facto by events in France from the European diplomatic game, he reasserted Douglas authority only briefly in 1429 and ceased to do so after James I imprisoned him for a few weeks. Yet he remained the wealthiest and most extensive landowner in Scotland, shorn a little perhaps of prestige, but a wiser survivor than his father; and he soon returned to royal favour.

How much Sir William assisted him, among his household circle, is impossible to calculate: the chaplain could not be more than a congenial, perhaps authoritative adviser among others such as his secretary John Cameron, later Bishop of Glasgow, once the erosion of Douglas power began, and as new patterns of affinity emerged, with the Red Douglas, Earls of Angus, encroaching on the East March. Yet in the regions, even the King's power had its limits. Having excluded Archibald from command of the assault on Roxburgh ("the foul raid") James I's own army broke up in disorder and he was constrained not only to release the fifth Earl from prison, but to appoint him Lieutenant-General of Scotland in 1431.

Before he died of plague two years later in 1433, Archibald did recover much influence in the East March and over the Church, so that he could replace the Bishop of Glasgow by his own nominee, John Cameron. But this revival owed more to his post as Lieutenant-General than his continuing position as a territorial magnate;[51] and much of it was reversed by James II (after James I's murder in 1437), before that king moved faster and more brutally against the power of overmighty subjects. [William, the young sixth Earl Douglas was murdered at the so-called Black Dinner with the King's connivance and the help of James the Gross, seventh Earl, in 1440, but the final reckoning was stayed for a few years.]

Before then, coinciding probably with the arrival of James the Gross as seventh Earl in 1440, and reassured by royal recognition of his Yarrow post in 1426, Sir William had begun to detach himself from the Douglas power, not out of disloyalty so much as prudence, and to search for an extra basis of support for his family and kin. Together with Pringles and Scott, masters of the two other wards of Ettrick, he thus survived the slow transition of the Forest back to royal supremacy, aided as this was by division and death among the Black Douglas. In the late 1430s, lands were reassigned, indicating new alignments: that part of Lempitlaw beside the Middlemastlands to Walter Scott, and the Sheriffdom of Roxburgh to the cadet branch, Archibald Douglas of Cavers, with Thomas Cranston as his tenant; each of these families were to be marriage targets for Sir William's kin later in the century. Once part of the Douglas retinue, kin-groups like Hepburns, Kerrs, Turnbulls, and Rutherfords, once "men of the Forest," took office and prospered in the King's service.

Sir William ceased to be Archibald's chaplain with his death in 1433, but continued to manage Yarrow and to occupy the fortified house of Schytinglee for the rest of his life. A tower house, built of stone unlike Glengabire, its foundations survive; and it was probably staffed by a reeve and servants, quite distinct from his clerical household in Selkirk. In the Exchequer Roll for 1434 there is an entry recording payment of £4 for 6 barrels of bitumen (for dousing sheep suffering from scab) delivered to him.[52] Forest management, of Yarrow and the magistracy, then passed on his death in 1449 to his nephew George, as the King had confirmed over 20 years earlier.

His passage as Vicar of Selkirk, however, was soon besieged. The living lay in Douglas hands, whatever the formal position vis à vis Kelso Abbey, and comprised a rich parish in a burgh soon to become royal, housing perhaps 1000 to 1200 people, with ecclesiastical influence far greater than he had had at Linton or Durisdeer. Earlier, there had been no question that Douglas power ensured safety and protection of both Melrose and Kelso abbeys – in so far as any monastery could then be protected – but by 1420, the fourth Earl appears to have extracted a high price from both, as well as Coldingham, through presentation of his household members to livings all across Roxburghshire.[53]

With the hiatus in Douglas power and James I's reassertion of royal authority in the late 1420s, Selkirk was a key appointment, with strategic political implications for the Forest region and the rights of Kelso Abbey. Despite the shortage of well-educated clerics after the Black Death (those giving comfort to the dying being at high risk of contagion) such a living, with its associated well-endowed St. Leonard's hospital for the sick, old and poor, together with space for lepers, pilgrims and travellers, naturally attracted competition: if Sir William was the Douglas nominee, there were rivals in court circles.[54]

*Battle Scene: siege of Newcastle, time of David I, but in early 15th century armour (Bibliotheque Nationale Paris)*

What followed became a game play for authority in the new royal borough and the Forest, involving the fifth Earl and the King, not directly but at one remove through their contenders, each with rights of appeal to the Pope, at exactly the time when James I was intervening in the Great Schism's final stage to try to decide where Scotland's ecclesiastical future lay. In the end he chose Martin V and rejected Benedict XIII, but Scotland still did not receive the long sought archbishoprics for St. Andrews and Glasgow – not until 1472.

Given that William was still, apparently, Vicar of Linton[55] and the Earl's chaplain till 1433, the substantial Selkirk burgh church[56] made demands which could not be met by a substitute. He would have held at least a weekly mass, distributed the sacraments, absolution and last rites, heard confessions (normally once a year at this period) and specific masses "for the salvation of the living and redemption of the dead", thus mitigating his parishioners' fears of hell and purgatory – even though by the late 15th century a plenary indulgence could be had for 10 shillings, basically a cash fine for accumulated sins.

All this in the Scot's tongue, which all lairds spoke in James I's day. He would have needed all his knowledge of theology and canon law as well as the secular legal expertise from his chaplaincy days, and the singing required by a sophisticated, if small, urban congregation. As yet, there was no heresy to contend with, Lollardy reaching the Borders only later in the century; but he would have noticed the slow transformation of the 13th century humanist view of God's majesty, explicit in Duns Scotus' writings, into a preoccupation with harsher concern with the inscrutable face of a remoter God, best approached via the Virgin Mary and innumerable saints.

This change may have been accelerated by the awful uncertainty of plague years; it was accompanied by a revival of magic, white rather than black, and may explain Sir Williams' own concern to found a chantry late in life (below). He would also have been responsible for all correspondence with and petitions to the Pope, as well as maintenance of ecclesiastical buildings, including his own vicarage and the hospital of St. Leonard outside Peebles. Knowledge of land management and the Forest must have been useful, and even much later he remained attuned to the Abbey's need for restoration after English raids.[57] Certainly, there was no opposition to his appointment to Selkirk from the Abbey itself, where he had been educated 20 years earlier.

Whatever had to be handed over, to the dioceses, the cathedrals in Glasgow or St. Andrews, and colleges and religious houses, parochial revenues underpinned the whole religious structure, apart from the vast lands owned by the church. Sir William had, for a cleric, a substantial income now; and owned lay property in Selkirk and Peebles, as well as receiving his (now-royal) salary as Master of Yarrow. Clearly also, incumbents filled in for him in his other parishes – Durisdeer being nearly sixty miles away.

His purview also included St. Leonard's hospital – probably for lepers – and shrine, by the bridge near Peebles, a place of pilgrimage (though not one of the first rank like St. Andrews, Glasgow, Tain and Dumferline, where the feuding families of Scott and Kerr were ordered to make penance for feud murder), and a source also of indulgences. This was one of the 13 shrines listed in John Knox's Reformation law of 1581, thundering against the old church and "the dregs of Idolatry that remain in diverse parts of the world, by using of pilgrimage to some chapel, wells, crosses and other such monuments of Idolatry."

All in all, Sir William lived well, his parishes bringing in at least £100 a year, cause in itself for jealousy. The system may appear corrupt to modern eyes. At the time, given the shortage of educated priests and the need experienced by both royal court and great magnates to ensure that the church positioned itself correctly vis à vis the English threat and the rival Popes,[58] its less attractive features, pluralism, and worse, simony and barratry (trading in vicarage futures), were understandable compromises. Those who suffered, in the short-term, were their congregations and in the long, the church itself, as the criticisms of Wycliffe and other reformers already demonstrated.

For men like Sir William, "the clerical elite who received major Douglas benefices, were an ambitious professional group," some of whom, such as Fogo and William Bullock went on to become bishops or in Fogo's case, the King's Confessor, a senior royal official.[59] Though the Schism had been resolved by the Council of Constance, its divisions within the Scottish church continued, particularly between the bishops of St. Andrews and Glasgow and their two colleges of clergy, both soon to become universities.

Selkirk provided a natural focus for rivalry, not least because Sir William was not, like the other contenders, a graduate. At first only Linton was involved, to which William Adeson was presented as his successor by Kelso Abbey in 1416, following a Douglas priest, John de Borthwick, inducted by the Bishop of Glasgow "and of noble race," MA and graduate of Paris. Borthwick had resented his removal; he denied the accusation he "had been a leper," and claimed his dismissal was the result of an affray inspired by nobles on the King's side.

This affair ramified, involving John Ewald, also an MA of Paris, who had held Selkirk till 1420, with dispensation to exchange the living for another; which he did, for several more, worth 600 merks in all. Robert Purves of St. Andrews then claimed the vacancy, but it went instead to Sir William, the Douglas nominee. The King accepted this; and twelve years later he was to ask the Pope, now Eugenius IV in Rome, for a dispensation for Sir William "that, together with the perpetual vicarage of the parish church of Selkirk, he might hold for life one other incompatible benefice, with power of exchange as often as he pleases."[60]

This appears to signify the start of a second round of political intervention, while the fifth Earl was still in prison, 1431; in that, the King wished to detach Sir William from Douglas allegiance, as Selkirk became a Royal burgh. Eugenius IV granted the request for three years, confirming the parish of Kirkandrew in Glasgow diocese and an £18 living, on top of the £8 Sir William already received from his tenure of St. Leonard's chapel and shrine.

Protests soon began, in May 1432, after the fifth Earl's release and his appointment as Lieutenant-General of the kingdom. Sir William was in fact caught in the middle of a devious game, perhaps suspected now of being a King's man, certainly open to charges of pluralism beyond the permitted range. But there were other legacies too, left over from Benedict XIII's days, among which needed to be settled, a matter involving the Scotts of Harden.

Whatever its real origin, the first salvo was fired by John de Mella, an official at the royal court.

One month later, the dispute started to threaten Sir William's tenancy of Selkirk, because he was accused of attempting to shoehorn his nephew, John Middlemas, a monk of Kelso, into the living of Stradbroke: "he gave a sum of money and arranged with John Middlemas that after obtaining it peaceably, he should resign it at the will and mandate of Sir William." This was serious: not only did John de Mella call him "alleged vicar" of Selkirk, but the crime of simony, trading offices for profit, threatened deprivation and probably excommunication.

Sir William had certainly opened himself up to charges of accumulating too many stipends, including the Prebendry of Duffus in Moray (and another in Aberdour and Pettokiss). These latter canonries and prebends (a Douglas gift in Fife) had already been proposed – again, presumably, to retain the loyalty of a key man. But he was also caught in a highly complex political struggle, where the interests played out behind an ecclesiastical front. John de Mella's attempt at a private prosecution came in the names of two other priests, John Benning and Thomas de Lawdor, both MAs, who asked the Pope to set up an enquiry, before depriving Sir William and handing all his livings to them.

De Lawdor was in fact the King's secretary, who already held five incompatible benefices, and claimed the same canonries of Aberdour and Pettokiss, worth £40 a year. The suspicion must be that he acted in the King's name, or at least with his acquiescence, making it a very dangerous attack. The accusers claimed that Sir William had only won Selkirk through their help (which was demonstrably false), and that Duffus and the other prebends had followed afterwards "by ordinary authority" i.e. by Douglas intervention.

The enemies added that William, as a non-graduate, "was ignorant of canon law...(and) considering his ignorance of law and simplicity" the Pope should therefore give him instead the Kirkandrew parish, while retaining the Duffus canonry and prebend. What seemed a compromise, of course, freed up Selkirk for a different royal appointment – a check on Douglas power, if one were needed, certainly antagonistic to the Lieutenant-General.

For the next year, de Lawdor pressed on, to get Selkirk vacated and himself promoted, "notwithstanding his defect of birth as son of a priest and an unmarried woman."

In the end, although de Lawdor won the Aberdour and Pettokiss canonry and prebends, and another vicarage at Erskine, Sir William held onto both Selkirk and the Duffus positions intact. By the time of James I's murder in 1437, the dispute had blown over. To a large degree, Sir William won, with papal favour, which extended to the grant of a plenary indulgence, *gratis*; and it seems highly improbable that he ever endangered the fifth Earl's patronage by disloyalty. Neither, however, did he estrange the King, despite the latter's long-term campaign against simony and barratry in Tweedale in the 1430s, and despite the feud over papal authority between John Cameron, now bishop of Glasgow (as a Douglas nominee) and William Croyser, archdeacon of Teviotdale, a self-appointed papal watchdog favoured by the King, through the same decade.[61] The whole episode should be seen as a remarkable diplomatic success, despite Sir William not possessing the passport of a university MA; perhaps gentle birth prevailed over de Lawdor's illegitimacy.

Such was early renaissance ecclesiastical politics. But one last round began in October 1444, still in Eugenius IV's time, when the papacy finally intervened on its own account. Kelso Abbey

> situate not more than 4 miles of those parts from the Borders and not more than 1 mile from a certain castle in Scotland (Roxburgh) occupied by the English, had by the long wars and the frequent visits of men at arms of both realms been so much burdened and suffered so much loss that the abbot and convent had long put off giving attention to the repair of the buildings; and that if the perpetual vicarages, of their patronage, of Innerlethan and Selkirk in the diocese of Glasgow, were united and appropriated to the said monastery, they would be able to give attention to the said repairs and better bear their burdens.[62]

The Pope suggested that if William de Middlemas was "reserved and assigned a suitable pension upon the fruits etc. of the said monastery, (he) would probably resign, whereby the said union and appropriation would more quickly take effect..."

*Monks at prayer, Henry VI's psalter (MS British Library)*

It was an offer Sir William could not refuse, if not for loyalty to his old school, then because he was now over 60 years of age, well beyond any medieval span of quiet retirement. Nevertheless (and even given the time taken to send a letter from Rome to Kelso), he took a year to accept – so that in 1447 Thomas Spens MA finally took the Selkirk living. As part of the deal – it can be called nothing else – William became Vicar of Ettrick and continued also to live in the fortified house of Schytinglee, dying there in 1449.

He had survived the tangled rivalry of Douglas and the King (first James I, then in 1444 as the young eighth Earl of Douglas struggled among other magnates for control of the next one, James II, before the new King's maturity arrived on his 14th birthday), together with court and baronial intrigue and ecclesiastical conspiracy. For a short while, and in a small world, he had been at the epicentre of a much larger game. Then he experienced in 1444-5 a greater, though wholly personal play, for his own immortal soul, in which the Pope's earlier plenary indulgence was only a single step.

***

Because of the general decline of monasticism and the arrival of mendicant orders of friars such as Franciscans in Scotland, there had been no new foundations since 1300, save the Abbey at Perth. Endowments and gifts of land by great lairds and nobles fell away, to be replaced by money settlements to pay priests or chaplains to celebrate masses for notable families: for which chantries were instituted, usually in cathedrals or burgh churches. Private chapels and this sort of living memorials, "pious foundations for the modestly rich", suited the heirs of old warrior elites;[63] [Priests performing this function could expect £5-10 a year, a much cheaper service than a monastery could provide, after the plague devastations.]Archibald the Grim set up two, at Lincluden and Bothwell Castle.

William Adeson, probably a descendant of the Ade who signed the Ragman Roll, was evidently an old friend of Sir William and had taken over Linton Parish from him. Together, the two decided to found their own chantry, with an altar dedicated to St. Michael, in the burgh church of St. Andrews at Peebles, now that William had relinquished Selkirk. The two already possessed four houses in Peebles, with some land and surrounding woods (confirmed by James II in 1436) and these were now given up to fund the new chantry.[64]

It is not clear whether the chantry itself dates from 1439 or 1444, or indeed whether it was a new building attached to the church, or a chapel within its nave or chancel; but it was probably started in 1439 and completed five years later and attached to the existing church. A lengthy document, the actual indenture with Peebles town authorities, sets out the terms of the endorsement and the duties of the priest in charge: [65] [This carries Sir William's seal in excellent condition (see illustration) but with a single bar on the cross, not the Lorraine version of 1296. This is for St. Hubert, like St. Eustace, the Patron saint of hunters, following the same 7th century legend of the hedonistic courtier Pepin, who went hunting on Good Friday instead of attending mass; but was converted when he saw the cross between the antlers of the stag he was about to shoot. The Hubert legend had become popular at the Scottish court since David I founded Holyrood, and it was mainly this version represented by artists of the 15th century. Sir William presumably followed the fashion.]

> To the service of a chaplain there perpetually to say mass according to the value of the rents and the possessions given thereto, in honour of almighty God, Mary his mother and St. Michael, for the health of the body and the soul of James King of Scots, for his forbears and successor kings of Scots, for the bailies, the burgesses and the community of the burgh of Peebles, and for the health of their own souls, their fathers' souls, their mothers' souls, their kin souls, and all Christian souls.

Sir William of course followed what was already a tradition among noble families and which was to be revisited frequently in the later 15th century: that of displaying what the living could do for the dead – and in due course themselves. So, twenty years later, did William Scherer ex-Provost of Aberdeen, writing in 1464, "sins are remitted and the pains of Purgatory overcome, and the souls of the dead very often liberated from them and placed among the joys of Paradise."

His formula is exactly the same, but excludes the good citizens of the town. There seems little doubt that Sir William Middlemas believed in what he was doing, and that his action would, in fact, speed his family on their journey towards Heaven. (He was fortunate too, at the time, for the same Pope, Eugenius IV made his grant of perpetual indulgence, circa. 1440 to Cosimo di Medici much more expensive: in return for the foundation of the monastery of San Marco in Florence, a massive difference of degree if not of kind.)

The document makes minute provision for holy books, chalice, and vestments, dedicated to this chapel alone; how to manage the endowment to keep pace with inflation, how and when to maintain the building, and provide it with candles; above all, how the chaplain shall make his service, in return not for a life salary, but a yearly one, reassigned after Easter according to good performance.

The post was open only to men of Peebles, for a fee of 10 merks, 6 shillings and 8 pence, with bread and wine and another 20 shillings for acting as manager/rent collector of the endowment. In return the chaplain was to guard the altar's furniture at his own risk; he must follow the vicar of St. Andrews' directions as to timing of masses, and be expert in plainchant; he shall be fined for non-attendance, even out of this small stipend, and if he fails to sing well enough, he shall be dismissed.

For the two donors' souls, families and kin, he is to sing the *de Profundis* and record the days of their deaths in each one's mass book. Until then, at evening, the *placebo* and *dirige*, and at morning, the requiem mass. After Sir William's death in 1449, the indenture was reissued, 3 September 1450, providing for other services in the Lady Chapel as well, the Pope to be included, with a *per dominum* "that God lend him grace to govern all Christian folk in secure and steadfast truth, and the bishop of Glasgow, and the Peebles community, *salus populi*."

Peace made with God, Sir William presumably died content. To remedy one growing criticism of the mid-15th century, that the church concerned itself only with the upper section of society, the two donors had also made provision for the common people:

an indication that Sir William may have been sensitive to their needs, which mendicant friars were already starting to meet. But the language remains that of the old elite, used to the church's role in providing magnificent display, in fostering authority, power and unity – and there is a strong argument that Scotland still needed such continuity.[66]

As at any time when local, regional and national loyalties conflicted, comparable to Italy (where tower houses were even taller), the kin-group provided recourse against outside threats. Sir William had sustained a long life with unusual success for a younger son; and some of this power and influence, he handed on to his family: a living for John, his nephew the monk of Melrose; the ward of Yarrow to his senior nephew George, now a master currour; and at one remove, George's descendants, through their enhanced marriageable status. In that sense, he was indeed the family's founding godfather. [As for the chantry, it survived for 120 years until the Reformers stripped it bare. It was never intended as a place of pilgrimage like St. Leonard's hospital, but only as a chapel for the altar to stand. Nothing of its furniture, missals, silver vessels, or robes survives; nor does the altar, and the body of the chapel can now hardly be distinguished among the ruins.]

As a laird, in the Forest like his father, he straddled the two worlds of landed gentry and the church – with an interlude of military service. An ambitious priest who clearly enjoyed the good life, and may have possessed a few books of his own, perhaps a Book of Hours, who read the poetry of other clerics such as Henryson and Gavin Dunbar, he managed to keep faith with the Douglas, even in decline, with the King (more or less), the Pope and perhaps with God. He may not have been learned, but he was literate enough for the fifth Earl's court and he knew about livestock and land management. In canon law he may have erred and he probably infringed the edicts on barratry, though less than some of his accusers claimed, and in common with most 15$^{th}$ century practice. Yet it is hard to imagine that, two centuries on, some of his family would fight their king, in defence of the Solemn League and Covenant.

But he had also been lucky, in enjoying Black Douglas patronage before its extinction in the 1450s. Thereafter, Middlemas lairds would need to rely on their own skills, political as well as agricultural; and though others of them became priests before the Reformation, none reached his eminence, or counted for as much in the circles of power.

*Hunting in the Late Middle Ages (MS Bodleian Library)*

# 5.

# Flowering Branches 1450-1540

More is known about Sir William de Middlemas than most members of the family until the 19th century; but in the 90 years between his death and the birth of Mary Queen of Scots, gaps still exist in the story. His side of the family, as it grew through his nephew George, is well enough documented; but the side represented by his elder brother Thomas is not, so that the dispersion from Middlemastwalls to Lilliesleaf, Eildon and Morebattle cannot easily be mapped.

That this generation was shaped by what Sir William had done for them is undeniable: he had set up a permanent placement in the Yarrow Ward of Ettrick, through his Douglas patronage, and the later extinction of Douglas influence did not prevent the Kelso Middlemases spreading in and around that area. Meanwhile, other Douglas lands became available in Tweeddale, while careers in the old church for younger sons remained, in that last Catholic century before the arrival of John Knox, trained in the harsh new discipline of Calvin's Geneva.

Rather more activities were also now recorded, by more literate clerks, resident even in small burghs, writing less in Latin, more in Scots, on durable parchment which, in accordance with the fashion of 19th century historiography, tinged with antiquarianism, were later set permanently in print: registers of the Great Seal, the Privy Seal, the Exchequer, as well as the Acts of the Scottish Parliament and the Lords' Auditors. Records, of course, by their very nature list what the better-off lairds and nobility did, not the "bonnet lairds" or husbandmen who served them, unless these appear as criminals, raiders or intruders on their betters' boundaries.

For some Middlemases, who led unadventurous lives, the 15th and 16th century details remain sparse, whether they belonged to what were originally the senior or junior branches. But as the pedigrees set out in appendix A demonstrate, that is not a useful distinction: Sir William's side, touching greater events, attracted more notice, whereas Thomas Middlemas's children and grandchildren recorded little until the third generation.

The final stage of Black Douglas regional power altered the context for a whole range of laird families who owed them their lands, wealth and status. James Douglas the Gross, successor in practice to Archibald (William's patron) who had died of plague in 1439, having incited the murder of his nephews at the "Black Dinner" in order to become Seventh Earl, died soon afterwards in 1443; and his 18 year old son, having apparently succeeded in his bid with other magnates to establish control over King James II during the royal minority, seemed to have re-established the glory days, after supervising James' coronation when the young King aged only 14 reached his majority. He took responsibility for diplomacy with France and Burgundy, rolled up a serious raid by the Percies, and sacked their main castles Alnwick and Warkworth – exploits set out lavishly in the *Boke of the Howlet*, an early essay in grandiose public relations.

But the eighth Earl was not a "real" Black Douglas by birth. He was also unpopular[67] and later, vulnerable to a more mature James II's onslaught, first to destroy the Douglas ally Livingstone, then in 1450, to assert royal authority over the Forest and Galloway. Douglas still held Newark but not Selkirk or Jedburgh, and though James II did re-grant him the Forest, the point had been made that the King ruled; and the royal progress to Melrose, with former Douglas associates such as Walter Scott of Buccleugh and Archibald Douglas of Cavers in his entourage, reinforced it. Having suppressed a revolt by the Lord of the Isles, at a dinner in Edinburgh on 22nd February 1452, the King himself like Brutus made the first thrust and his courtiers finished off the Earl.

Parliament duly absolved its King, as Bruce had been absolved of Comyn's murder. James then toured the Marches, gathering up lairds' loyalties. It did not help the Douglases that the ninth Earl made tentative approaches to Henry VI of England. But madness engulfed the latter as the Wars of the Roses ran against the Lancastrians, exacerbated by English defeats in France and Spain; and the Earl, deserted even by the Scotts, Maxwells and Johnstones from the southwest, went down to defeat at Arkingholme in 1455. Afterwards, James II set out to finish the whole business with the English begun by Edward I, besieging Berwick in 1457, Roxburgh in 1460, and renewing the alliance with France. The newly forfeited Douglas lands gave him a wealth of patronage to hand out, while the Red Douglas Earls filled the Black ones' places. As Brown comments,[68] "Barons, lords and freeholders of the south no longer needed the kind of military leadership provided by the Douglases." No magnate in Scotland ever re-established such territorial power in his own right, without an office such as Regent in a royal minority.

Widespread transfers of allegiance which this upheaval caused presented no moral challenge to Sir William, 11 years dead, nor apparently to any others in the family, whose transitions had mostly been made earlier. For the lands they held now, they paid the King direct. But James II died at the siege of Roxburgh when a wedge holding one of his new cannon blew out and hit his thigh, causing a fatal haemorrhage. When the castle at last fell, to be demolished in the Bruce tradition, however, the long-held English enclave vanished and the lands along the Tweed south and west of Kelso were released from English domination.

Fifteen years of peace followed, a truce broken only in 1482 by Henry VI's recapture of Berwick, itself followed by more negotiations and treaties, through Richard III's time, until Henry VII, when the Tudors reached the English throne; and that farsighted, calculating monarch, in pursuance of an agreement dating back to 1474, married his sister Margaret to James IV in 1503. [The future James IV had rebelled against his father and the latter's death in 1488 after the engagement of Sauchieburn ended a national struggle for power between them.[69] James IV's rebellion, however, was conditioned as much by local politics as national ones: many lairds and nobles committed themselves to him in pursuit of their own interest, and the Humes among others benefited from the outcome, even if reallocation of lands and offices sometimes stimulated new feuds.] James IV was already evolving a bureaucracy that reflected the Tudor style, matching Henry VII's Morton and Fox with Bishop William Elphinstone; and it is not unfair therefore to see the later 15th century, once James IV had completed the wholesale ejection of his father's court officials, as a time of success – but also as a foretaste of the sort of triumphalism, which would lead the Scottish King to the disaster of Flodden.

Part of that successful rebalancing of power between magnates and King, perhaps more effective than in England, included the imposition of a post-Douglas order in the Border shires (which on the one hand allowed the Middlemases to spread out from Kelso, but on the other, ended their almost hereditary official position in the Forest, since the post of Master went as a reward to the Humes in 1488, together with some of the land in Yarrow. [Which in turn reflected national politics and James IV's need to bolster his authority via à vis the Humes who had supported him against his father, while allowing Thomas Middlemas to retain one-third of the barony of Glen within Yarrow.] Yet feud, disorder and violence, and "Jeddart justice" (summary execution) still continued, though not as much as in the West March, where James IV took on the reiving clans, hunting down the Armstrongs in particular, in the 1500s, using the Hepburns (later Earls of Bothwell) to enforce his "letters of fire and slaughter". (From the Middlemases perspective, this must have seemed like retribution for the sack and murders at Plora by "thieves of Levyn" in 1491, below.)

Even Flodden, 1513, for all its tragic implications, with the King's death in battle surrounded by his shield of pikemen, remnants of one of the strongest Scottish armies ever raised, and the "Flowers of the Forest" (men of Ettrick), celebrated in that most mournful of pipers' laments, made surprisingly little impact on Scotland as a whole. In the period 1450 to 1520, a sense of Scottishness was finally defined and implanted, an ideology of nationhood first adumbrated at Arbroath, documented by the subsequent clerical chroniclers, Fordun, Barbour, Wyntoun, Bower.

After so long a struggle against England, a sense of order was being established, even in the Marches. Unfortunately, Flodden's other legacy, the long minority of James V, ensured that central authority remained weak throughout the 1520s and early 1530s. Scotland had been too easily caught by its commitments to France, as well as the enticements offered by the Pope and the Italians. When he did rule, James V was not a pleasant king, greedy for riches (largely by feuing monastic lands) and palaces like Linlithgow, which charmed his first wife with its echoes of the Burgundian renaissance.[70] Scottish leaders of the early 16th century failed to learn, even from Regent Albany's retreat from the siege of Wark in 1523 when faced by

Henry VIII's far more mobile army, that French support was not enough to counter English military mobility.

Henry VIII had tried to impose Mary his daughter as a bride for James V; but James turned instead, first to a French treaty and then, to Henry VIII's great displeasure, to a French marriage. But finding he disliked the lady, he married another, daughter of Francis I, with a magnificence typical of his lavish palace building in the 1540s. Her dowry had been worth £166,000 Scots but she died, six months later. Only in 1538, from marriage to Mary of Lorraine, did he achieve a legitimate heir, Mary – soon to be Queen of Scots, as a child, after his own death at the Battle of Solway Moss. Full-scale war with England once more developed out of raids and counter-raids and endless political conflict, opening a way for the English "rough wooing" of the infant Mary.

***

Given this uncertain context, how to tell the Middlemas story? In the 1420s, Sir William had found a way to establish his nephew, but George was himself a younger son. About the head of the senior branch, Thomas Middlemas (born circa 1380) William's elder brother, nothing is known apart from the 1438 Sprouston retour, but that he had other sons as well: John, the monk of Melrose, who graduated MA from the newly founded University of Glasgow in 1440, and an elder brother, name unrecorded, who inherited the Middlemast lands still held nominally from Kelso Abbey.

That they did not actually hold Douglas lands but were lairds associated with them, seems clear from the fifth Earl's charters of the 1430s and 40s, allocating lands in the Sprouston area to the monastery, and from others to his cousin Thomas Cranston who, in turn with John Rutherford of Hundalee, witnessed a grant by William Douglas of Cavers in 1449 to Walter Kerr – all of whom were Thomas Middlemas's neighbours, and some from families into which his would later marry.

The generation of Thomas's elder son (born 1405?) passed in complete obscurity, before the line reached John Middlemas (born circa 1438 died circa 1505-10) who witnessed a Kelso Abbey charter in 1457 and styled himself Middlemas of Middlemas: the style being equivalent to "of that ilk," indicating that he regarded himself as head of the kin-group.[71]

John's son (or possibly his younger brother) Peter was involved unsuccessfully with William Haig of Bemersyde in a "vexatious disturbance" with James Newton of Dalkeith and his tenants in 1494;[72] the next in line, William Middlemas (circa 1480-1530), the first to call himself "of Lilliesleaf," found himself sued in 1503 by Robert Kerr, a neighbouring laird aggrieved by Williams's tenants there.[73] From this scanty evidence, one can deduce that the family had already extended its holdings to Eildon (next door to the Haigs of Bemersyde) and Lilliesleaf, seven miles to the southwest. This can be confirmed by a 1531 grant (James V) when Archibald Middlemas, probably the father of Hugo Middlemas of Midlem and Thomas Middlemas of Eildon (see Chapter 7 below) was recorded as holding two husbandlands in Bemersyde from Jasper Cranston of Crosley, as part of the estate.

These land acquisitions were fortunate, because on the day after Flodden in 1513, Andrew Kerr of Ferniehurst, taking advantage of spreading disorder after the King's death, expelled from office the Abbot of Kelso, Andrew Stewart, and installed his own brother Thomas – a disastrous switch for the Middlemases, whose friendly feudal lord, the Bishop of Caithness, protested but finally caved in, later in the year, accepting the need to appease the Kerr family. The usurper Thomas received formal recognition four years later, and matters stood so, until James V at the age of 22 appointed his own five-year old illegitimate son as lay commendator – in charge both of Kelso and Melrose.[74]

Meanwhile, as the great abbeys fell into decay, with their estates feued (sold off) to lay relations and lairds, the Middlemas family, identified since the 1460s with the Scotts and therefore at frequent feud with the Kerrs, had lost ownership of their original estate, the Middlemast lands, probably in the 1530s. Thomas Kerr, the new Abbot (as former vicar of Yetholm) had been a rival of theirs and in 1524 he gave the house and mains of Middlemast walls to his brother Ralph Kerr "and all the Brooms [heath land, growing the broom that were used to roof most houses of the period] excepting Medilmestis lands"[75] onto which they hung for a few years more.

Nevertheless, they still farmed as tenants that part of the original knight's fee south of Kelso (which was still marked on a map of 1831) by Easter Softlaw. By the mid-16th century, there were at least three groups of the same family farming there, at Sharprig and Lempitlaw (Lime Pit Hill) and Morebattle, at the northern end of Kale Water. (see Appendix A5 for an assessment of their line of descent.) The fact that Andrew/Dand Middlemas (1540-1590) styled himself Middlemas of Middlemas indicates that he had re-established his family as the senior branch, even if the actual lairdship had been diminished.

The Kerrs recovered Kelso Abbey from the King in 1559 and held it for another seven years. Meanwhile the Abbey itself suffered, near-fatally, at English hands: first in the raid two months after Flodden in which they burned out the Abbot's house, the dormitories and the Virgin's chapel, and again at the will of the Earl of Surrey in October 1522: "I had decided that, within three nights, God willing, Kelso shall be burned with all the corn in the same town; and then they will have no place to lie any garrison nigh unto the Borders." So, despite the entreaties of Margaret Tudor (James IV's widow and Henry VIII's aunt) it was, even the great gatehouse.

The last of that generation, the youngest brother, Alexander Middlemas (circa 1480 to early 16th century) graduated from St. Andrews with his MA – having no doubt learned from Sir William's experience – in 1498. Nothing more is recorded of him, though Cuthbert Middlemas, also a priest and graduate of St. Andrews (St. Salvator's College) in 1512, joined a mendicant order of friars and took his MA, 7th out of 12 on the list of licenciates. Such a choice characterised that side of the late medieval church concerned with personal devotion and service direct to the poor, of whom the Franciscans were already the best-established. Cuthbert probably joined St. Francis's order at Roxburgh or Jedburgh as an Observant friar, a preacher.

William Middlemas's son, John of Lilliesleaf (born circa 1505) married Elizabeth Scott in the 1530s[76] after a wild, misspent youth, entirely typical of the uncertain period. A letter of pardon from James V, given generally to a motley assembly of Scotts, Kerrs,

Hoppringles, Turnbulls, and Rutherfords, quoted "illegal assembly" with George Hume and other Humes, threatening the King both in Edinburgh and Stirling. John was specifically cited, along with friends of the Grieston branch, such as Walter Scott of Haining, William Stewart of Traquair, Scotts of Harden, and Branxholme, Andrew Kerr of Primside, and John Cranston of that ilk – a roll call of Roxburgh and Peebles lairds that also demonstrates how closely knit still were the two branches of Middlemases.

***

George Middlemas of the Selkirk/Peebles branch (circa 1405 to 1455) took over from his uncle Sir William as master of Yarrow Ward,[77] having served as currour (or ranger) under him since the original Douglas grant, ratified by King James I. While his elder brother held the Middlemast lands, he managed Yarrow [Yarrow Ward comprised a large area, approximately 45 square miles, not as richly endowed with trees or fertile as Ettrick, but which since 1320 included Traquair Forest with Glengabireburn, Whitehope (the master's own stead) Glenpoyt and Plora – much larger than the Pringles' Ward of Tweed. Ettrick (the Scott's ward) had the Forest bailiff's house at Kirkhope and all three major castles, Newark itself, Oldwark and Selkirk], giving primary allegiance to Thomas Cranston of that ilk as Baillie (Head Officer) of the whole Forest; with Pringles and Scotts as his neighbouring Masters in the other two wards.

In this capacity, and presumably from the tower house of Schytinglee, as well as the more modest stead at Glengabireburn, he had to cope with a royal visit in 1452, after the King's murder of the eighth Earl Douglas, at the head of an army several thousand strong, to overawe any Douglas attempts at reprisal. The same delicate task of entertaining the King recurred in 1455, as the Douglas empire finally crumbled, when James IV and his household hunted in the Forest more peaceably, and in a different sort of demonstration of regal power; and on both occasions George would have presented his own son William, shortly to take over as Master and receive the King on his next progress in 1457-8.

This William (circa 1430-1475) married the sister (first name unknown) of his father's friend and neighbour Robert Scott of

Haining, an estate just outside Selkirk. Scott was in turn younger brother of David Scott of Branxholme; and their father Sir Walter headed the whole Scott kin-group.[78] This hugely advantageous marriage can be seen as the logical extension of the earlier relationship with the Douglases, where a family's future – land, office and sometimes maintenance for a household official like Sir William – depended less on a written bond than an unspoken social contract. But now, after the Black Douglas' decline, such security had to be found within a wider confraternity where kin-groups as small as theirs might rely on the support of more powerful families, given that they all, as "lairds of good birth" formed part of this elite and exclusive social group.[79]

David Scott had, in fact, married a daughter of the Earl of Angus (Red Douglas), whose dowry included the sombre fortress of Hermitage. Already he had national status, having raised men for the King's army in the 1450s, negotiated truces with England in 1449 and 1464, and fought for the King at Arkingholme. It was he who witnessed Robert Scott's charter giving Grieston Tower to William's son Thomas in 1476.

Such a link had very long consequences, not only because the Middlemases were to marry Scotts on several occasions over the next century, but also because it committed them, as kin by marriage, to the long feud that was to start with the murder of Kerr of Cessford in 1526; which broke out repeatedly thereafter in spite of all attempts at settlement.[80]

From William Middlemas' marriage to a Scott sprang at least four children, Thomas, William, Robert, and Marion. His father's death at a relatively young age made William Master of Yarrow Ward with Robert Liddell as his second in command, giving him the same status as both his father-in-law in Ettrick, and George Pringle, Master of Tweed. It was Liddell as currour, on his behalf, who handled the King's household expenses on the 1476 tour, the wages of royal servants coming to £87-1/8, paid by the Exchequer.[81] In addition, William authorised £6 for 12 bowls of oatmeal to feed "Scotis silvestribus," an itinerant band of players disguised in wild animal skins which he had organised to amuse the King and his troops.

So good were these players that William recalled them for the King's revels on his next visit, to Melrose in 1458. Accounts for the peregrination include £5 – 5/6 for farrier's expenses and repairs to saddles and bridles; and the next year, 21 shillings for hire of horses bringing victuals and £22 for constructing a temporary reception hall with two bed chambers at Newark Castle – royal visits being costly in any century. William's own fee as Master was £9 in 1456, £3 in 1457, settling down to £6 for the decade 1458-67, when his elder son Thomas took over the office – possibly because by then his father had become infirm.

There were penalties for such service: William had to accept the King's order to demolish the small former Douglas fortalice of Schytinglee in Yarrow – of which only the outer earthwork now remains – where he was living; and so much damage had been caused to the Forest stedes that he was freed of two year's rental. But military logic demanded it: 1460 saw one final Douglas revolt, with Percy support from Northumberland.

1460 also brought the King's death at Roxburgh Castle and William would certainly have attended the coronation at Kelso Abbey of his nine-year old son, James III; of which there are two accounts, the formal one, that bishop Kennedy of St. Andrews officiated, the informal, that Angus impatiently seized the crown and fitted it on the boy's head, declaring "now it is upon your majesty's head by my own setting, let us see who will be bold enough to take it off again". Red Douglas had inherited Black Douglas's over-weening pride.

William's last appearance came in 1476, as witness to the Scott's sale of Grieston, with the land of Gillishaugh, to Thomas his son.[82] Meanwhile, his younger brother John (circa 1420-1500) had taken his BA in Theology at Glasgow University, in the presence of the bishop (an archbishop still being denied to Scotland by papal authority). He then became a monk at Melrose Abbey, rising to sub-Prior under the former Douglas adviser, Abbot John Fogo; being recorded as a witness to two abbey charters, in 1484 and 1497. It was a bad time at Melrose, if the chronicler Lindsay of Pitscottie is to be believed, of slothful easy days after Fogo, under his successor Andrew Hunter who combined the office with the truly incompatible post of Lord High Treasurer. No doubt the sub-Prior had to fill in on the business side of estate management.

Thomas (circa 1450-1499) succeeded his father as Master of Yarrow Ward in 1465 and held it for over 20 years until relegated by the King in order to reward the Hume family who had backed him against his father James III. Thomas's fee remained at the old rate of £6, rising to £9 in the 1470s – when the ward, and his duties, were enlarged.[83] Afterwards, albeit without the title of Master, he retained the tenancy of Yarrow lands and the ones added in 1478 for at least another decade. Meanwhile, the Scott marriage seems to have brought not only Grieston but land at Lempitlaw near Kelso, where Middlemas was established by the 16th century, (unless, that is, that Lempitlaw had been part of the original abbey lands held by the senior branch).

Thomas's first marriage (circa 1475) to a daughter of John Murray of Falahill – a family long-established in Peebleshire – built on the network affinity with neighbouring lairds, partners in running the Ettrick Wards; an understanding which may have been stimulated by the fact that James III had married in 1469 Margaret, daughter of Denmark's king, who brought as her dowry Orkney and Shetland and received as recompense lordship over much of Ettrick Forest including Newark. Being a wilful, flirtatious lady, she gave offence to the Ettrick establishment, upsetting the local balance of power.

Having taken over as Master, still with Robert Liddell as currour, he engaged himself in managing the ward, supervising the markets and agricultural goods and cattle, and extending his own estate along his border with the Murrays, by two half steads in Plora, the hilly area above the Tweed east of Traquair. Liddell himself by 1475 had become Sir James and was supplying the King's army with spades and shovels, made by John Murray's workers, for Newark's fortifications.[84]

The Yarrow accounts show rents paid in 1479 amounted to £20 each for Liddell and Murray and the same for Plora, now apparently divided between Thomas and Ninian Lowis – these lands of course being distinct from his office as Master in charge of the whole ward, with Murray now promoted as his second in command. When the Mastership was handed to Hume, they remained as tenants; and in 1492 he won a case against John

Robson to recover a third of the lands of Glen which the latter had wrongly occupied.[85]

Evidently, once Schytinglee had been pulled down, Thomas needed another proper stone tower house, and this is what he bought, at Grieston, high above the Tweed, looking down on his neighbours at Cardrona and Traquair – neither of which was then fortified. Grieston (or Greviston as it was sometimes spelled) Tower had passed through several hands already in the 15th century, from its original building in 1422 by the Regent, Albany, to Robert Scott in 1463; and Scott sold it with Gillishaugh, to Thomas on a feudal tenure of one silver penny, 13 years later.[86]

Thomas's land was increased by purchase from the Auckinlech family in 1481. Such acquisitions may be seen not only as a late part of the marriage settlement, but an element in the Scott's binding in of the family, including William's widow; with the long-term aim of stabilising this part of the old Douglas lands. It is known that the King was also involved, because in 1489, for reasons which remain obscure, Grieston's feudal tenure from Scott "fallen into the King's hands" was granted to John Murray, his brother-in-law, and at once handed back to Thomas, who then consolidated it with Plora.

Grieston consisted of a simple square stone fortified building, surrounded by a walled enclosure, of which only the oval-shaped defensive earthwork now remains and the water course and well. Plora, rebuilt by Thomas, was grander, with six farm steads, imposing enough to be also called Bold Castle after the nearby village. Much of it, tower and great hall, survived into the 19th century and was sketched in 1831 (see illustration). Very little stands now, it having been quarried for dressed and rubble stone over many years, but the three terraces remain. They were not a garden in the modern sense, but tilled lands, perhaps for fruit trees and vegetables, together with a barmkin (farmyard) and an early grain dryer, presumably for the oats grown on three large fields above the Bold Valley.[87]

It may be that, by 1490, Thomas had overreached himself financially, to fund what was, for the time, an extravagant lifestyle; certainly the contents of Plora, from the 1494 inventory, were unusually lavish for a Border laird – even one with his extensive estate. But the set-back was more likely the sour result of marrying his daughter Jonate to Gilbert Williamson of Cardrona, on the next door lands west of Grieston. Gilbert was a burgess of Peebles, probably a rich corn merchant, and his brother John was a burgess of Edinburgh: between them, they had either over-borrowed, or owed as a debt to the Exchequer the substantial sum of 500 merks – and Thomas, who had stood as guarantor, was ordered to pay or suffer distraint.[88]

Large as this burden was, it was not Thomas's only debt. He owed cattle and £38 to other members of the Williamson family, despite his protests that he had already paid them; there was a suit by Hay of Yester for a debt to Sir James Crichton of Cairns, incurred by Thomas's younger brother Robert, and another for £100 by his neighbour at Plora East, John Lowis in 1491. It is known that his procurator (lawyer) resigned lands on his behalf at Roslin, near Edinburgh and that he had also that year sublet part of the Plora estate.

The appearance of financial distress and family embarrassment may be no more than the results of taking responsibility unwisely, as head of the family, a role which also involved him on the head court roll of Peebles and as the magistrate for the barony of Glen; it is impossible to gauge. But a far more serious disaster occurred, later that year. We have only the lawyers' account of what happened, from the first court record, 1491, to the later process in 1494; but it seems that "thieves and traitors of Levyn," (the standard phrase describing raiding bands out of Liddesdale, led by Armstrongs, Elliots and Forsters), ambushed Plora when the laird was away, murdered his wife and his two younger sons, Ninian and John, and looted the house of its entire contents.[89]

Analysing the Lords of Council Decree of 1491, in which Ralph Kerr, as surety for the accused, David Turnbull, was ordered to pay for the theft of 11 horses and mares, 44 cows and oxen, and the entire stolen contents of the house, it appears that the Turnbull family became the first suspects. Ralph Kerr did not attend court and was ordered to be distrained. But David Turnbull was not then accused of the three murders.

Three years later, presumably because nothing had happened, Thomas's suit reached the Selkirk assize judges. There, two

*Pillage of a house, (MS British Library)*

*Plora ruins in the 1830s (RCAMS)*

other Turnbulls, Alexander and Andrew, stood accused with the Liddesdale raiders as associates, of both murder and "treasonable stouthrief" (banditry). What happened to them is not known, nor whether Thomas ever got satisfaction, nor even whether Ninian and John were still children at the time of their deaths or whether they defended their mother and the tower. But the inventory, in Scots and Latin, identical in each case, is indeed a remarkable index of his wealth in moveable property, and the social standing that such possessions and the house must have conveyed.[90]

xi horses and mares, price 100 merks
xliij oxen and cows, price £88
ij le standis armorum (suits of mail or armour) £20
Gold and silver coin, £40
6 silver spoons, 6 merks
A great dozen of pewter flagons, £7
6 men's gowns (togae virorum) £8
11 women's kirtles, £22
12 scarves or veils (flammeae) £12
5 blankets (?) (cadurcae) £10
5 bows, 50s
6 lances, 6 pole-axes, £2, 10s
2 gold rings, £5
3 le tykis de feddir beddis, £5
22 pairs of linen sheets, £11
22 worsted coverlets, £10
16 sheets, £6
20 trinaclia, 20s
5 swords, £5
1 daker (10) of tanned hides, £3
Riding boots, etc., £5
5 Flanderscaps, £2, 10s
2 webs of gray cloth, £10
3 webs of linen cloth, £3
5 boxes, £2, 10s
4 coffers, 26s. 8d
5 duplii camentorum bistmiti (?) £2, 10s
3 ells of English cloth, £3
3 Handkerchiefs, (towels?) 6s

"Which goods were despoiled and taken by the said David Turnbull, for which he took them to our sovereign lord, in front of the justices of Selkirk..."

Three years of "ongoing enquiries" may not have been unduly long by 15th century Border standards, but it was long for a laird who had lost his wife and two of his three sons. What follows suggests a certain lack of judgment, for his choice as second wife of Margaret Cockburn, daughter of another near neighbour Sir William Cockburn, turned out to be as problematic as his earlier debts (of which, after the Plora massacre, nothing more was heard, implying that at least some recompense was paid to him, and that his rentals were enough to settle the rest).

Cockburn, of a notable laird family established over 200 years, was at that time elaborating his tower house of Skraling in the early renaissance style. Son of a Parliament member, who married into the nobility, and one of the ambassadors to England in 1424 to negotiate the release of James I, Sir William held a much greater estate than Thomas; he was also mean and highly litigious: his daughter's marriage contract, February 1493, provided a dowry of only 80 merks.

Thomas may well have been impatient, and when that dowry remained unpaid, he sued his new father-in-law. Cockburn responded with his own suit for Thomas's alleged "wrongful detention and withholding from him of 20 score (400) sheep" worth rather more than the dowry itself.[91] No record of payment by either side exists, but as Cockburn's many lawsuits against Murray of Traquair and others show, he was a dangerous man to have stirred up – especially since the Cockburns held the other part of Glen, two-thirds to Thomas's one-third.

Feuding at law continued till Thomas's death in 1499, in spite of the fact that he had helped to set up one of Cockburn's nephews, Vicar of Ellen, as a tenant; and when he died, his Cockburn widow promptly married John Murray of Blackbarony in 1500, leaving him 12 years later in her will the lands of Easter Plora, which had been entailed originally to Thomas's elder son George. The two children born of Thomas's second marriage (Adam/Alan, circa 1493 to after 1530 and Ninian, circa 1494 to after 1520) were taken into Murray's guardianship until their coming of age – following yet another lawsuit by Cockburn over a previous tutelage by Sir John Hay of Sned (1505).

Among that generation's other Middlemas siblings, the records are silent about his younger brother Robert, once Thomas had paid his debt to Crichton. Marion, his sister (circa 1460-1500) held land as a tenant in Traquair from the Stewarts. That she managed her own estate can be guessed from the fact that she and others sued John Earl of Buchan and the Murrays over unpaid rents: the latter failed to attend court and the Lords Auditors ordered them to pay her.[92] Jonate, the other sister, as a widow also managed her late husband's Cardrona estate and went on to buy the former church lands of Swinhope, near Peebles, feued to her from the Cranstons.

Thomas's eldest son George had escaped the Plora raid, presumably because he was with his father; from whom he inherited Grieston and Gillishaugh with their 20 husband lands beside the

Tweed and his share of Glen, confirmed by the King in 1500. His good fortune was that the Auchinlecks then resigned their over-lordship of the whole of Glen, not to Cockburn who held the larger part, but to George in 1505. He and his half brother Adam had already survived yet another Cockburn suit, set up by his step mother and her new husband John Murray, for "taking certain beasts" from the lands of Glen, and it is possible that Auchinleck so disliked the Cockburns that he chose George instead.

Whatever the reason, George's tenure was short. In the summer of 1512, he was murdered in the streets of Edinburgh, and two Dicksons John and his son John, were convicted of "slaughter of the laird of Grieston...committed in forethought and culpable felony" and beheaded at the Tolbooth in Edinburgh 12th November. A third assailant, William Dickson, was caught later and also executed. Even in a violent age, which had witnessed the murder of one neighbour John Porteus in 1500 and another John Forde a year later, premeditated assassination (which is what it seemed to be) counted as headline news.[93]

The obvious motive was assassination in pursuit of a feud, rather than robbery: there had been a legal dispute with the Dicksons in 1501, resolved in Middlemas's favour. But the consequences, when George's son Thomas (circa 1500-1566) was still a minor, were serious for the family's estate; Easter Plora being handed over to John Murray with the house, while Glen was reassigned, at the Peebles head court, into three: Thomas (then aged 12) Gilbert Cockburn and Janet Murray (who sold her share on to James Stewart of Traquair). This may also explain why there was no Middlemas in the roll-call at Flodden, and no effective kin support for the senior branch's eviction from Middlemast lands at Kelso after that defeat.

On his coming of age, 1517, Thomas was vested in what were now the 18 husband lands of Grieston and Gillishaugh, with the tower house and the village (toun), together with the one third of Glen, salmon fishing rights in the Tweed, and Wester Plora – a fair sized lairdship, but by comparison with his neighbours, no longer in the first rank. Nevertheless, he inherited some of his ancestors' political weight, and rather more than his share of their disreputable youth: being one of those accused of the 1526 murder of Kerr of Cessford, brother of the lord Warden of the March.

*Musicians in the 15th Century (MS Bodleian Library)*

*Dining entertainment, 15th century,(MS British Library)*

This was not a crime to be ignored by the authorities or by the Kerrs.[94] Fortunately, after the first indictment, with its sentence of outlawry, the justice clerk told the assize in August "that it is understood to my Lord of Angus and to the laird of Ferniehurst (Mark Kerr, the Warden) and the rest of the friends of the (late) Lord of Cessford that "these persons underwritten (the list including Thomas) are innocent thereof and were not of the committing of the same." Thomas was free again, never actually having been imprisoned.

But the affair left a question mark, and only four years later, his name appears among those pursued by James V, after the Earl of Angus's treason.[95] The King's crackdown set heavy penalties "to keep good rule within their respective borders." Some lairds were actually hanged, as was the raider Johnny Armstrong from the West March, others banished for a time, including Bothwell, various Humes, Scott of Buccleugh, Kerr of Ferniehurst, and Lord Polwarth – and the record, 18-19 May 1530, sets out a long list of Border notables who gave signed sureties before the Selkirk justices. Thomas's was in the substantial sum of 500 merks.

His more respectable life in middle age belongs in Chapter 7. But this much sets the tone for the period of James V, before the latter's death at Solway Moss and before the ruthless English incursions of the mid-1540s, with their devastation of Roxburghshire and Berwickshire. The Borders may, as modern historians tend to argue, have become generally less violent; but well-to-do individual lairds, especially when young, pursued land, women, status, and wealth in an environment where aspiration easily succumbed to arrogance, status to flamboyance, courtesy to extreme hostility.

Almost as if in reaction to the quarrelsome intemperate Border lairds' feuding, litigating, even murdering, the first tremors of the coming earthquake-Reformation began, unsettling men's minds and daily habits and cutting short, not only the life of the old Church, but the habits of late-medieval Scotland. The Reformation came later but more abruptly than in England and there was no need for a Thomas Cromwell, since the monasteries had already been undermined by their lay commendators' sales of lands and by the slow drying up of religious vocation.

There would be no more Middlemas vocations under the Catholic Church, as the linked families experienced the transition from a lairdship still redolent of feudality (despite the existence within the formal feudal system of elements of a cash market in land) to the early modern opening-up of a market economy. They started with the handicap of losing Glen and much of the original Kelso land – their marriage bond with Scott of Haining being inadequate to defend them against Abbot Kerr and his powerful brother – but their new association with the Humes, begun in Ettrick, brought its own benefits at Lilliesleaf, Eildon and Midlem and in the valleys of Kalewater south of Kelso.

During this last medieval century, the kin-group as a whole seemed to have solved the inherent problems of transition and survival. They had established relatively secure title to lands, albeit still under feudal tenure, and born adult male heirs to inherit it. They had survived events that caused other families to fail: collapse of the Douglas fiefdom, plague, years of bad harvest, raids and rebellions, without much help from what central authority existed in the years from James I to James V. But the problem remained, that land, the only real measure of wealth, was a positional good, since there could never be enough to satisfy ambitions, certainly not of junior branches descended from younger sons. Neither were they important enough now, in the increasingly centralised politics of Mary Queen of Scots, to merit grants from Royal authority, as Sir William and the first Thomas had done. History's lottery condemned them to survive as provincial lairds, unless they acquired education, or access to the Court.

Marriage remained the best answer, and indeed, with the Hume marriage in 1567, this did pay off. But, apart from that benefit to Lilliesleaf, those of the 15$^{th}$ century could not, realistically, be repeated: Cockburns, Murrays, Scotts already aimed higher, and only their younger sons' daughters were available. Even these marriages might put them in the front line of Border feuds; while the Williamson experience militated against toying with the risks associated with commercial wealth in a pre-capitalist economy.

This did not prevent them having their daughters educated, and Jonate in one generation, Margaret and Malie in the next (see Chapter 7) demonstrated the ability of women, especially widows, to survive on their independent rentals. Yet even these did best by marrying again because, for the core family, marriage was often a weaker link than kinship, with its multiple obligations and group mutual aid. Worse, even though daughters retained the name, their children bore other names, and meshed with other kin – as did Margaret Cockburn's, taking Middlemas land with them.

In the later 15th century and through most of the 16th, bonds of manrent formalised some of this kin structure with its extensive, almost tribal safety nets. [96] Most defined the relationship between two men of differing social order, providing service in return for security and support.[97] Between equals in status – a better measure for the time than wealth – there were agreements, bonds of friendship with neighbours, or legal ones, sanctified by the church to prevent feuds or assyth (placate) their results, as in the 1530 attempt to settle the Scott-Kerr long quarrel.[98]

For the Middlemas family with its small numbers, extending as yet no further than 3rd or 4th cousins, all the name-kind (still spelled with a final t, *mast* or *most*) needed to be involved. Hence no written bonds were used, and by the time that kinship began to break down generally in the mid-17th century, the conditions which had earlier held them together, also began to erode, leaving at the end only the honour code, last legacy of the medieval past.

As the kin-group widened, especially in the dangerous early 16th century, the style Middlemas of Middlemas was regularly used, both as a badge of status, and a guarantee of kin headship,[99] not essentially different from the code in southern Italy in the 17th century or *Pushtunwali* in modern Afghanistan. Pride lay not just in lands, expensive chattels like Plora's contents, or fine clothes, but lineage and heraldry, following a patrilinear line whether mythical or real. There is of course no way to know whether 16th century lairds remembered their origins or Sir William's provision for them. The "de" had long vanished, but the heraldry remained, at least as far as the crest is concerned, the stag's head appropriate to their position in the former ward of Yarrow.

# 6.

# Living Like a Laird: The Early Modern Borders

To the historian, all periods are ones of transition, between ever-fluctuating definitions of beginning and end; which may account for the continuing need for narrative to leaven analysis. Time moves, or history would merely revolve like a man-made mobile oscillating between light and shade. What Huizinga, in a famous study in the 1930s, called "the waning of the Middle Ages," offers perhaps the best mode through which to approach the transition to the early modern age, for nothing abrupt occurred and the Borders remained deeply conservative, both in farming and domestic life. Yet between 1450 and 1600, the patterns of living altered profoundly, so that the old landmarks of work or faith began to disappear.

Rampant misbehaviour by the younger Middlemas lairds was only froth on this *longue durée*. Nevertheless, it signified the responses to change within families by men who faced economic and social risks different in quality from those of their grandparents, which in turn forced them to act more aggressively, even outrageously to ensure survival. Their reaction set a new, often physically violent tone, captured by Elizabethan dramatists such as Webster or Marlowe, or in Scotland itself Sir David Lyndesay.

Who then was, and what were lairds, the landowners who north of the Border equated to English gentry, and who can also be compared to the Spanish *hidalgo*? Definitely not the nobility, with their hereditary titles, and indeed owing obligation to those who remained their feudal superiors; yet with no defined lower social limit; and to compound complexity, different from the nobility only in degree of wealth and power, not in kind. A laird did not normally work his land with his own hands, yet his younger son might, without losing immediately the dignity; and in times of famine or devastation by war, all would labour for survival. For at least one generation after dropping out of the landowning elite, a man might retain the manners and style of the laird, yet a well-off laird might dress habitually in the same rough jerkin and trews as his cottars or husbandmen. Only after Mary Queen of Scots' time, and under French influence, would he follow Pepys' advice "I must go handsomely, whatever it costs me" and spend more on his clothes than did his wife on hers.[100]

One social historian of the Border counts 307 laird families, defined as those holding a minimum of two husband lands (52 acres).[101] Most had much more: the average seems to have been about one thousand acres, if one counts *total* land, aggregating what really counted, the arable, with pasture and waste – of which 200-300 acres might have been the ploughed infield; slightly smaller than the usual criterion in Northumberland. By the 1500s, however, a class of grander laird families, Douglas of Cavers, Scotts, Pringles, Kerrs, Cranstons, had achieved local dominance, among whom the Middlemases still just ranked when Mary became Queen. On the other side, in Northumberland, they can be compared with Dacres, Ogles, Grays, Herons, Fenwicks, and Widdringtons. But in terms of wealth and power, rather than status, the differentiation between greater lairds and the rest grew rapidly, so that in the early modern period, the former might aspire to be part of the nobility, the latter remained part of a rural gentry class.

So long as he held land, whether by the remnants of feudal tenure or increasingly, by purchase and feuing, the head of a family counted as a laird, most of his medieval military obligations having been commuted for cash or rental much earlier. What then defined him was his occupation, his pursuits and pleasures, and his birth – the last implying not only social status but place in the kinship group. In one as small as this, there was originally no need to rely on the style Middlemas of Middlemas, and the fact that this emerged in the 16th century indicates not only how small the group still was but how dangerously it was often exposed.

Even so, by the 1600s, some at the lower end were already emigrating and it is fair to assume that several, of whom there is no record, had been on the way down in terms of status and occupation for a century already. Yet they were also kin, whether plain soldiers or husbandmen, as the events at Dumbarton Castle under its constable William Middlemas in the 1610s demonstrated. The close family were direct kin by blood, the extended family beyond second cousins could be defined by name; and perhaps until the mid-17th century by geography.

Land-holding being the criterion, lairds managed what estates they had, enjoying a leisure which clearly separated them from those that had little or none. Nothing changed radically in land management between 1450 and the 1600s in Tweed, Teviot, the lands ringed by the Cheviots, Southern Uplands, Moorfoot Hills, and Lammermuirs; as late as 1799, John Fuller in his *History of Berwick*, noted the bad roads and the deleterious effects of the run-rig (strip) system of cultivation in which "for mutual security and defence, every man's lands were so interwoven with those of others as to resemble the teeth of a comb... the greatest obstacle to the improvement of agriculture."[102]

Yet most historians now emphasise how much had been done by the later 17th century, in advance of the great wave of 18th century "improvement," by lairds' slow accumulation of expertise. This was despite the inertia of inhabitants restricted by the short-term nature of their tenure and complete absence of capital to invest, living as they did in small, scattered rural communities or "touns," on a subsistence diet of bere (barley), and oats, leavened by wheat, kail, beans, and peas, with crop returns of 1:3-4 compared with today's 1:20. Pigs, sheep, and cattle and of course horses – the only means of land transport – counted as moveable wealth, even if fleeces weighed as little as two pounds, and a cow gave only 100 gallons a year. There was of course no other source of manure.

A laird's management consisted of allocating land on his estate in accordance with customs dating back centuries, policing the run-rig boundaries, deciding when stock should be moved between waste and arable land after reaping, how best to balance the crop-growing infield and the less good outfield, when to start transhumance, when to get in hay for those animals set to survive the winter for the next year's breeding, which ewes and cows to slaughter in the autumn for salted beef and mutton, and how to police the salmon catch from the Tweed, what drainage improvement might be attempted, or what trees cut or planted. He would be directly involved in his own home farm, the mains around his house, and preside over toun life or many touns on his estates. In his own baronial court, like Thomas Middlemas at Glen, he would adjudicate on trespass, encroachment or theft, maybe even what we now call GBH. He might, if humane, extend "kindly tenure" to a son after a father's death, assist a widow, or remit rent in time of disease, English raids, or dearth.

One would have to be a farmer and an agronomist to assess the balance between soil and climate on one hand, health, live birth rate and contentment on the other; a crossing point for his people being a full stomach and a good night's rest. He lived in a stone-built house, they in two-room bothies made of wooden beams, wattle and daub, easy for raiders to burn but equally easy to rebuild. Well-to-do lairds like Grieston and Lilliesleaf after 1571 might have as few touns as 10 or as many as 20 on their land. Touns might have 10-15 such primitive lodgings, in a still sparsely populated countryside: all four southeast Border counties held only 100 to 110,000 people in the 16th century.[103]

By the early 17th century, in the cold period sometimes called the "Little Ice Age," the old differential between the upland valleys and the richer lands of the Merse had grown more acute: barley could be cut in August on the plain but not till a month later upstream. Kelso Abbey had maintained one of its granges at 1,000 feet in 1200, impossible thereafter (despite a remission in the early 16th century) until the 20th century. Harsh conditions shortened the growing season after very bad winters, as in 1564-65, and agriculture in the southeast did not really escape this distress till the mid-18th century. The 1690s were the worst, with seven crop failures out of eight years in Tweed and Teviot; and it was in those years that the farmers' debts piled up, to the detriment of even long-established laird families in the early 18th century.

Given these constraints and the fact that longer winters, bad roads and lack of capital militated against radical improvement, a family's fortunes rested to a large extent on whether they held land in the better economic geography of the coastal plain. Those who did best, of course, were merchants and traders, whether in the small burghs or growing cities, men like Gilbert Williamson and his brother, whose grandchildren by the 17th century were again buying land. Yet markets remained small, compared with

Edinburgh and Berwick (the latter before 1603 often not open to Scots) and restricted by local traders' monopolies at Peebles, Selkirk or Roxburgh. Wool continued to be the main trade, exported to the Flanders staple till 15th century wars diverted it to Walcheren. By the 16th century, cloth, fish and hides became major exports, and later on salt and coal. Scotland was, in short, a primary producer, not yet a manufacturer except of cloth and linen.

All trade patterns linked the Borders closely to Edinburgh, by 1530 the centre for 90% of the wool trade. Landowners took on the role of sheep farmers, replacing the monks of Melrose and Kelso as the owners of vast flocks. Yet the selling price of wool fell steadily, exacerbated by currency debasement's effect on the pound Scots.[104] [Although this was not so dramatic as Henry VIII's debasement of the English currency in the 1540s, the deliberate Scottish debasement lasted longer, from 1470-1600, reducing parity with England from 3:4 in the 1350s to 1:12 by 1600], leaving lairds little better off, beset by costs of transport, prey to guild monopolies, war, theft, scarcity of labour, and price inflation – the latter having the most grievous consequence for lairds who, for one reason or another, could not or did not raise their tenants' rents, or who failed to turn them off the land for sheep, by the mid-17th century.

Conversely, husbandmen and small farmers did well, if they hung onto land at old, fixed rents or lived close enough to developing markets, as towns replaced touns as centres of prosperity. Many landlords failed in the 16th century to do more than hold their own. As for the cottar or labourer, Sir David Lyndesay in 1550 portrayed them

*whose raiment was all raggit, revin and rent,*
*with visage lean, as he had fastig lent, and*
*fordwest fast his wais he did advance*
*with ane richt melancolious countenance*

The point, for the peasant, being that 'they,' the lazy, richer landlord "live through me and I die through them."[105]

It is not easy to assess how the Middlemases did in this period. The fact that Cockburn sued Thomas for 400 sheep in the 1490s, does not prove how many he had in all, compared say with Alexander Hume of Dunglass who possessed 2,618 in 1424. The only two valid measures of wealth are land itself as *property*, the security of their tenure from generation to generation, and the size and condition of their houses.

We know only what thc 'landit men' held, principally the two main branches, Grieston and Lilliesleaf, but also including the rest in Eildon, Midlem and the small farms around Hownam, up Kale Water. South of Kelso, John Middlemas in 1657 had 29 separate run-rig strips to farm. Subdivision, of course proliferated the numbers of holdings in small touns like the Middlemases' old lands of East and Wester Softlaw or Sprouston, between co-heirs and portioners; but John was an exception in the second half of the 17th century since lairds used every means they had to rationalize holdings, albeit tempered by the fear of creating social discontent.

Grieston was still held by the formal feudal payment of the silver penny but had in fact been acquired by purchase; Glen had been reassigned after George Middlemas's murder in 1512. The main accretion came via the Hume dowry in 1571, with the 18½ husbandlands (500 acres infield, perhaps 1,000 outfield, at Lilliesleaf, which derived originally from the land feued by Melrose Abbey).

The latter was certainly good, fertile land, farmed for centuries by monks; the same was true in Eildon. The valleys in Glen, Plora and Kale Water were less good, some of Grieston's hills and moors, marginal. Other Middlemas holdings were mostly heritable, but some of the kin-group had clearly become husbandmen by the later 16th century, possessing either tenure for life (extendable by kindly tenure but not of right) or on short-term tacks (leases), a difficult slope to be on, in bad years. Some acquired special skills, like the Middlemas family of professional shepherds at Longformacus in the mid-17th century.

One cannot sum up the kin-group as a whole in the early modern period, even if relations between laird-owners and their tenants appear to have better in Scotland over the whole period than in England. There were no peasants' revolts. But if one part of the family declined to the status of cottar, they lacked any security

*Export of wool, Late Middle Ages, (MS Biblioteque Nationale Paris)*

of tenure, and if below that, as labourers, they had nothing. In what remained of the vernacular agrarian society, by 1600, many lairds' farming depended on day labourers in a cash economy, which worked to the detriment of those on second-grade land, or embedded in older, possibly kindlier ways.

The lairds held office, as *nobilitas minor*, in baronial courts like Glen or Lilliesleaf, and in smaller estate ones dealing with local matters, and they presumably had working knowledge of the law as custom. With the Humes taking over the Mastership of Yarrow, their duties of keeping order in the Forest (Justice ayre in Yarrow and Glen), overseeing justice and the *vert* rules, and ensuring that there would be plentiful supply of stags to hunt by the King and pasture for his herds, had vanished.[106] Indeed, medieval royal hunting was also disappearing, as James IV resorted more and more to the Forest's potential for rental revenue or feu-farming, and as the original steads were deforested to provide more land for pasture.[107] [The original husbandland denomination did not change, even when large tracts of former waste were incorporated in the 16th century, which makes it hard to tell the actual extent of a holding like Glen or even Lilliesleaf. The latter was technically about 500 acres, but once waste had been incorporated into the infield-outfield system, the Middlemases may have held 1,500 acres or more, with probably 10-15 small touns.]

Within the baronial or burlaw courts, lairds carried out the local bureaucratic duties, regulating mills (usually their own) and breweries, adjudicating on land holdings, crop rotation and the collection and payment of teinds to the priest (or post-Reformation minister) and the diocese. But apart from these really local matters, after James VI's assertion of royal jurisdiction, more serious matters in the later 16th century such as offences carrying the death penalty, were steadily being withdrawn from the jurisdiction of individual lairds.

Some were of course judges of assize,[108] others becoming notaries (solicitors); and in terms of status, the titular kin heads maintained the style Middlemas of Middlemas within the group and in legal documents. Inheritance does not appear to have failed for any branch until the mid-17th century at Grieston; for the other branches, problems came later and were of a different sort.

Military service as part of tenure had vanished long before, being replaced by cash rents (mails). (Enlistment in the Bishops' War in 1638 occurred for reasons of religion and ideology.) So land had become property, with a mixed economy of landlord and tenant linked to local markets,[109] even if feudal vestiges survived. Within the southeast as a whole, the greater families of Scott of Buccleugh, Hume, Kerr of Cessford, and Kerr of Ferniehurst, Douglas of Cavers, Murray of Philliphaugh, by 1600 had established district or even regional estates; and Middlemases, from being once comparable to those families' cadet branches, had, apart from Grieston and Lilliesleaf, become subordinate, straightforward owners and lairds on hereditary tenures. Their 17th century comparators would be Pringles, Turnbulls, Rutherfords. Nevertheless, as late as 1581, they were significant enough in Border politics to have signed the Scott of Buccleugh bond (below, page 112).

As for their houses, what survives indicates their effective wealth. They fall into two categories: simple pele towers, square or rectangular, built of stone with one room on each of three levels, and a narrow stairway in the angle of two walls, with an open fire and a downpipe for lavatory and waste; and larger peles with attached buildings, a hall for dining, domestic offices, perhaps a larder. Both were roughly fortified, not against a marauding army, but enough to stave off rievers' attacks or armed forays for a few days, as prescribed by the Royal Edict of 1535 "for saving of men their goods and gear in time of war, and all troublous time." Both needed a source of water, either a burn or well and a kailyard – though a few livestock might be held within the tower at ground level under the vaulted ceiling, if the door with its iron yett (grid) were on the first floor.

Comfortable these were not, but they served in rough times, far more substantial than the houses of the tenants, with their single hearth and no chimney, whose walls and roofs were finished off in brush, wood and mud. But by the late 16th century, and even more after 1600, a great rebuilding began, as lairds followed the pattern set by kings and nobility, driven not only by fashion, but fashion's twin, competition with other lairds. As numbers of families who bought feued lands from the monastic reserves rose, counting themselves as lairds, they needed a better style of dwelling than what were beginning to be seen as primitive survivals. Houses of the $17^{th}$ century would be for living, for guests, for display, not safety from attack; and the 20,000 or so tower houses all over Scotland, noted by every medieval foreigner, either slipped into long decay or were incorporated in more grandiose rebuilding – often beyond a laird's final capacity to pay.

As a result of what is fair to call "upward mobility," licences to build rather than to fortify or aggrandise became the norm, with dressed sandstone courses, quoins and architraves, renaissance precursors of the $18^{th}$ century classical revival. None of this was cheap and the rebuilding of Plora may be what worsened Thomas Middlemas' finances in the 1490s. [Thomas would have paid for infeftment, a down payment on the land, then grassums and Crown confirmation – perhaps interspersed with bribes, then feu-duty assessed on the lump sum, all before he began the rebuild.]

An English visitor in 1591 commented, "the houses....are but one little stone tower, garretted and slated or thatched...such be all the lairds' houses in Scotland."[110] That would describe Schytinglee of whose earthworks a few mounds remain, marked on Blaeu's map late $16^{th}$ century. (Glengabire may have been an unfortified timber structure or barmkin. Of Eildon and Glen there is no trace.) Grieston was larger, contained in its rectangular triple ramparts which are still extant 120 yards by 42 yards with remains of a stone outer revetment and a 10-foot wide entrance gate in the diagonal,[111] and by the early $17^{th}$ century it had been extended, probably by the Thomas Middlemas who married Katherine Stewart of nearby Traquair, as a "mansion, fortalice, etc."

By the 1620s, however, the Stewarts themselves, recusant Catholics (as Thomas almost certainly was also) were lavishly extending Traquair into the great house of today; in sharp contrast, once the Middlemases of Grieston had died out, the house was quarried for its dressed stone after its own nearby quarry had been worked out.

If Grieston was of intermediate size, the two towers at Lilliesleaf and Lilliesleaf Chapel fall in the same category, but taller, with corbelled roofs and courtyards. But nothing of these remains,[112] although the sites and farm buildings and the ruins of the much earlier chapel, are shown on Stobie's map of 1772. All three can be compared with Cramond (Douglas, late 15th century), Corbet (15th/16th century) and Lanton (Douglas of Cavers 15th/16th century).

The one exception is Plora, one of the steads of Ettrick Forest (see illustration and site plans), high up above the village of Bold. With its massive 4 foot-thick walls of the main tower, 25 by 20 feet interior, two apartments 54 by 20 feet, and great hall 40 feet by 20 feet, together with outbuildings, offices, and a substantial courtyard surrounded by complex earthworks, it falls in the same category as Smailholm Tower (Pringle, then Scott of Harden), Tranent (late 15th century) or Minto (Turnbulls then Elliots 16th century).[113] That it was improved further in the 17th century, when the terraces became gardens, like those of Neidpath Castle, is suggested by a 1722 description of it as "a gentleman's house betwixt two hills with a great deal of wood."[114]

The 1535 edict set out basic elements of design. Built of stone with lime mortar, the vaulted stone ceiling protected those above from fire; servants slept on the ground floor with the cattle in time of attack. A narrow circular stair led up to the living room and then to the sleeping room above, both with open fires of the French pattern. Every landit man with a hundred pounds a year:

> Sall big ane sufficient barmkyn apoun his heritage and landis, of stane and lyme contenance thre score futis of the square, ane eln thick, and six elnes heicht for the reset and defenss of him, his tennents, and his gudis in troublous tyme, with ane toure in the samen for himself gif he thinkis it expedient. And all uther landit men of smaller rent and reuenew big pelis and gret strenthis as they plese for saifing of thare selfis, etc.; and that all the saidis strenthis, barmkynis, and pelis be biggit and completit within twa zeris under pane.[115]

There is obviously no single date by which a need for comfort took priority over security behind the iron yett; Thomas Middlemas of Plora may have made the error of embarking on it half a century too early – and the Plora inventory certainly lists richer contents than most houses of the late 15th century. Craig-Brown assessed the typical tower house as much simpler, even cruder.

> The hall would contain trestle tables, benches, possibly a high-backed chair for the chief, a side table or compter, and a chest for linen. The upper room would contain a bed, a clothes chest, and possibly a stool. The floors would be covered with rushes, the walls bare masonry. Hangings would be very unusual at this period. Lighting in the evenings would be practically non-existent, or at best by a wick floating in oil. On the roof there was an outlook or barbizan with a brazier ready charged with wood to blaze the alarm of attack.[116]

Such a tower house could be built in the 15th century for around £300. Plora's rebuilding may have cost twice that, more if there had been renaissance carving on the architraves and roof cornice.[117] All of which indicates that Thomas' income would have been more than £300 to 400 a year; but it is impossible to be more exact. His wealth was built up of house and contents, flocks and land, and in different combinations the same is true for all his kindred down to cottars with their tiny vegetable gardens, two-roomed huts, and scant store for the winter snow time.

The clearest line between laird and tenants was leisure, which he had and they rarely if ever enjoyed – though the late medieval Sundays and Feast days gave occasion for "gamin and gle" absent from the dour Presbyterian Sabbath that encroached steadily after Mary Queen of Scots' time. Leisure meant sports, dining (starting midday in the winter), some reading, music or song, and the pleasure of company, guests, family, passing notables like Piccolomini. Royal visits to the Forest, on the other hand, counted as very serious business. Music in fact had become an essential element in lairds' houses, often based on tuition, even if the instruments were fewer and cruder compared with noble houses: lute, viol (or fiddle), flute and harp (clarsach).

Sport, apart from the anarchic football of whole touns, spread over miles, or shinty with few rules and often extreme violence, or curling and skating in winter, common to all, meant horses and hounds and frequently, like archery or jousting, derived directly from war. Hounds might be for hunting, equally for sleuthing and chasing thieves. Being the only form of transport, horses were valued as are modern motorcars, the finer and faster the better:

heavy horses for war, lighter ones for the chase.

Racing had emerged as a well-organised sport, one of the earliest references in Scotland being from Peebles Burgh Court book in 1569, asking one winner from the previous year to restore his prize of a silver bell and an arrow from an archery contest. By 1608, crowds at the Peebles May meeting forced the Privy Council to consider a ban, fearing trouble "from the great numbers of people of all qualities and ranks....betwixt whom there being quarrels, private grudges and miscontentment."[118] Fifteen years later the main race was won by a black gelding, property of Sir John Stewart of Traquair. It is hard to imagine that his neighbours at Grieston failed to attend this and earlier races, along with Murray of Blackbarony and other relations, recorded as winners.

Municipal racing was organised enough to involve wide advertisement, family colours, proper weight handicapping, minimum number of horses and a well-defined course. But there were also matches between individual lairds, usually as a result of wagers: in one 1576 case John Hume staked his silver bell and £10 against a friend. An essential part of this was the care and time devoted to breeding, although before the arrival of 18th century Arab stock, their standard must have fallen short even of naïve 17th century hunting paintings.

In Robert Wedderburn's 16th century *Complaynt of Scotland*, his heroine Lady Scotia complains: "a man is not reputed for a gentleman in Scotland, unless he makes more expenses on his home and his dogs than he does on his wife and bairns" – a lament echoing down to modern times. A fine horse might be worth a fair part of his fortune, as a racer or a sire: and several Acts of the Parliament attempted in vain to curb gambling and its consequent disorders.

Gambling and cards had existed in the late Middle Ages and would frequently have taken up much of the long winter evenings after dining, accompanied probably by some music, on the lowland pipes (common on both sides of the Border) or a primitive stringed instrument. There is no evidence of a musical culture in the family after Sir William's death but it is hard to imagine it absent from a dinner where guests were present.

Other spectator sports included wrestling, prevalent all along the

Tweed, and cause of many disturbances as at the Berwick Bailiff's Court, 28 February 1572. Hill or fell-running occurred regularly, as it still does in the North, and less dignified games like sack races. Afterwards, as at Berwick, "at 5 o'clock 30 gentlemen members of the games sat down to dinner in Mr. Cockburn's tent."

But the mixture of revelry and rout, inflamed by wine, among a provincial elite still not habituated to the use of the fork, sometimes went wrong, ending up in court: one of James III's favourites, William Roger, a fine musician, angered other courtiers who, led by the jealous Earl of Angus in 1482, hanged him over the side of Lauder Bridge – 70 years before David Rizzio met a similar assassination for over-familiarity with Mary Queen of Scots. Yet conventions, what would by the 19th century be called "fair play," did evolve, from a distant origin in the medieval tournament, to distinguish between sport and trial by combat: *à l'outrance* became *à plaisance*, in boxing, fencing or golf and it is the exceptions that were recorded in the courts.

No theatre existed south of Edinburgh or Haddington, but travelling players circulated, with Scottish versions of morality plays, till banned by the renascent Kirk. Otherwise, in the little burghs, there were the alehouses and the occasional oyster house. No real tennis court existed before James V's one built at Falkland Palace, but golf was already well-established along the North Sea coast, as were primitive forms of squash. Nevertheless Reformation ideology worked against the leisure of non-laird families and did away in the end with Holy days and most festivals, although James VI stood up against the theocrats for football and tennis. Leisure suffered dismally, for all classes in the mid-17th century.

It is not an easy question to answer, whether Border lairds were what Jane Austen called "educated men." In terms of courtesy and behaviour, following the French codes of Mary's court, yes; literacy was widespread among 16th century lairds, though less common among their women folk; very few, even of "bonnet lairds" were unable to sign their names. An Act of 1496 had imposed Latin as an obligation for all lairds' eldest sons from the age of eight, and tutors were common enough in their houses – especially recusant ones. Generally, education in a laird household came from a local priest or later the manse; but its quality depended on its provider, ill paid and possibly barely literate himself. As in England, education took a hard blow with the dissolution of the monasteries. Such were the Kirk's financial straits in the 16th and early 17th centuries, that Scottish rural-provincial education may have been worse in 1650 than in 1450.

In terms of manners, southern Scotland never ceased to be part of a European tradition, and in some respects, deliberately so. The Middlemas of Lilliesleaf judge who tried witches at Selkirk in the 1620s knew, if only from his Privy Council instructions and what the King had already written, how the obsession had spread across the whole Continent already. Middlemas lairds probably knew the literature of the period and the Border ballads (in their original form), some of the chroniclers like William Dunbar or Gavin Douglas, and perhaps John Major's *History of Kings and Kingship* (printed in Edinburgh 1507-8) and the 16th century social critics like Lindesay. They are unlikely to have known much science outside agricultural practice; painting, beyond medieval scriptural scenes in parish churches, remained the prerogative of only the very grandest houses.

As for their wives and daughters, the question is purely speculative. Women's role – in so far as we understand it from the very scarce sources available,which say nothing about intimacy, tenderness or love – existed in and through the family, essential for its future transmission through birth, upbringing and, if widowed, through safeguarding the endowment that remained. They, almost as much as their husbands, helped to maintain the kinship ties, expectations and obligations essential to the proximate family itself. A woman did have legal status, especially if she were a portioner in lands in her own right. Daughters were worth educating if only to make their prospects more attractive – though a laird had always to calculate the balance between an influential match and the cost of a bride's tocher (dowry); for which reason, roughly one-third of lairds' daughters never married.

For women below that class, whether wives of husbandmen or simply labourers, the pattern was and would remain set until the 19th century: hard, rural labour, milking, feeding, shearing, spinning, gathering hay and peats, dung spreading, carrying, cleaning byres and stables; but not men's work, such as scything or ploughing. Courbet and Millais painted such women, even in the 1850s. Then came all the household tasks. In the burghs, one could add, shopkeeping, alehouses, and trading – albeit for wages only half or one-third those of men.[119] By the early 17th century, surplus women were already migrants in Edinburgh and Tyneside.

Women of the upper class might, however, wear a few items of gold, even jewels, though their dress, in the Borders, was barely finer than their mainly homespun husbands'. Men, apart from farming dress of jerkin and trews, had long abandoned the mail sleeves and head pieces associated with light cavalry and, if in a town or city, would go in doublet and hose, under a fleece-lined coat or cloak – and by 1600 no longer "well horsed and wholly armed, as a gentleman should be." Such were the sumptuary laws and the Kirk's criticism that even Edinburgh went less lavishly than most English cities.

Servants were another sign of a laird's status and wealth. It might no longer be appropriate to call it a retinue, but a laird's household staff could vary in the Borders between 10 and 20. Middlemas of Lilliesleaf probably had the former in the 1580s, Middlemas of Grieston the latter. George Middlemas of Gosswick, just south of Berwick, attended the Northumberland muster in 1583 with 10 men at arms from his own staff, as befitted a gentleman, and the lord High Treasurer paid Robert Middlemas [probably of the Grieston branch] for the service of eight men to fight the English c. 1550.[120] James VI's late 16th century limits were set at six armed men for a baron, knight or laird.

But a laird would still know how to use his sword; perhaps, Italian-style, with a dagger in his other hand, and how to shoot both pistol and a rifled-barrelled gun. Border necessity reinforced skill at arms: 16th century penalties for non-attendance at shire musters remained harsh (though not always enforced) on both sides of the Border – 10 merks minimum in 1585. Most lairds would also have known how to load and discharge a culverin, and one early 17th century Middlemas migrant considered it fine for a gentleman to be apprenticed to a noted Edinburgh gunsmith.

Such knowledge, such ability to defend against, or overawe

an enemy, remained a vital element of male survival well into the 1600s. Risks to life and limb are the easiest to categorise: raiding, feud, reprisals, all-out war; and the limited means to ensure against them are also obvious, in an age before either police force or even a standing army. Yet, despite what English northerners thought about the Scots in general and the Borders in particular, the East March was not, according to modern historians, an especially violent place; certainly less so than its counterpart the West March. Much of its reputation as a haunt of reivers, thieves and worse can be ascribed to post-Enlightenment historians' views that everything dating from before the 18th century was "primitive and horrid."[121]

Thus Sir John Forster, English Commissioner of the East March, could write to his opposite number in West Teviotdale in February 1576 complaining of "great and sundry rieffs made by the broken people of Liddesdale and the inhabitants of East Teviot, for that the keepers of these countries are not known and thereby, I am not able to know at whose hands I should ask redress."[122] This at least presumed that there *was* such a possibility, although as another Commissioner pointed out, all depended on the Border guards and watches "where men must needs be, and continue in their seat for service...and at all times have their horse and gear kept."[123]

Almost as bad as the West March were the Northumberland upland valleys of Tynedale and Redesdale. Yet since the 1460s, mixed Scots and English juries had met to settle reparations regularly and evolved rules, which by the late 16th century could be styled Border Laws, part of the Tudor framework,[124] to moderate raiding and deal with tribes of persistent offenders. Even before the 1603 union, this had become ancient custom, vital to the administrations of James IV and V, Henry VII and VIII, to the end of preventing eruptions of violence becoming real wars (though probably nothing could have prevented the folly of Flodden).

Slowly the culture of private armies, freebooting or chevauchèe, declined, surviving by 1600 only in isolated valleys and remoter uplands. The Borders remained porous, fugitives and criminals fled both ways. But the reiver, trucebreaker, blackmailer, grew isolated, more often than not to end up like the bandit Johnny Armstrong "hanged on a growing tree." Custom and law, the establishment of quasi-modern centres of government, increased rural and burgh prosperity, consigned them to the status of ballad heroes or mere "broken men," to be replaced by the habitual early modern *villain*, the sheep and cattle thief, the smuggler, the illegal fisherman, the occupier of his neighbour's lands.[125]

Reiving, followed by "hot trod" (pursuit), of course continued, usually once the harvest was in, committed by impoverished lairds as well as bandit families.[126] But the great reprisal raids were not repeated after the "rough wooing" of the mid-1540s, when for example the English under Lord Evers and Sir Brian Latham in 1544 rampaged from West to East, killing 403 Scots, taking 816 prisoners, over 10,000 cattle and 13,000 sheep, in a campaign of deliberate destruction of economic and social assets. In that sense, later 16$^{th}$ century lairds were never faced with the sort of warfare that blighted Continental Europe in the 30 Years War.

How to curb, if not quell the habit of reiving? As Wormald shows, much of the trouble came from the young, men trained to arms, aspiring to wealth, but lacking land to fund a renaissance lifestyle – in literary forms, Scots' equivalent of Montagus and Capulets. Bonds of varying sorts therefore evolved, both to purge quarrels over slights and to defuse larger feuds or arrange compensation. These might be state-imposed (the "General Band") or set up by kin-groups to prevent violence and land disputes, or to settle intractable feuds like that between Kerrs of Cessford and Scotts of Branxholme, started in 1529, unsettled till 1598.

No other sort of insurance existed then, against what Pitscottie described in 1455 as "spoliation of their beasts, corn and houses destroyed and burned, and sundry gentlemen and commoners hurt and slain for the defence of their goods and gear." Signature of the General Band indicated status and often conveyed remission for past offences; but failure to observe it might lead to severe penalties. James V began the practice in 1529 among "head men of the Merse, Teviotdale, Selkirk, and Peebles" and followed it up in 1551 and 1561, the toughest of all being in 1602. Grieston and Lilliesleaf signed some and their effect appears marked.[127] But it was the kinship bonds, notably with the Scotts in 1589, that gave more prospect to security and redress at local level. Feud was easier to catch earlier, and prevention (assythment by local

Border lairds) did sometimes work – though not in time to save George Middlemas's life in 1512. The role of lairds in itself tended towards better order and though overall the Border may have been no more disciplined at the end of James VI's personal rule than it was in the 1450s, in the sense that violence remained endemic, the region was certainly less actively *lawless* than its later reputation suggests.

But none of this reduced the burden of self-preservation: avoidance of risk, maintenance of secure houses, armed defence of one's lands, the need for prudence as well as access to law, together with able-bodied sons and like-minded responsive kin. The bond created by Sir Walter Scott of Branxholme "and his friends one with another" in 1589 was signed by 43 Scott lairds, William Middlemas of Lilliesleaf and three other names; it repeated an earlier, similar "act and ordinance" of his grandfather's day and bound them all "for the avoiding of controversies, debates and plays among Sir Walter's friends.." to act "in amity and friendship and familiarity and like as brethren and friends ought to be amongst themselves."

In substance, none were able to take or encompass title or enter on each other's lands, and if they did, Branxholme himself would adjudicate and with four others pronounce legal sentence. So would four of his own kin if he were the accused. Local law enforcement at the end of the 16th century evidently still had a better chance than that of the King.

***

What then did kinship mean by this early modern period? Obviously, it was as it always had been, agnatic – based on the male line, linking all of the same name to the head of the dominant family branch, linked to common understanding by cadet branches or migrant offshoots. [It is of some significance that the spelling of Middlemas often contained a final "t" until the mid or late 18th century, whether "mast" or "mist" or "most." Only by the early 18th century do the modern endings "mas," "mass," "mis," and "miss" predominate, and some still used the final "t" into the 19th century.] The title Middlemas of Middlemas meaning "of that ilk" was used in the 16th and early 17th century first at Grieston, then at

Lilliesleaf, and finally at Morebattle, appropriately for the period when kin loyalty provided an effective dimension of security.

Its generic value can be read in the history of much larger families, where bonds and testaments added a quasi-legal validity, though these were rarely necessary among the small numbers of Middlemases. Kinship relations with other families by marriage (enhanced by written bonds such as that of the Scotts in 1589), widened the basis of insurance against disaster, while "to possess distinguished sons-in-law added greatly to a laird's worship, and his worldly repute. Disposal of the hand of a daughter was his chief opportunity to forge a valuable connection."[128]

Marriage reinforced other bonds of mutual support: most occurred within 10-15 miles distance, rarely lapping over from east to west March, and was actually illegal across the Border. Within that narrow geographical band, just as central state power seemed far away, compared with local jurisdictions, so the King's justice needed reinforcement. Better still, kinship covered a whole range of needs: money-lending in time of trouble and security for debt, care of children (tutorships), the old and widows, and refuge in emergency. Moreover, loyalties tended to be stronger at the base, especially when the centre was disturbed, as it was throughout Queen Mary's reign and into the 1590s.

In a small group then, kin were a natural source of help, if only as witnesses to documents or executors for testaments (wills); and the likelihood of serious division, like the Hume's factions, pro-French or pro-English under Regent Morton, or internal feuds, was small. (The Middlemases gained from the 5th Earl Hume's favour, but were put at risk when the 6th Earl rejoined Queen Mary and by his subsequent forfeiture in 1573; the danger only lifting as he recovered favour with James VI in the 1590s.)

There is a resemblance to the 19th century Sicilian godfather, in the style of headship and tutelage, not least in the significance of the child's baptism and parent's choice of godfathers, whose role was to assist in binding the family within the kin group. Unlike English practice, Scottish baptism defined the social and legal as well as spiritual status of the father, and his position within the kin group.

Thomas Middlemas of Mangerton acted as guardian for the

Lilliesleaf children as late as the 1650s; and protection extended to illegitimate children, whether among the Humes with Mariota's settlement in 1576, or through political leverage, ensuring Queen Mary's legitimation of George Middlemas in 1547. In one sense, the 1638 National Covenant itself represents a kinship bond, voluntarily undertaken by a confraternity not of names, but of minds, ordered by degree: nobility, lairds, burgesses in that order, in defence of a common interest and identity (recalling the Douglas-Albany Bond of 1409) embodied in the collective religious commitment – even if the outcome was a major war.

But there were other risks, connecting all the kin, rich or poor, against which there might still be an insurance. Towards the end of the Middle Ages, and under the old Church, Sir William – a relatively wealthy priest – had provided for his soul's immortality by selling his town properties to found the Peebles chantry. In the 16th century, and as the Reformation gale blew through Scotland, later kin had to make harder choices: whether to stay Catholic, as a handful of Border families did, including the Stewarts of Traquair (and probably Middlemas of Grieston) or join the new Kirk with its troubling Calvinist assumption that faith and works were not enough, merely overt signs that one *might* be part of the predestined elect.

Rome still had final authority till 1560, long after it had lost to the Anglican settlement south of the Border, though the challenge had already begun with John Knox's arrival in 1547. It would be an error to judge the old Church by what its Reform accusers said, and there is evidence that, reinvigorated by the designation of two archbishops in 1487 by the Pope and the designation of "special daughter of Rome," it was far from moribund. Families were still sending monks to the universities of St Andrews and Glasgow in the 1540s, while the mendicant orders flourished, as did Catholic reformers like Bishop William Elphinstone (1431-1514). Abuses may well have been no worse, mid-16th century, than mid-13th century,[129] and the Church's contribution to learning, even to science and medicine, continued up to the 1550s with Archbishop Hamilton's Reforming Councils.

Until the Mass itself was abolished, 24th August 1560, no ultimate crisis of conscience presented itself to existing laird families; and long after, if they kept a discreet profile, Catholics could practise if not in the Merse, at least in Teviot and upper Tweed. For the Middlemases of Lilliesleaf who seem to have chosen the Kirk without great trauma, the crisis came much later with the "Bishops' War" of 1638, the period of Cromwell's rule, followed by Charles II's Episcopal reaction (Chapter 8). It may well have been that the Border lairds, remote from the Edinburgh religious fever, looked at what the enragés said and did in Knox's time with surprise and even disdain. Only one actually got caught up in the armed quarrels for and against Mary Queen of Scots and he was a younger son, and did it not primarily for a religious reason.

Few lairds were ever accused of heresy and the Lollards who were burned at the stake came from a different level of mainly urban society.[130] Under the new Kirk, whatever political alliances were formed between landed families and the Reformers, serious tests of conscience were avoided until the moment of choice, February 1638, signature of the National Covenant. Even then, the motives of many – perhaps a majority of signatories – were as much patriotic protests against interference in Scottish religious practice by a largely English King's misguided advisers, as profound convictions of belief.

Yet between Huizinga's "Waning of the Middle Ages" and the printing of the King James Bible in 1612, a vast unease had developed, a preoccupation with death and divine punishment, appropriate enough perhaps in the plague years, a search for remedies within the personal soul, a xenophobic focus on outsiders, and what may be described as an early culture of blame – not just the malevolent English or the old Church's abuses – but Jews, witches, and all the paraphernalia of magic and diabolism. It affected all classes and most obviously the King himself, James VI, with his obsessive crusade against witchcraft.

Out of this matrix, and from plain evidence in many parishes about the inadequacy of underpaid, often ill-educated priests, grew a public demand for reform, for an educated parish clergy, responsible to a Scottish religious authority, determined neither by Pope nor King. Knox's brand of Calvinism may not have provided the right doctrinal answer but what mattered was how his words were heard by his contemporaries, not the precise theology behind them. It pointed the way, and if financially it demolished the Catholic version "nae penny nae paternoster," politically it offered the hope and peril of an individual response, based on personal and communal understanding of scriptures in the people's own language, freely printed in Edinburgh or imported from England, interpreted but not enforced by legal authority.[131]

It was this, not heresy nor abuse, which undermined Catholicism from within, after the old Church's final failure to reform in 1558-60. It called into being a remarkable alliance between rural lairds and the urban working class; and since (in the later 16th century at least) it offered the promise of mediation with God rather than punishment, adherence to the Kirk can be seen as another form of insurance, offering survival in another world. Tragically, Scotland's political institutions, within the two-kingdom structure after 1603, and under the rule of Charles I from London, were not adequate to translate this complex balance between individual judgement and state authority into the sort of settlement already provided in England under Elizabeth I.

***

More than this century and a half would be needed before James VI's "middle shires" took real shape, not in fact until the 1630s, only just before war drove the two kingdoms apart again. The Border identity and its kinship "honour code" enjoyed a late redefinition and survived into the 18th century, even the 19th, as the reliance of emigrant Scots, including Middlemases, on their original families at home indicates.

Its last collective expression was perhaps the assertion of Border lairds to be a *fourth* estate in the Parliament of 1587, confronting the dual challenges of a centralising monarch (James VI shortly to be James I of England) and a partly-liberated Kirk, testing its powers of discipline in the regions. In the process, they had to defend their old ideals of kinship and lairdship against the theocratic justification of a new order by both the external forces claiming divinely-inspired central direction.

Since both King and Kirk, for very different reasons, needed the Border lairds' support, these retained collectively a much closer link with the Scottish court and General Assembly than their counterparts in Northern England had enjoyed with London since the end of the Wars of the Roses. But after 1603, the needs of both changed, steadily diminishing not only the region's significance but its way of life. Transfer of power to London matched the end of bonding, creating a sort of social and economic transhumance, as lairds of uplands and valleys in their peles gave way to the landowners of the Merse and the Lothians in their newly-built, unfortified mansions.

*Poultry feeding, from the Luttrell Salter (MS British Library)*

*Agriculture in the early 16th century (scene from the Georgics, (MS British Library)*

# 7.

# Court and Country: The Late $16^{th}$ Century

Mary Queen of Scots' reign appears, in popular accounts, to dominate Scotland in the late $16^{th}$ century, as Queen Elizabeth's does for England. But while the latter perception is largely accurate, the former is not. Mary was an infant when her father James V died, having failed to re-establish full royal authority in the 1530s and having lost another full-scale war with England at Solway Moss in 1542.

Mary's Scotland then had to endure the so called "rough wooing," as Henry VIII launched the devastating Hertford Raids of 1544-45 in pursuit of another Tudor-Stewart marriage alliance. This was followed by the Regency of Arran and Cardinal Beaton; and when Mary was married to Francis II of France she was removed altogether. Only with her return, after her first husband's death in 1561, was she actually Queen of Scots, and that for only six years, until her imprisonment in Lochleven Castle ended in escape and final defeat at Langside.

It is the long time of confinement in England, a perennial threat to Elizabeth, that gave her symbolic importance for later historians; and it was the stormy years of James VI's minority and slow, subsequent establishment of his personal rule, after her execution in 1587, that mattered for the great tracts of Scotland outside Edinburgh and the declining numbers of "Queen's men."

As James V's widow, Mary of Guise, established a benign influence over court and government during Mary's infancy, after the murder of Cardinal Beaton, religious protests by Reformers grew; among whom southeastern nobles and greater lairds took a leading part: Hume, Cockburn, Kerr, some of them in receipt of Henry VIII's pensions. Yet Mary of Guise skilfully maintained Catholic predominance and strong links with France, while preserving Scotland from the unyielding fervour and persecution launched in the southern kingdom by Mary Tudor.

This delicate balance between civil and religious government, linking court and country magnates, ran clean counter to Henry

VIII's earlier intent to join the two kingdoms indissolubly through a Tudor-Stewart heir from Mary and his son Edward; a policy which was continued by Protector Somerset during Edward VI's brief reign. The Hertford raids were intended, quite simply, to coerce the Scots into submission, using the sort of devastation once employed by Edward III. May to September 1544 saw the sack of Edinburgh and the ravaging of the Merse and Teviot, quite different in extent from the aftermath of Flodden; of which the destruction of Kelso Abbey offers only the most notable example. Hertford's report noted coldly how he dealt with the monks' defence:

> Persuaded with their owne folly...they did refuse to render and deliver it...Whereupon I caused the same to be approached out of hand with ordinance and within an hour a grette brech was made...the Scots by and by driven into the steeple but the way being so dangerous and of good strength and night being at hand I decided to leave the assault till morning setting a good watch at night about the House, which was not well kept that a dozen corners with no lytell daunger to their lyves...When the day was come the steeple oftsonnes assaulted it was immediately won and as many Scots as were within slayne.

The Abbey was then gutted, the lead from its roof stripped, and Hertford rode with his army away to do the same to Melrose, Dryburgh, Jedburgh and "all the villages and crops on the way."

The Scots, like the monks, were not persuaded; and although Somerset established a sort of English pale for a time, after his victory at Pinkie, this was steadily eroded, with French help, until Mary's marriage to Francis II. The arrogant assertion of Henrician power had been wholly counterproductive. But the Border counties, their houses and economies suffered grievously, only the upland valleys escaping the worst. Not surprisingly, as they had done in the $14^{th}$ century, many lairds took English bribes and pensions and trimmed, becoming "assured Scots" out of sheer necessity.[132] They were in an occupied territory and undefended by their own government, especially in the Lothians and Berwickshire – and had to, as King Ibn Saud was to say in the 1920s, "always kiss the hand you cannot bite."

The 1540s and 50s then, gave rise to all the old vices of treachery, betrayal, spying and coat-turning (Kerr of Ferniehurst turned twice), but also gave a stimulus to Protestantism, partly because of the damage done to Mary of Guise's compromise. By the time Mary returned as Queen, reform had already gathered momentum, Border lairds' gatherings having formed part of the movement which produced, spectacularly, the Reformation Parliament of 1560.

Lutheran sympathies had been fostered by foreign, usually Flemish traders for over 30 years, undermining the extended life given to medieval religious practice by the limited Catholic reforms of the 1550s. With William Tyndale's vernacular bible in hand (permitted by an act of 1543) and emboldened by Mary of Guise's relative tolerance, literate lairds and what may be called the urban middle class resisted pressures to recant, and extended their criticism to practical matters: payment of teinds, inadequacy of schooling and failure to maintain parish churches. Inflamed by a bizarre combination of John Knox's preaching after 1559, and Queen Elizabeth's order covertly to circulate the English Bible and the Elizabethan Prayer Book, Scottish Border society faced a radical wave, part religious, part political, in the regions as well as the capital, long before peace with England was sealed with the Treaty of Berwick.

Product of two extremes, the 1560 Reformation Parliament was in fact not that radical; and Mary, returning home in 1561, could perhaps have capitalized on a growing sense of national separateness. It abrogated papal authority (as Henry VIII had done 20 years earlier), it prohibited "idolatry" including the mass in Latin (while making an exception for the Catholic queen at home), and repealed all laws restraining the Protestant faith – all within seven days. But it did not create a revolution and Mary took seven years before accepting its edicts. Some churchmen, including a few bishops, simply switched sides, incurring none of the sufferings of Cranmer and the English martyrs under Mary Tudor.

At the Edinburgh centre, radicalism did flourish far more than in the periphery. Border lairds probably remained in the minority among the "godly men" in the early 1560s. But although

Knox raised the stakes (offending Queen Elizabeth with his tirade against "the monstrous regiment of women" actually aimed at Mary of Guise) and sought to establish a theocracy of the elect, it was not he nor his preachers who signed the Band of Lords of the Congregation in 1557, but the Protestant magnates. These held together in pursuit of a settlement, united on the need for reform, ousting of French influence, and defence of their own social order against the dangerous religious revolutionaries like Knox and Andrew Melville.

As a result, the enragés took another quarter century to establish the Kirk's supremacy and then only within a settlement that provided for James VI's claim to rule by divine right. The non-negotiable claims set out by Parliament in the First Book of Discipline 1560 vanished in the face of mundane reality. Outside Edinburgh there were simply not enough ministers, money, or fervent local support to offset the King's opposition to government by Presbytery.

It is to the laird class, the nobility and the urban elites that Scotland owed its escape from what happened in France in the 1790s: there was no Thermidor, and no overthrow of monarchy by a dictator in the mould of Cromwell or Robespierre. This occurred partly because argument concentrated on real needs, in mainly rural areas and small towns, partly because James VI understood far better than the Bourbons how to re-establish civil government, and how to manipulate synods and the General Assembly of the Kirk itself. Episcopacy remained an integral part of his settlement and that climactic battle was postponed until after the 1620s and James VI's replacement by the far less experienced, dogmatic Charles I.

Queen Mary might have gone that way. Initially, she conceded much, without alienating her conservative supporters. Most of the early troubles were local, or remote from the centre, and could be settled by a clever mixture of force and assythment, as used in Border feuds. But she remained isolated, often badly advised by her courtiers and favourites, and her charm, wit and generosity failed to penetrate the public sphere beyond.

Worse, her choice of second husband, Lord Darnley, that "empty-headed fop of nineteen" ended the prospect of accommodation with Elizabeth, because Mary's reaffirmation of papal authority assisted Knox's recovery from his low point of the early 1560s. The majority of nobles and godly lairds stood by their allegiance but remained suspicious of her return to Rome; and the murder of Darnley in October 1567 made problematic the succession of his son, the future king James VI.

Mary's third marriage with the tempestuous Earl of Bothwell, after a passionate too-public affair, set off the explosion, to which both Queen's men and King's men contributed, forcing the majority of her supporters to a harsh choice: which divided the southeast and the Kerrs and put the Humes' whole power base at risk.[133] Such a period of local rivalries, fuelled by a central government dilemma, had not occurred since the late 13th century; and this contributed to Mary's deposition in 1567 – followed in due course by her escape and final defeat at the battle of Langside in May 1568. It also affected very many local affinities and the distribution of influence, including all branches of Middlemases' relations with the Humes and Scotts.

Even so, Mary had managed to raise 6000 men in only 11 days – but the Border contingents arrived too late to fight. The game was not finally lost until her flight to England, the 20 years' imprisonment there providing only a mournful epitaph. Meanwhile, conflicts between the two sides ramified and in turn fed off kinship quarrels and divisions, sparking new feuds and reviving old ones. Infighting at the political centre mutated into a struggle for control of the infant James, accompanied by murders of high ranking nobles and exacerbated by a stream of financial assistance from London, aimed to fund the King's party.

Publication of Queen Mary's incriminating correspondence in 1571, branding her as accomplice in Darnley's murder, ended the last hope that Elizabeth might collude in a restoration, even if this had been possible on English terms. Two year's later, the English captured Edinburgh Castle and handed it to Regent Morton to hold for King James; and Morton proved so efficient at detaching Mary's remaining supporters that a settlement was achieved in a relatively civilised way, with few executions.

On the Borders, Hume was released, while Scott of Buccleugh suffered only the demolition of his house at Branxholm. But quiet lasted only until Morton's downfall in 1580, and disturbances and a Catholic revanche continued: one reason among many for Elizabeth to sign Queen Mary's death warrant. At local level, for example, Jedburgh burgh joined the King, together with Kerr of Cessford, against Kerr of Ferniehurst, one of the Marian leaders. National and local rivalries entwined, and for much of the 1570s, Ferniehurst kept up raids on the burgh, which in turn defended itself, using the English garrison to harry Ferniehurst's lands. When the garrison was withdrawn, the latter with an armed troop swept through the small town, killing as they rode, and nullified the Privy Council's attempts to impose a bond of peace. The feud continued, at the burgh's expense, till the 1590s and beyond.

Various Middlemases were involved here: Andrew Middlemas of Middlemaswalls and his brother John, Edward and George of Mylrig and Lempitlaw, Robert of Sharprig, in the years 1571-76, all on Ferniehurst's side, he being their feudal superior in the ancient Middlemastlands. These, all smaller lairds south and east of Kelso, were heavily fined later for "inter-communing with rebels," "fire raising and pursuing and overthrowing the King's faithful subjects and inhabitants of the burgh of Jedburgh."[134] All four and various Middlemas subordinates were of the Queen's party and evidence from the 1590s confirms that their kin at Grieston and Lilliesleaf were involved on the same side.

Once James VI had signed the Negative Confession, after his mother's execution, a Lutheran compromise developed, in which bishops formed the administrative structure, while the Kirk's clerical oligarchy, bolstered by its own independent legal court, ran in parallel to the three estates in Parliament. Despite all the theocrats' attempts to exclude the laity, the latter continued to manage civil society under the King's authority, and Scotland avoided becoming an English satellite, in its dealings with the rest of Europe.

Attempts to control the King, morally or physically, continued – notably with the Ruthven Raid inspired by Arran, ostensibly to separate him from "undesirables" in 1582. But slowly a core of highly professional royal administrators grew up in the hands of the great lawyer, Maitland of Lethington, who managed the alignment of kinship, patronage, ambition, and loyalty (in that order) with a skill envied even by Elizabeth's first Minister, Lord Burghley. Such statecraft was embodied by George Buchanan in a description of limited monarchy which, if adopted, might have saved the house of Stewart from its 17th century downfall. But James VI, as he came of age, would have none of it: he was King by divine right, a thesis he was later to set out in his remarkable political-religious tract, *Basilikon Doron* 1599.

This may, however, have been the only way at the time to defend civil society against Andrew Melville and the extreme Calvinist theocrats. Similar debates were already dividing European kingdoms, from Spain to Bohemia, where James VI's sister's husband ruled in Prague, in the wake of the Catholic Counter-Reformation, and in advance of the 30 Years' War. At the level of theory, where he took the lead, the King could not admit the right of any estate, or the Kirk to correct him; but in practice, he could only maintain this if his personal rule was stabilised, and if his King's party subsumed what was left of the Queen's one in an undivided civil estate, without alienating the same people and their followers in their new religious affiliation.

James VI's experience predated much of the development of European monarchies; as the gilded court around him showed, with its favourites, perquisites and preferment, launched in sumptuous new palaces, providing a foretaste of Versailles by detaching the Scottish nobility from their regional bases – preparatory to the long march south to London in 1603. Those who lost out in the last twenty years of the 16th century were the Catholic families, and the less grand lairds who for whatever reason, failed – or did not try – to gain purchase at the Court. Thus Scott of Buccleugh was no more than a lord of Parliament in 1595, while the King's favourites and officers – often the same thing – achieved status by preferment rather than extent of lands.

Older, less grandiose families retained their place in the local hierarchy, even after the great move to London. But they found themselves separated by a divide which could hardly have been foreseen: the short political distance to Edinburgh was to become a vast, unknown passage, in which direct royal favour rather than local eminence provided influence, especially after an English anti-Scots reaction developed, to the detriment of the new hangers-on in London.

*Ploughing (above) and Sewing (below), both from the Luttrell Psalter (MS British Library)*

Failure to see that this transition was occurring, from a position where continued Scottish currency depreciation[135] militated against any move to, or even trade with the south, among families whose ability to understand what was occurring in Edinburgh, let alone its English and European dimension, was limited, may have reduced the capacity of Border lairds to adjust to the transition. Yet this was the most vital element for lairds' survival into the modern world; and it was not, perhaps, the King's fault; for his advocacy of the "middle shires" and real *political* union in 1607 was to be defeated, not by Scottish reluctance or nationalistic feeling but by English incomprehension and derision.

There were some who saw what might happen and this may be the best way to read the story of the next Earl of Bothwell, Francis Stewart, and his apparently ungovernable ambition to control James VI in 1591. Promoted earlier to the earldom voided by Mary's third husband, Francis was the illegitimate son of James V, with estates in the Borders and the title also Sheriff of Berwickshire. But the two quarrelled and the King accused him of witchcraft – a devastating charge, given the royal obsession, even pathology on the subject. Imprisoned, Bothwell escaped, was outlawed and hunted down.

But he was not alone and the origins of this feud may reach back years. He had worked with Kerr of Ferniehurst in the campaign against Chancellor Maitland, with support from some of the wild Liddesdale clans, and the Catholic Earl of Huntley, not to do with religion but in defence of local autonomy against a centralising state. As Lord Burghley commented: "the (Border) nobility are not acquainted with absolute government of their King but, rather, are themselves in a sort absolute." A violent man with a mafia-like honour code, he tried to carry off the King in June 1591, assaulted Holyrood House in December, and set out in June 1592 finally to capture him at Falkland Palace. William Middlemas, younger brother of Grieston (circa 1550-1592) joined him, together with many other Border names.

As the spy reported to Lord Burghley,[136] Bothwell had had 300 horsemen, whereas only 60 defended the King. But despite their assumption that the Earl of Erroll and Colonel Stewart would open the Palace gate for them, these two had been imprisoned before the raiders arrived. Having failed to batter the gate down, Bothwell rode off, pursued by Lord Hamilton and the King's men. Only one horseman was killed in the shooting – William Middlemas. Bothwell was hunted down and after two further engagements, including a raid on Edinburgh, fled Scotland altogether in 1596.

Long before then, Hume had made his peace with the King, rendering the alliance with Maitland even stronger. Hume was to be rewarded with the rich revenues of Coldingham Priory and the temporal lordship of Kelso. The repercussions hit Thomas Middlemas the younger of Grieston (circa 1535-1603) financially, as the bullet had hit his brother William. In November 1592, together with a cousin by marriage, James Stewart of Tinnis (a cousin of Traquair), he was forced to stand surety for 300 merks, both for Thomas and his uncle George as warrants were issued to round up Bothwell's supporters, with an injunction to stay 10 miles away from Edinburgh on pain of death. [137] Thomas and George were lucky to avoid the list of those attainted for treason – which included the dead William and a brother John, and a cross-section of lairds in Teviot and Tweed, all of whom were forfeited.[138]

The origins of this foray can be linked, not only with the repeated raids by Ferniehurst and his allies on Jedburgh, but the origins of one of the classic Border feuds in 1526. Then, Thomas Middlemas of Grieston had been accused with many others of the murder of Kerr of Cessford, but set free of charges on the evidence among others of Mark Kerr of Ferniehurst, then Warden of the March, to whom Thomas evidently owed some allegiance[139] (see Chapter 5).

Like the Scotts' feud against Kerr of Cessford (which also called in the Middlemas loyalty), a feud between Ferniehurst and Cessford branches took many forms and can be seen in the warring factions for Queen Mary's favour and Maitland's attempt to create a centralised state for James to rule. It was not just the small lairds around Kelso who supported Ferniehurst. So did Grieston, which explains perhaps why William Middlemas rode with Bothwell, and why the whole family – indeed the kin-group – were put at risk by James VI's reprisals of 1592-4.

Not only did the two major Border feuds affect their security. Ferniehurst was also Baillie of Kelso, Roxburgh and Lilliesleaf. At the same time, the family depended in some way on the Humes, because the Lilliesleaf branch owed most of its land to the marriage with Mariota Hume in 1576 (see below). The fact that the sixth Earl Hume adhered to Queen Mary and had been forfeited and imprisoned, affected all his relationships, as did his switch to the young King that restored his family's influence in Roxburgh and Berwickshire.

It is in this context that the late 16th century history of the Middlemas branches should be seen – a time of multiple feuds (Scotts versus Elliots or Armstrongs for example or the renewed outbreak of Scott-Kerr hostilities in 1577), which were fostered and subsidised from London even after Queen Mary's execution, with peaks in the 1580s 90s and even 1600s.[140] Similar, but more local feuds and rivalries embroiled them in the Morebattle-Hownam/Yetholm area where they had re-established themselves after losing the Middlemastlands. Yet Pringles, Davidsons and Rutherfords were all potentially hostile and William Middlemas of Lilliesleaf's first wife was murdered there in 1574 by Hoppringles from Hownam.

Successive lairds of Grieston had recourse to frequent emphasis of the Middlemas of Middlemas title and this must be understood in the context of alliances operating at all levels of society, which lasted well into the next century. The King might see through Parliament the 1598 Act "Anent deadly feuds" (which did at least help to separate local feuds from rivalries at Court); but, like his own sumptuary legislation, it needed a quarter of a century to take effect. Meanwhile the local musters, ostensibly for Border defence but more often occasions for jollity and gossip, continued up to the end of the 1590s, and served to keep alive lairds' (and that of gentry on the other side) preparedness to use their weapons seriously against their enemies, if not each other.

The need for alliances as political insurance or leverage extended across the Border. In 1571, Walter Middlemas of Sharprig and Lempitlaw complained that William Kerr the younger of Cessford, then Warden, had not defended him against an East March suit by Sir Thomas Grey of Chillingham for the theft of four oxen and a horse: Walter had been fined by the Warden £220, but was then acquitted on new evidence and had his fine repaid in 1577. But Cessford, who was openly hostile, went on to claim both his expenses and offset the slight to his honour; bringing other witnesses to try to overturn the acquittal. In the end, Cessford failed to make the charge stick and he had to pay the market value of Grey's loss – £11 – and accept the £220 repayment to Walter Middlemas as a write off.[141]

Right up to 1603, the closer to the Border, the more disturbed the peace was: upper valleys of the Kale and Jed Water were as remote in behaviour from the Merse or Tweed as Tynedale or Redesdale were from the Northumberland plain; and in this sense, Bothwell can be compared in lawlessness with the later Percies who, after the Northern Earls failed in their revolt in the 1560s, found it expedient to live in the south of England.

***

Thomas Middlemas of Grieston appears to have settled into respectable middle age by the 1550s, becoming one of three sheriffs in Peebleshire, under the overall sway of John Lord Hay of Yester. (Various sasines [transfers of land] that he witnessed in the 1550s are in the Yester Papers; including Lord Hay's inquest, and he may have acted as a legal adviser for the family.) Apart from his adjudications in land disputes, little more is known about him, till in 1566 he conveyed the estate to his son, Thomas the younger (circa 1540-1603) "with the tower, fortalice and mansion," its salmon-fishing in the Tweed and the remaining one-third of Glen.[142]

Queen Mary confirmed this (at a cost to the family of £160) styling the younger Thomas Middlemas of Middlemas. Of that generation, his brother John and William (killed at Falkland Palace) were evidently Marians until the Queen's execution, as was the now-legitimate George – presumably his uncle. [George Middlemas (circa 1540-1595) had been born the illegitimate son of Thomas Middlemas the elder at Grieston, and had been legitimated by a warrant in the name of the infant Queen Mary in 1547.] Of Robert Middlemas, perhaps another son of the elder Thomas, we know only that he was paid with others £18 8 shillings for the supply of eight men at arms, by the Lord High Treasurer in 1550. Of James Middlemas, only that he had been a prisoner of the English in 1535, and engaged in a lawsuit with his cousin Scott of Haining in 1554 and 1561, ranged once more, against Kerr of Cessford, concerning six stolen horses out of Berwick.[143]

The younger Thomas married circa 1565 Katherine Stewart of Traquair, daughter of Sir William Stewart, then engaged in the vast extension and decoration of his house. The connection between the two families seems to have been friendly and was to lead in 1605, after Thomas's death, to the transfer of Wester Plora to James Stewart of Traquair (Easter Plora having gone to Murray of Blackbarony a century earlier).

Thomas and Katherine had three children, Thomas (circa 1565 to circa 1630), Margaret (circa 1565 to 1626) who married first Patrick Murray of Falahill, Sheriff of Peebles, then after his death, Robert Scott of Huntley; and William (circa 1570 to mid-17th century) later Constable of Dunbarton Castle. But Katherine died and he married again, Marion Sinclair, having two children, John and Marion. The latter married yet another Murray, John of Syndhope and it was to her that Thomas left his one-third part of the Glen estate.[144] Thus was continued the intricate web of local connections.

Other than that, the legal record suggests an element of feuding left over from the Cockburn-Middlemas earlier lawsuits, in which two notable local families, the now-related Stewart of Traquair and Porteus of Glenkirk were on Thomas's side, together with Alexander Horsburgh of that ilk (1591-2). In 1599, as a judge, he presided over a General Band subscribed at Pettinween and three years later signed the General Band of 1602. He may well have been a good neighbour, since the year before his death, he donated, together with Sir William Stewart and John Sandilands of Melrig, four acres each to set up a glebe field for the new manse at Traquair.

The most successful marriage of the period, however, took place at Lilliesleaf, where in January 1576, John Middlemas (son of William of Lilliesleaf) and his wife Elizabeth Scott gave their consent to their own son William's betrothal to Mariota Hume, illegitimate daughter of John Hume, lay Abbott of Jedburgh and brother to the fourth Earl of Hume.[145] Her dowry comprised an estate the same size as Grieston in its original form: eleven and a half husband lands in Raperlaw, a neighbouring toun to Lilliesleaf, and extra plots, in all with a feudal payment of £12; which was increased shortly afterwards when William Pryor, lay commendator of Glasgow diocese, confirming the dowry grant, added the judicial office of Barony of Lilliesleaf, five librates and seven husband lands (plus two in Bewlie nearby at a feu rent of £5 10 shillings) together with the castle, the mill and woods.[146]

In terms of total size including outfield, this may have been over 2000 acres. Coming on top of the tower house and land John Middlemas already held, it made the family wealth into a substantial and economically coherent unit; and one needs to ask why such an arrangement suited the Humes. The answer must lie in the later stages of Marian politics, and Lord Hume's need for support, beset as he was by Regent Morton and trying to re-establish himself with James VI after imprisonment. It may also be an echo of earlier local strategic politics from the 1560s. William Middlemas (circa 1545 to 1616) had been married before, to an unnamed Eccles, murdered in 1574, and the family were already long-established in Lilliesleaf Chapel at one of the tower houses "furnished with loopholes for the discharge of missiles," with a much earlier sanctuary chapel built in part of the fortalice. The "castle" that Mariota brought with her was presumably the tower with outbuildings and barn whose remains could still in the 1850s be found in the town of Lilliesleaf, "a principal fortress on the highest point of the village, fortified with a mere [moat]."[147]

He and Mariota had at least three children who survived to maturity, William of Lilliesleaf (circa 1577 to 1632), James of Raperlaw (circa 1580 to 1620), and John, later called "of Jedburgh," dates unknown. But he had had also a son James from his first marriage (circa 1565 to 1604) who settled in Morebattle, southeast of Kelso, since he had no claim on the newly-acquired Raperlaw estate. (The fact that the first wife had been murdered by a family from that area confirms an earlier, if dangerous, kin-connection to the Kale Valley.)

By the 1560s, Kerr of Cessford had taken over what remained of the original Middlemast lands, rejoining it with Middlemastwalls, now called Mains of Softlaw, and passing it on in the 1620s to Sir Thomas Kerr of Cavers.[148] That was now an irrecoverable loss; but Middlemas branches had proliferated, in Softlaw, Sharprig and Eildon near Newstead. Thomas Middlemas farmed in Eildon c. 1580-1595 and had at least two brothers nearby, Robert (born c. 1580), and William (c. 1580-1650) who farmed in Minto south of Lilliesleaf. Melrose Abbey records show Newstead as larger in 1564 than Melrose itself, a nucleated village with 33 feuars, rural traders and craftsmen, under their own birlayman/mossgrieve, acting for the regality. The Melrose Abbey land of Newstead was feued in 1564 among others to John Middlemas of Newstead[149] who by 1567 had become one of the larger tenants of the Abbey, according to its cartulary of that date.[150]

Thomas was presumably son of that John and grandson of Hugo Middlemas of Midlem, (circa 1510-1555); and John styled himself "of Newstead," as did his eldest son Thomas (1575 to 1638). Their descendents held the land there until the early 18th century[151]. The second son, John (c. 1575-1630) held land in Melrose, Newstead and Kelso (perhaps part of the original holding); he married Janet Marshall in 1609 and had seven children; a third son Robert (circa 1580-1641) who in 1602 married a local land owner's daughter Margaret Vair, had three daughters Janet, Margaret and Marion and after her death married again. This completed a family network remarkable only in the numbers that reached maturity. All the daughters married local men, George Mein, John Lillie and John Kyd, with whose families the Middlemases of Eildon were to marry, ally or quarrel throughout the 17th century.

Hugo himself also had two daughters, Malie (later 16th century) who is recorded as a tenant at the Abbey's remaining feudal lands, and Margaret (c. 1545 to 1625) who married a neighbouring laird, George Douglas of Friershaw, later seventh Lord Cavers, and continued to hold the land in her own right after his death in 1623. Their son Andrew duly became eighth Lord Cavers and married Jean Hume of Polwarth in 1640, complementing in a sense the Hume-Middlemas match made at Lilliesleaf in 1576. (Margaret, being a tenant of two husbandlands called "the Burlands," held of Thomas Kerr of Cavers, was thus actually the last member of the family to farm the original Middlemast lands, assigned in the $13^{th}$ century.)

If the Eildon-Newstead-Midlem branches can be seen as rising in the social scale, those south of Kelso found it harder. Three are recorded in the 1570s, of whom Watte (Walter) of Sharprig, William and Edward Middlemas of Lempitlaw (now a farmhouse in Sprouston Parish, but then a toun of some importance with its own ancient parish church) and Sharprig can be called the senior branch, holding at least something of the original estate, which they inherited in 1571. On his death in 1601 this passed to his son William (1565-1621) also of Lempitlaw and Sharprig. A younger brother George appears in 1577 styled in the same way, and another, John, who inherited in Sharprig and Grubet in the early 1620s and died in 1627. Grubet was a stone tower house (like Corbet across the valley, which still survives intact after Victorian restoration) near to a much earlier circular defensive enclosure faced with a wall of large stones.[152]

These are clearly members of the same family, as are a clutch of relatives in Sharprig, identified only by their association with Kerr of Ferniehurst's assaults on Jedburgh. Those further southeast, up Kale Water derive from an earlier generation: James held land worth 20 shillings in Morebattle in the 1550s; Andrew David Middlemas still called himself Middlemas of Middlemas in 1576 and 1588; and owned land at Morebattle and Grubet, as well as property in Kelso. A brother George is recorded in Grubet Haugh in 1576 and 1608 and another brother John, who with Andrew David, were also tenants of the Rutherfords of Hundalee in Grubet, and owned some land in Morebattle.[153] These may be related to James Middlemas, first son of William of Lilliesleaf. (The table in Appendix A marks possible lines of descent.) [Andrew David was sued and put to the horn by John Kerr of Greenhead for not removing from Middlemastwalls, and although he held on in 1576-7, he lost his tenancy of the east half of Greenhead, the whole of Easter Softlaw and Grubet, and half of Wideopen near Morebattle – in effect three useful farms.]

Records are scarce for Kale Water even at the turn of the $17^{th}$ century (apart from criminal ones, both Sharprig and Lempitlaw families being accused of the grievous bodily harm by shooting of Gavin Ford in 1599), but it is clear that several families were well-established before the Civil War as tenants either of Stewart of Traquair or Kerr of Oxnam in that narrow upland valley, stretching from Morebattle and Yetholm in the north, up river to Hownam and Hownam Grange, along the line of the Roman Road, Dere Street, and the well-known "dry march" for reivers into Northumberland. Some of their extra-farming occupations can be guessed at from the fact that Thomas was slain in 1592 and Jock was accused of stealing horses both in 1599 and 1601. But some of them held on as lairds in what was an administrative free barony linked to Kirk Yetholm, under the Earl of Morton.

***

These four family groups comprise the kin who witnessed and lived through the last phase of the medieval-early modern transition. As the 17th century began, the extended family group was becoming more diverse, indeed divergent; and family interest, occupation and migration demonstrate the long process in which kinship itself was eroded. It was also conditioned by a new sort of lottery: who benefited most from the Kirk's commitment to educate at least those who had the time left over from duties on the land.

Quality of education available varied greatly in the period before the union of the two crowns, depending on what endowments the Kirk and landowners were able to provide for the new order of ministers, whether indeed the manse's occupant was ordained,[154] or a reader-preacher only. (Hownam had only the latter.) Better education may still have been provided in Catholic households served by Jesuits, despite the problems of recusancy in a Protestant kingdom; but Catholic profession tailed off after the 1600s.

Emigration already provided alternatives to the problems of what to do with younger sons, a problem only now showing itself among Middlemas kin members (none of them are found in the records of 15th and 16th century mercenary armies on the Continent, nor did their descendents settle in the Baltic countries, Germany or Poland, where local versions of Scottish ancestral names proliferated). At least one, Thomas Middlemas became a notary (solicitor), practising at Pettinween by 1599, and others were to follow him into what was rapidly becoming a profitable career in the 17th century. Others bereft of education, simply left, seeking work in the early stages of a vast, largely unrecorded outward flow, at first primarily seasonal, to the farms of the Merse or north Northumberland, then to the cities, mainly Edinburgh, and by the 1630s to the new industrialising regions of Tyneside.

When exactly this migration developed is hard to say. In farming, there had been local flows at harvest time even in the Middle Ages, and trained artisans like blacksmiths or wheelrights, and of course shepherds, possessed skills always in demand. As for crossing the Border, perhaps two to three thousand Scottish lived at any one time in the English East March, despite late 16th century complaints, despite prejudice, heavier taxes, and frequent arrests.[155]

By the 16th century, it suited many Northumbrian landowners to have Scots as tenants, despite all the Elizabethan prohibitions and restrictions, since they were less likely to be attacked or raided by their Border kin, and hence might be more capable of paying higher rents.

It may be in this sense that George Middlemas – the illegitimate son of Thomas of Grieston legitimated by Mary Queen of Scotts in 1547 – acquired enough land at Gosswick, south of Berwick, to qualify him as a gentleman in the 1579 and 1584 English Muster-Rolls of the East March; or Edward, just over the Border from Yetholm, with his kinsmen, the Strothers of Kirknewton.[156] At least among lairds and gentry some degree of social contact or "trysting" obtained across the Border line, under the relatively lax regime of John Forster the Warden, pointing up their shared interests, even marriage, despite prohibitions. Many others would follow them once the Border disappeared in 1603. But those few who went to Edinburgh appeared to have gone, if male as apprentices, if female as domestic servants or shopkeepers – thus, Bessie Middlemas who in 1602 married first John Allen, keeper of the Canongate tolbooth, followed six years later by Hew Williamson, a merchant.

Others are recorded in the early 1600s in Kelso. But this was a local, much older dimension, highlighted by the appearance of parish registers of births, marriages and deaths; any earlier patterns of urban settlement are far harder to document. The first two families in Newcastle established themselves in the years 1615-20; those in the coal-mining parish of Wickham, in Durham in the 1630s, almost certainly after a recruiting drive by early coal-owners in what was to become the great northeast coal-mining region.

At least those who went south after 1603 experienced less of the anti-Scottish discrimination, racial hatred and xenophobia, still rife in the 1590s when the Corporation of Berwick on Tweed endorsed a harsh range of bylaws based on the common presumption that all Scotsmen were thieves and liars, and all Scotswomen whores, both being purveyors of forged coin.[157]

George Middlemas may have escaped this by what was called "denization," Edward may have avoided it, living at the porous edge of the Border. Such laws and prohibitions were scarcely surprising, given Berwick's importance, its role as centre for Burghley's spying operations, and the presence of an English garrison of 600 men costing £15.000 a year on which, according to the Border Laws, no Scotsman was allowed to serve or indeed live in the town. Even the "Scotch market" on whose produce the town depended, was kept firmly outside the fortified centre – though customs evasion and illegal fishing in the Tweed continued, as they always had.

*Gambling (Grimani Breviary, MS Bodleian Library)*

# 8.

# The Middle Shires

As James VI travelled south in 1603 to take over authority of his new kingdom under the title of James I, there was no reason for Border lairds to feel uneasy. No Middlemases were among those who had chosen to accompany him, for reasons which were obvious: tied to their estates, secure in their rentals, and with ambitions limited to the Border, they could have seen no advantage in the heterodox politics and rivalries of London. If anything, as William of Grieston's younger brother found, the removal of so many seekers after court favour in Edinburgh made it easier to find royal preferment at home; while those in Eildon or Kale Water did not aspire at all.

King James has had a bad press in England, then and since, especially from 19th and early 20th century historians who recognised him as intelligent and cultured – albeit as extravagant – but saw his judgment as erratic or pig-headed, criticised his vanity and pedantry, and misread his assertion of divine right: in short, "the wisest fool in Christendom," accompanied by foppish favourites surrounded by assertions of homosexuality. Guided by Macaulay's judgement, they ignored James' long experience of re-establishing central government in Scotland, his firm philosophical defence of civil power against an all-encroaching theocracy, and his contrast with absolute Continental monarchs.

They discounted also his intense desire for a real union of the two kingdoms, for strategic, diplomatic, and cultural reasons, far beyond the contemporary union of Poland and Lithuania, because his efforts of 1607 were defeated by English incomprehension or hostility, and deferred for a century until England itself sought it. Yet union of the crowns on its own gave England not only a male king with a son, resolving the Tudor succession dilemma; but a monarch with a European mentality, that is, a history of pro-French sentiment without being anti-Spanish, and allied by marriage to a Danish princess. But the latter advantage could not survive the counter-Reformation's legacy of religious strife, the annihilation of

Bohemia's golden age at the Battle of the White Mountain in 1620, and the onset of the 30 Years War.

Other European regal unions, between Spain and Portugal or Poland and Sweden, broke up in the mid-17$^{th}$ century and James' one was by no means predestined to success. As Jenny Wormald points out "The Scots and the English did not like each other before 1603, and relations when they actually met thereafter were characterised by violence, hatred, and jealousy rather than affection."[158] Even in religion, there was little connection between the 1560s Elizabethan settlement and the uneasy truce between James' defence of bishops, Episcopalians in the main body of the Kirk, and the enragés of Melville's persuasion.

So the grounds for repudiation of full union on the claim it represented an assault on Englishness already existed, while James' courage and wisdom demonstrated before and after Queen Mary's execution, was simply not appreciated by courtiers offended at Scots' pride and their new King's cultural aspirations; which, like his son Charles I's collection of European paintings, were above the heads of most of those around him. Lacking an English sense of humour, he in turn found it hard to subvert English prejudice, of which a fair sample can be found in one (English) courtier's diary for the sole visit home in 1617: "to be chained in marriage.. were to be tied to a dead carcass and cast into a stinking ditch."

James was not adaptable to government via private secretaries, even if he claimed he could rule Scotland by his pen; and Robert Cecil was not Burghley. Neither could the King commune directly with his magnates as he had done in Scotland: personal rule in the south had ended by the 1580s. He chafed at Elizabeth's assertive, long-experienced Parliament, found his dependency on it for taxation a severe restraint, and its boredom with his political theory humiliating. But an innate political sense kept him from the dogmatism and the high-handedness of his son Charles.

Worst perhaps, in the 1607 debate about union, was the evidence of contempt. As Nicholas Fuller put it, the rich English pastures would "be inundated by lean and ravenous Scottish cattle, whose English equivalents would scorn the miserable facilities open to them in Scotland." So it was all put aside, and on that basis, for the

*April, Simon Bening, (MS Biblioteque Royale de Belgique)*

rest of James' life, there seemed a reasonable prospect of avoiding the Spanish-Portuguese split. Yet this was partly because James, apart from the one visit, left Scotland alone, ruling by decree and letters through his ministers, as if with the 1607 rejection he had lost interest in avoiding what he himself had feared would become "the northern Shires, seldom seen and saluted by their King."

What to most English was an undifferentiated north, included his hypothetical "middle Shires" where, as local lairds soon found, Edinburgh was no longer the centre of power for a King 400 miles away: easy access to their sovereign had been relegated to a mere memory of a pre-modern era. Of course the Scottish parliament survived, as did its separate courts and legal system, taxation and church structure. But the English rejection of full union meant that for another 100 years Scotland would be shut out of the vastly profitable trade with the English West Indies and the North American colonies and confined, in a mercantilist age, to its traditional economic resources.

What Scotland did gain was less tangible: equal citizenship in Great Britain for those born after 1603, access to the Bible in the epochal King James version of 1611 and, at least in the southeast, a slow end to Border disputes and the institutionalised racism prevalent in northern England. Of more immediate popularity, Ulster was opened up to settlement by Protestant Scots farmers. Peace brought its own dividend; no new internal threat occurred except for the rebellion of Patrick Stewart, last Earl of Orkney in 1612, an illegitimate son of James V who was soon forfeited and imprisoned.

James was even more successful in tying down the Kirk, reducing its Assembly to obedience and forcing Melville into exile. Bishops' rights and revenues were slowly restored – yet the Presbyterian system held out and James found it expedient not to enforce new injunctions such as kneeling to receive Communion; the full extent of his Episcopalian reforms was postponed until 1621 in the Five Articles of Perth.

As his Scottish administration became more formalised, Sheriffs and their deputies began to control more of shire affairs, except at the level of lairds' hold over baronies and regalities; even these lost ground to the Courts of Session. For those who sought court appointments, the way now lay through the nobles who administered on James' behalf rather than direct royal favour. Influential appointments, for example to the command of royal castles, depended on it; and as the heads of families were drawn in towards the new centre, a combination of the imposition of civil law, the rules and practice of Presbyterianism, and the institutions of a modern state, eroded not only the need for bonding, but the significance of kinship itself.

True, the Kirk did not aggregate effective civil power until the 1640s; but with its own court sessions drawing in local lairds, rather than the nobility, it had both a centralising and disciplining effect. Establishment of the idea of public authority, as against unruly individualism, benefited local elites even if the price was a certain social harshness, directed against pleasure, leisure, sex, and sport (witness the disappearance of Christmas and Easter celebrations). It also had the effect of keeping peasants and the urban working class in their place, which appealed to all godly men, notably what can already be called the professional middle class, or lairds co-opted as elders of Kirk sessions.

The social tensions which inevitably accompanied the enforcement of godly discipline, whether by state or church, may explain the continued high level of violence, especially among younger men, and the climate of fear engendered by the witch panics, first in the 1590s (which so disturbed King James) then again in the 1620s, which the Kirk fostered as avidly as did Protestant and Catholic churches in Europe or North America. Trials had taken place in Berwickshire, for demonic possession, but this initial fervour had died away. What revived it was the concept of a demonic *pact*, which flourished in the 1620s and 30s – in which William Middlemas of Lilliesleaf had to serve as a judge, being Sheriff of Selkirk.

Increases in taxation to sustain this Jacobean administration bore hardly on local landowners by the 1620s (even when it was used, charitably, to pay for famine relief in 1623) and there is no doubt that William of Lilliesleaf suffered severely in the years 1610-15. Nevertheless, it was a good time for lairds, despite the injunctions against extravagance, as John Taylor the "water poet" observed in 1618:

a great time of rebuilding, refurbishing, notable for new industries, glass making, better quality beer, better clothes and furniture – albeit all bought from industries under control of the merchant monopolies. Science, mathematics and geography might still vie for attention with alchemy and magic – but so was it in London or Prague or Paris in the heyday of the "Rosicrucian Enlightenment." And there were substantive advances in education, literacy, the universities and music – even if the latter came mainly via the Scottish psalter and at the expense of older ballads and drama.

Much of this delayed renaissance was in fact a modern European, largely Protestant overlay on Scottish 16$^{th}$ century culture, not to be questioned consciously until the 18$^{th}$ century admiration for Robert Burns. The fact that it was couched in English did not mean that it was an English implant: Henryson's English had been as good as Chaucer's 150 years earlier. Rather, it signified a growing conformity around the principles of modernity to which, in political form, James' VI and I had failed to instil a common approach in 1607.

No laird could be free of this, the latest formation of cultural and economic life which governed how he behaved, how he farmed his estate, how he treated his tenants and labourers. As the difference grew in the 17$^{th}$ century between the practice of estate management of ever-larger estates, that of small farmers, and the world of cottars and labourers or seasonal migrants, the family branches have to be described separately.

***

At Grieston, Thomas Middlemas died in 1603, having survived his second wife Marion Sinclair by four years; [By her will of 1599 she left her possessions, an agricultural inventory, which suggests she retained rights over the property she had brought on marriage, domestic equipment, furniture and clothes worth £509, before deducting debts of £283 6/8, to her children John and Marion. Robert Scott of Huntley was surety for the testament.] his last recorded act had been to sign the General Band "against thieves, murderers and oppressors" in October 1602.

> We nobleman, baronis, landit gentlemen, and utheris undersubscrivng, deiplie considering with oureselffis the wrackfull

> and intolerable calamities sa lang sustenit be us, oure freindis, oure servandis, and inhabitantis upoun oure proper landis and heritages, at the handis of thevis and murtherars within the Heylandis and Bordours, quhairby oure bludis hes bene cruellie sched, oure guidis be oppin depredations violentlie reft and spuilyeit, and oure maist plentifull and profitable rowmes, for feare of thair incursionis and oppressionis, left desolat and desert without tenant or inhabitante, to oure inexcusable reprotche and schamefull wrack gif we sall ony langer neglect to use sic lauchfull and allowable remedies as God, oure honoure, and the memorable examples of oure worthie predicessouris still extant in the recordis for thair dayes, cravis at oure handis for the repressing of thair insolence.

Fifty-five Border notables signed that day[159] (only three of whom could not write), 65 on the following days, a roll-call of landowners in the four counties.

Thomas' son by Katherine Stewart, also called Thomas, and husband of Janet Kerr took over; and signed the last General Band in 1617. But they had no son, only a daughter Marion. It was possible therefore that the estate could pass to his half brother, but it seems that John had predeceased him, and his half-sister Marion had no claim. His own sister Margaret had married first Patrick Murray, then Robert Scott of Huntley (see Chapter 5) and their son, James Scott, inherited the lands of Longhope in Ettrick in 1609.[160]

Lack of a male heir was a calamity which the Middlemases had managed to avoid for nearly four centuries. The only other claimant, if Thomas died, would have been his younger brother William, soon in an exercise of considerable royal favour to become Constable of Dumbarton Castle, the second greatest fortress in Scotland after Edinburgh itself, which commanded the whole Clyde estuary and protected the central lowlands in Glasgow from a possible Spanish or French invasion.

Promotion to such an office, which had previously been held by one of Stewart of Traquair's relatives, put William in a powerful position which ill-luck, his own presumption, and the character of the next Traquair combined to undermine. Perhaps more important, however, was continuing shortage of financial support for Grieston (which did not prevent Thomas standing surety for a friend, Dixon of Ormeston in 1610 for 2000 merks).

Seeing that there would be no son to follow him, Thomas in 1611 sold part of Wester Glen, and in 1618 a third of the remaining barony to his daughter Marion, now married to John Murray of Syndhope, in return for 6,000 merks, a sale converted to a gift when he renounced the reversion.[161]

At the same time, he provided for his wife (who would lose her holding in Grieston when he died, £100 per year out of the rents of the Mains of Grieston). Two years later, he transferred another 5 husband lands of Bold beside Plora, to Sir John Murray of Philiphaugh and William Sandilands to offset a £470 debt, and this part was sold to Traquair in 1624. On Thomas' death in 1630, the whole estate, the remaining 18 husband lands at Grieston, the lands of Gillishaugh, the tower and mansion of Grieston, the fishing rights in the Tweed, and the 10 librates of Bold/Plora, passed to John, now Lord Stewart of Traquair.

That there had been an estrangement with John Stewart at some point seems certain but its origin is obscure. Thomas' father had been a friend of Sir William Stewart up to 1603. John Stewart, however, born c. 1590, was of a younger generation, who had been given rapid promotion by James VI: Commissioner for Tweeddale in 1621, Deputy Treasurer and a Lord in 1628, then Lord High Treasurer under Charles I. Later, in the 1640s, having managed the early stages of Charles I's struggle with the Covenanters, he was to be challenged – turning out to be a trimmer, trusted by neither side. (In the Civil War, he showed himself a poor commander, was dismissed and fined; he refused refuge to Montrose, to shouts of treachery, and died in obscurity before the Restoration.)

None of that explains the dislike, and Craig Brown's *History of Peebleshire* speculates that the cause was more personal. The most likely answer is a mixture of his cousin's quarrel with William Middlemas over Dumbarton Castle, plus local jealousy: a laird with Traquair's ambitions was unlikely to welcome being flanked on both sides by the lands of an older family in decline.

William Middlemas the Constable (c. 1570-c. 1640), husband of Agnes Cairncross, had three sons, Thomas, William and James, and had a fair claim to inherit after Thomas' death.

*December, Simon Bening (MS Victoria & Albert Museum)*

Long after it had ceased to be the main west coast defence against the Highlands, Dumbarton had become a political appointment in the late 16th century under William Stewart of Cavers (whose main prisoner had been the Regent Morton before his execution) and to that extent, it fulfilled the same function as the Tower of London. William's prisoners after 1611 were to include not only the rebel Earl of Orkney, but the Catholic priest John Ogilvie "the Blessed" soon to become a martyr. But his tenure began with an unpropitious outrage in his own household, the murder of his "master cook" by a servant, Robert Guthrie "apprehended with a bloody hand."[162]

Dumbarton still stands impressively on its 240-foot high volcanic plug. It had an ancient history, being main stronghold of the Strathclyde kingdom, mentioned by Bede in 730 AD; and William Wallace had been held prisoner here before his last journey to London and execution. It held out longer for Mary Queen of Scots than anywhere but Edinburgh Castle itself. A 17th century antiquarian wrote:

> On one of the tops of the rocks there standeth upon a lofty watch tower a keep. On the other, which is lower, there are sundry strong bulwarks. Between these two tops on the north it hath only one ascent, by which only one by one can pass up, and that with a labour by tiers and steps cutt out a slope traverse the Rock. Instead of ditches on the west side serveth the River Leven, on the south Clyde, and on the east a boggy slate, which at every tyde is wholly covered over with waters, and on the north side the very upright steepness of the place is a most sufficient defence.

The Constable's quarters were probably in what is called the Windy Hall and noble prisoners would have been lodged in the White Tower or the Wallace Tower. None of these now stand among the 18th century fortifications. To William as Constable was committed the flamboyant rebel Patrick Stewart, third Earl of Orkney, not in fact the last Lord of the Isles, but aspiring to that title. Given the courtly custom of the time, they sometimes dined together and may have become friendly. It is unlikely that William did not know what would be his prisoner's fate.

Orkney was at risk not only as a rebel and traitor to James VI but as the object of an ancient feud with the Earl of Caithness, who was now ready to revenge a wrong done to his ancestor nearly a century earlier. The King being determined to ensure peace in the northwest, Orkney's enemies in Edinburgh, mobilised by Caithness, wanted only his death after a short show trial. William had to deal with both as well as his prisoner's botched attempts to escape.

That elaborate escape plan of 1612, given to the Crown as evidence by James Lyon, an illegitimate son of the Master of Glamis, involved too many people, too many deceptions, and fell apart over money.[163] After it was found out, the Constable was ordered to make no more acts of friendship or courtesy, but "to keep the Earl of Orkney close prisoner; to remove his own servants from him and to appoint one of the Constable's servants to attend him; to suffer none to have access to him, nor conference with him, nor no letter to be carried to or from him, as the said Constable will answer upon peril of his life."[164]

It can be assumed that William carried out this first order, but the next one imposed too much: to deliver up the prisoner "to such of the guard as shall bring him to Edinburgh and to appear before the Council." He must have known that the result was foregone: a show trial, followed by execution. Whether he acted out of a sense of what would now be called fair play, believed him innocent, or simply from friendship, cannot be known.

As the report noted, "Having earnestly entreated:

> the said William to delyvar the said Erll unto thame, the said Williame very disdanefullie and proudlie refuisit to delyver the said Erll unto thame, and thairby has done quhat in him lyis to frustrate and disappoint suche of his Majesteis affairis and busyness quhairin the said Erll is to be delt with, in heich contempt of his Majestie, and to the neglect of that dewtie whiche the said Williame aucht to his Majestie in the faithfull discharge of that place whilk be haldis of his Majestie: Thairfoir the Lordis of the Secreit Counsaill ordainis letteris to the direct charging the said Williame Middlemast to delyver the said Patrik, Erll of Orknay, to suche of his Majesteis Gaird as salbe thair reddy to ressave him, to the effect he may be transportit and broght heir to this burgh, within three houris nixtefter he said Williame beis chargeit thairto, under the pane of rebellioun, & c..[165]

This he could not ignore. Orkney was dispatched, given a five-day trial and duly executed, with Caithness boasting of his role. William's first – public – refusal may have helped to ensure a more open trial but it did him no good with the King's Secret Council. He was dismissed and replaced by Sir James Stewart. But by a private contract made in October 1615, this fate was delayed until Sir James had paid him the sum of 3,000 merks. That this debt contract was recorded in Edinburgh suggests that the sum represented all the back pay due to William since the affair began – not an unusual arrangement, given the state of the King's Exchequer.

The sum being unpaid, William waited till Stewart was in Edinburgh and in February 1620, with the help of various kinsmen and former retainers still in the garrison, came back to the Castle:

> upon old familiarity and acquaintance and made himself master and commander thereof, seized upon the ports and gates and upon the munitions, ordnance, and weapons being therein, and upon the parts and places of strength.. and there he violently thrust the servants (garrison) to the gates and now keeps the said Castle as a house of war against his Majesty, and it is very likely that he has some purpose in head concerning the said Castle which may be prejudicial to his Majesty.

This was, undeniably, high treason. Yet, oddly even for the early 17$^{th}$ century, the Council dealt with it as a matter between two rival lairds. Both appeared in person, William relying on the earlier contract, Stewart claiming he had paid at least the interest on the 3,000 merks; and the Lords of Council, judging that neither should have entered such a bargain "anent his Majesty's house and Castle," gave William one month to withdraw but ordered Stewart to pay the debt.

Thereafter it became more formal. Since the debt remained unpaid, William sued Sir James and two of his kinsmen, and the King, who appears to have been kind to his former protégé, became involved, ordering the Lord Treasurer to satisfy William for the arrears of pay "if equity so demands," following this up with a warrant in November 1625 to the Earl of Mar to pay "the sometime keeper."[166]

The dispute had become a matter of high politics: on one side the Duke of Lennox who had appointed Stewart, on the other William with a case to which the King seemed not unsympathetic. William was, after all, a well-known judge of assize who had served on notable tribunals and had much local support.[167] But Sir James Stewart won in the end, whereupon William finally left; and Stewart reviewed the condition of the Castle in 1627 with predictable prejudice:

> At his entry within the Castle he found only three men and a boy in ordinar guarding of the same. The walls in the chief and most important parts were ruinous and decayed; the houses wanting doors, locks or bolts, and nather wind nor water tight; the ordnance unmounted, and little or no provision of victuals or munitions (except a few rusty muskets) within the same.[168]

It is impossible to disentangle fact from assertion in what had become a deep quarrel. Long after James's cousin John Stewart's own downfall during the Civil War, William's widow Marion continued the suit, petitioning the Council in March 1649 for payment of 1,900 merks out of the 4,500 (with interest) due to her by Charles I, since the Earl of Orkney's imprisonment 24 years earlier. The Council gave a surprisingly benign response "that the Parliament seriously recommend the supplicant to the Commission of the Treasurer and Exchequer in respect of her necessity."[169] Whether the bill was ever paid is not recorded.

The bill that was paid occurred at home. There were reasons for the Middlemases at Grieston to dislike Sir John Stewart of Traquair apart from this, and his rapid rise to political eminence clearly put them at risk. There is no evidence as to how William and his sons were cut out of their main estate: it may be that Thomas had already made irreversible provisions excluding him, before the late 1620s. At least William's three sons inherited something: parts of Spittelhope which the two brothers had owned jointly, went to them in 1611 and two, William and Thomas, were active as small lairds at least till 1645, when they sold out to Andrew Hay, a lawyer related to the Murrays.[170]

Their descendents remained in the Peebles area into the 19th century. But the house of Grieston vanished, apart from its 300 x 100 metre outer earthwork, probably quarried for its stone. Traquair had no need for the old fortalice on its neighbouring hill. It could not be converted like Plora and was too near for the now elaborate Stewart house. After Lord Stewart's death, it was all sold to James Earl of Southesk in 1656, two centuries before the Tennant family head Lord Glenconner commissioned the architect David Bryce to build what is now the vast baronial mansion of Glen.

***

At Lilliesleaf, William Middlemas, having married Mariota Hume, ended the 16th century as a judge in the baronial court, appointed by James VI in 1596. Most records of him are concerned with estate management, as befits the substantial acreage he now possessed. But the years 1609-11 brought very bad harvests as well as heavier taxation and he had to wrack up debts to carry on, that were heavy even for a well-to-do laird. He was, for example, assessed in 1607 £2 16 shillings primary taxes and £25 12 shillings for the Bewlie and Lilliesleaf estate, as heavy a burden as that on his neighbour Andrew Kerr of Ferniehurst.[171] These debts became so severe that in 1615 he temporarily resigned his barony and sold some land in Bewlie to Andrew Riddell, his neighbour.

His elder son, also William (c. 1577-1632) was involved briefly and probably erroneously, together with his brother John married to Margaret Turnbull and two other Turnbulls, Hector and Mark, both of Bewlie and neighbours of Lilliesleaf, in the sombre consequences of the Ferniehurst-Cessford feud. The case was as serious as the earlier involvement in the Kerr feud: on this occasion, the slaughter of Thomas Kerr of Craling, brother of Sir Andrew Kerr, laird of Ferniehurst. Having initially been accused, denounced for non-attendance and fined 1,400 merks, they were exonerated; the trial records suggest that either the Turnbulls were guilty or William Kerr from the Cessford faction. Thomas Turnbull of Minto nearby had to stand surety for the fine.[172]

William inherited on his father's death in 1619 the barony, which had been reinstated, the Raperlaw and Bewlie lands, Lilliesleaf Chapel and its towers.[173] At the same time, there was some redistribution of boundaries with the far longer-established family of Riddell around Bewlie–part of the original land belonging to Hugo Middlemas of Midlem; and his sister Isobel, wife of George Douglas of Friershaw inherited her portion in 1620. William had already married Bessie Pringle and had at least three sons (out of five children), the elder being also called William (c. 1600-1647), then Walter of Lilliesleaf Chapel (c. 1600-1650) and Thomas (1605-1660) of Mangerton, a farmland south of Hawick, but still in Roxburghshire (who became a Major in the Civil War). John (c. 1605-1672) of Purviven (married to Agnes Thompson), was either another brother or son of John (c.1580-1620) and Isobel Scott.

Feuding did not simply die away in the first quarter of the 17th century, despite the introduction of a slightly more efficient judicial process. Verbal and physical assaults remained common especially among lairds' sons, together with property destruction – though theft was, by the 17th century, largely confined to the criminal fringe. Underlying the feud itself was the need to preserve the integrity of one's name and also its credit worthiness, while against it, increasingly, with full intervention by the Kirk, was the need to maintain good neighbourliness in the community.

The elder William experienced – and perhaps fostered – his brother James' set of local assaults on George Douglas of Friershaw 1616-17, which at an earlier time would itself have created a new feud. Meanwhile, indeed at Grieston, Thomas Middlemas had been involved in a complex lawsuit to evict Marion Kerr and her son from his land, made more delicate by his blood relationships with two of the three Peebles sheriffs who had to try the case, James Lord Hay of Yester and Alexander Horsbrugh of that Ilk.[174]

According to the Privy Council Record in January 1616, James rode with John Rutherford and one of the Lilliesleaf house servants to seek out Douglas "and sought to have slain him... having tried to tempt him outside (the honour code frowning on murder inside an opponent's house) they passed directly to his yard and maliciously and despitefully cut twenty of the best ash trees, thinking by that means to have caused him to come out.." Five months later, they went to Douglas' house in Lilliesleaf itself, "invaded and pursued him, presented hagbuts to have shot in at his windows and ran at his doors to have forced the same." Failing there, they went on and shot up Friershaw again.[175]

That was settled in the traditional manner when the younger William's sister Isobel married the brother, Sir William Douglas of Friershaw, five years later. But peace on one front did not prevent a second round of hostilities against another neighbour, George Turnbull of Belses (a village between Lilliesleaf and Eildon), when William and two of his sons, and his brother James, with their servants, went fully armed one February night to his house "where he was with his family in their naked beds taking their night's rest," besieged it, firing in at the windows, until the arrival of some of Turnbull's neighbours sent them off.

In May, the same servants burst into the Kirk at Belses and attacked some of Turnbull's herders "and unhonestly struck and hit them and broke their heads to the effusion of their blood." Later that month, William and Walter went back to Belses, cutting him off from his defensive gate, and "in very swaggering manner, upbraided him with many injurious and reproachful speeches and proudly and avowedly appealed to him to the combat."[176]

Trial by combat being somewhat outdated, the parties went to court, where the Lords of Council committed both to the Edinburgh tollbooth "at their own expense during their Lordships' pleasure"– but dismissed more serious charges of carrying and shooting firearms. [This feud appears to have been settled when Margaret, sister of John Middlemas of Jedburgh, married Robert Turnbull of Bewlie (next door to Lilliesleaf)]. However inflated the language used in the trial, it is hard to avoid thinking that they were a lawless lot, and in 1619 they met a serious civil reversal when sued by Archibald Kerr in Bowden: £1,100 and 500 merks expenses.

None of this seems to have impeded William's career as a judge after his appointment in 1622. [That year saw the last of their disorderly incursions, when Walter with George Kerr made a "violent entry" on Sir William Oliphant's house on Lochtaw, on the pretext of searching for two rebels (Sir John Kerr of Jedburgh and John Kerr of Longnewton). There is a possibility that they were acting, in effect, as bounty-hunters, hoping for a reward from the Courts.] Two years later, he took over from his Riddell neighbour as an assize judge, and in 1629 was one of three Baillies of Selkirk, with Sir James Pringle as sheriff and George Kerr. That same year, he was also appointed sheriff of Selkirk, and set by the Earl of Mar and the Privy Council (with Pringle and four Scott and Kerr judges) to try a group of five suspected witches. Their names are known[177] but the verdict is not: given that it was guilty in the majority of cases in Scotland in the 1620s witch fever, where the supposed charge was demonic possession, with its threat to procreation, legitimacy and health, it is likely that they were executed.[178]

The Lilliesleaf branch was evidently still close to Grieston, William having been called in on the basis of his local knowledge in 1628 to adjudicate in a boundary dispute in Ettrick Forest, on behalf of the Lord Chancellor, in which many of the Border lairds including Hume and Buccleugh were involved. That he knew the ground well, and was trusted by them, as well as by the Riddells, is self-evident; the inquest *ad valorem* called him "one of the trusted and faithful men of the county."

He died in 1632, his son William being infefted with the estate "with houses, buildings, towers, fortalices, orchards, fields, pendacles, and pertinents, and the lands of Bewlie £5 lying between the fountain of Saint Quintigern from the east, to the boundary of the corn mills and the byre from the west, the lower quarters of the town north and south and Lilliesmoss."[179] Nothing more is known of this William before the Civil War, except that his son James, married to Isobel Scott, with three children, took over on his death (after a brief interlude) in 1648. He too died only eight years later, leaving the children in the tutelage of a cousin (see Chapter 10).

In spite of their disorderly youth, caused by local disputes blowing up into affrays at a time when the Borders were definitely not settled by the union of the two crowns, this period may be seen as one of relative prosperity, even affluence, comparable to what Grieston had enjoyed in the late 15th century. Their sometimes outrageous behaviour has to be seen in a context where the Catholic modes of authority and restraint had finally broken down, but where the Kirk had not yet established its godly rule to replace the old honour code; where violence remained endemic, accompanied by a very Renaissance habit of competitive display, and where primogeniture and high land prices caused by the acquirers' bidding-up, cut off siblings from careers they thought appropriate to their pride.

The ways out differed. With the end of the Grieston branch, it might seem that the Lilliesleaf one had inherited their status, as respectable judges, enjoying a similar measure of local power and influence, distinguished by income if not behaviour from other branches such as the families at Eildon, Newstead, and Melrose.

***

Here in Newstead, Thomas (1600-1647) farmed, following his father Thomas (c. 1575-1638) whose land he had inherited; and whose widow Agnes Mein, helped to manage it for another decade or more. In the same years, Robert was farming in Eildon and John (1611-1673) in Myneholm by Kelso, both being cousins. Thomas added two husband-lands from Melrose Abbey; while John seems to have been a successful entrepreneur, starting as a mere in-dweller, ending up as one of the larger Abbey tenants, and a substantial corn merchant in Kelso (see Chapter 10).

Meanwhile, south of Kelso, descendants of the original senior branch, deprived of their estates held from the Abbey since the 13th century, by the Kerrs' takeover after Flodden (see Chapter 7), continued to hold land in Sharprig, Lempitlaw, Morebattle, and Hownam, despite the appalling English depredations in 1544, when Robert Collingwood burned Hownam Grange and Sharplaw, which Hertford repeated the next year. These were all interconnected, as they were to the family of Lilliesleaf, for William of Lilliesleaf's first wife, a member of the Eccles family, had come from Kale Water and was murdered there, in pursuit of a feud by two members of the Hoppringle clan in 1574.

It is not easy to disentangle any direct line of inheritance here, but it is known that in 1576 they were tenants of Sir Thomas Kerr of Greenhead, near Morebattle–he who was recorded in the Roxburgh Retours in 1629 and in the Inquisition of 1678, concerning the feu-farm of 4 merks of land (35 acres) near Kelso with the Broomcroft "called Midlimslands, with pasture on the moors and lands in Wester Softlaw, Bowden and Belses and Raper Law toun, part of the barony of Cavers"; and salmon-fishing in the Tweed – while his son John Kerr of Cavers got land in Grubet, Bowden, Midlem, and the remaining Middlemastlands, together with Mylnerig.[180]

How much of that had once belonged to the Middlemas family, as the original knight's fee from the Abbey, cannot be accurately mapped; but it does indicate a continuing close link between their early 17th century farm holdings and the overall kin structure. There were, by then, four distinct families in Kale Water, some at least being sons of the murdered Eccles' wife of William of Lilliesleaf: James (c. 1570-1604) of Morebattle; Andrew/David (active 1576-1590) in Easter Grubet, Middlemaswalls and Morebattle (who was expelled from some of this including Easter Grubet in 1577 by Kerr of Greenhead [see Chapter 7] the land being given to the Rutherford clan; Walter (mid-16th century to 1601) of Lempitlaw and Softlaw; and finally George, active in Grubet in the 1570s whose brother Thomas was "slain at night in his own house" (a serious breach of the honour code that a man should only be killed *outside* his private defences) by Peter and Jock, "the bastard," Pott in 1592.[181]

How uneasy was the relationship between them, the Rutherfords of Hundalee and the Kerrs of Cessford, can be judged from the tangled affair of the theft of cattle and horses from Grey of Chillingham in 1571 [see Chapter 7] and the near-murder of a Kerr associate, Gavin Ford by John Middlemas in Sharprig in 1599.[182] But a degree of appeasement came in 1608 to 1611 through an arrangement with the Rutherfords: Andrew/Dand sold 2½ husbandlands (65 acres) which had been bought earlier on a 19 year lease for 1,000 merks from Nicol Rutherford, to John Middlemas of Grubet "with the houses, biggings, outsets, yards, barns, tofts, crofts, pendicles, and pertinents of the town, worth £312.6/8 pence" with rents and assedations till 1628, when George Middlemas, styling himself of Hindlaw, was to inherit.

Another portion, 1¼ husbandlands in Grubet valued at £205, was later allotted to Andrew and John, younger sons of Andrew/Dand. (Andrew/Dand had lands at Wideopen and Heuchhead, as well as Grubet Mill and two husbandlands in Morebattle.) At the same time, Andrew/Dand, evidently head of the kin-group here, sold another 2½ husbandlands bought from Nicol Rutherford and Martha Stewart in 1608, to his brother John on his marriage to Isobel Kerr, daughter of Kerr of Greenhead – presumably as a dowry and perhaps in settlement of the ancient feud between them.[183]

A similar arrangement was also reached by William Middlemas of Lempitlaw and 17 others with Sir Walter Scott of Branxholme (father of the future Earl of Buccleugh) in 1621 to return lands that Sir Walter had mortgaged to them and in William's case,three merk lands redeemable for £240; and Robert took over a 20 shilling land in Morebattle in 1648 from the Earl of Lothian, head of the Kerr kin, which James of Lilliesleaf had held in the mid-16th century.

What all this meant was that although their holdings had diminished since the early 16th century's losses to the Kerrs of Greenhead, and had become more marginal, being further upstream from Morebattle, the Middlemas family network had survived and was probably increasing its modest wealth in the first half of the 17th century. They remained lairds, lesser ones than their Lilliesleaf or Grieston kin, and mainly tenants of greater landowners, but they were by the Civil War at better peace with their neighbours. [184]

For smaller lairds like these, nothing changed greatly until the War came. None of them appears to have held to the old religion and from the evidence of signing of the Covenant in March 1638, all had moved easily under the Reform umbrella, as interpreted by the laird fraternity rather than the Kirk itself.

Of all these it was still true, as Camden had written (1595) of their Northumbrian counterparts "There is no man among them of the better sort that hath not his little tower or pele," an observation confirmed by Fuller in 1662, "all houses of gentry...either being castles or castle-like, able to resist, though no sullen siege, a tumultuary incursion." By the later date, however, after the Civil War, there would be no more incursions; and Lawrence Stone dates the greater rebuilding in the north to after 1610, their new edifices either incorporating the now-useless towers, or building what should now be called the country house from scratch.

Lack of roads and bridges (the ferry at Kelso being able to take only three horses at a time), the backwardness of upland agriculture, and a continuing element of physical insecurity, meant that Middlemas kin had no surplus for extravagant house-building. That lack and their vulnerability to bad harvests, and consequent debt to richer lairds meant that they would slip back in the competition to increase estates by purchase which changed the relative social balance between middling lairds and greater ones, whose drive for supremacy, briefly checked under Cromwell's regime, picked up again in the 1660s and was to erupt again, decisively, in the early 18$^{th}$ century.[185]

The alternative was migration, still following the late 16$^{th}$ century modes, but far more easily documented through better kept registers of births, marriages and deaths. Not by chance, those Middlemases searching for rural employment or tenancies followed the lines of the older traditional geography: their new settlement areas lying mostly in the Merse and within the ancient rentals of Kelso Abbey as set out in 1567 in the two archdeaconates of Teviotdale and Glasgow. Those with artisan skills or trading aptitudes moved into Edinburgh, the would-be legal professionals to Lothian towns like Pettinweem or Haddington on the Berwickshire coast. Some certainly became tenants in north Northumberland, others set up in Newcastle, and a small group took advantage of the exponential rise in coal mining in Whickham, north Durham, just across the Tyne.

The parish registers now begin to reveal the establishment of *clusters*, defined as a few settled urban or industrial families, first, naturally in Kelso and villages around like Sprouston and Duns, then in cities or large towns, Edinburgh, Berwick and Newcastle; finally in the 1630s, as coal prices peaked and drove up demand for sinkers, hewers, horse drivers and keel men along the Tyne, above all in the early relatively shallow and very productive pits in Whickham. Their implantation belongs to the later 17$^{th}$ century, but Whickham is unusual in that it seems to have lasted no longer than the 1630s decade, ending when the boom burst with the digging of too many pits, followed by occupation of Newcastle by the Covenanting army in 1640-42.

What happened to the pre-war migrants is hard to say. Those from Whickham, hired during the labour shortages after the 1580s (sparked off by the Grand Lease in 1578) tended to be sent home again in "the Hobbesian war of all against all beneath the fields of Whickham."[186] But those who stayed, lived in the little cottages (despite suspicions of them during the Civil War) and became locals; endowed with miners,' drainers' or keelmen's skills, they moved into the growing towns of Newcastle, South Shields, Gateshead – that is the rapidly-extending mining areas of the northeast, regrouping as clusters also in Durham: Tanfield, Lamesley and Chester le Street. However squalid and stinking, the towns and pit villages' streets offered an element of free movement, even aspiration, absent from the stifling nexus of rural poverty and village isolation at home.

At whatever level these migrants surfaced, they seem to have kept contact with their Scottish kin, even if only to pursue old debts, but that story belongs first to the Civil War, then to the late $17^{th}$ century and to those who did not fight at all.

# 9.

# Civil and Religious War

Did the Civil War affect the whole of Scottish society in the 1640s? Obviously there were some who actually fought, like Major Thomas and Cornet James Middlemas; there were those, especially in the southeastern counties, who were caught up in it as the armies passed through, needing food, fodder for horses, munitions, or whose houses were billeted and lands pillaged. As Royalist and Covenanting armies raged across Scotland, followed by Cromwell's New Model Army, even those whose lives were not at risk had to react to alien ideas, alien interpretations of how a man should believe or be governed, if only to reject them – even after the Restoration–when set against personal convictions, sanctified in most cases by belief in God.

How much the years from the first Bishops War in 1638 to the Restoration of Charles II in 1660 and the contentious thirty years that followed, shaped the evolution of a kindred made up of increasingly disparate families is impossible to gauge. That they changed Scotland is undeniable, but in ways different from their impact on England, as much as history told from the Scottish perspective differs from the Anglocentric version. Both nations, however, like the kin themselves, had to face the unresolved questions left over from the Reformation period about the proper forms of religious worship, the way society should be governed, and how relations between the two should be conducted.

Some general account is required, if the particular residue of Middlemas activity is to make sense. In the good years before 1638, it seemed that James VI's claim to govern his northern kingdom "by a clerk of the council, which others could not do by the sword," might continue under his son. After all, James had taken note of the opposition to his Five Articles, at Perth in 1621, to ensure the fragile basis on which consent for Jacobean episcopacy rested. After James's death in 1628, Charles I initially seemed minded to accept the same "decent and comelie order," including the deepening of Presbyteries and Kirk sessions; despite the Assembly's tough response that kneeling at Communion (the fifth Article) counted as "rank popery."

Devout in the Anglican mode, Charles had his father's intellectual arrogance without his wisdom, tact or capacity for manoeuvre. He knew little of Scotland, appearing essentially English, even in his encounters with Europeans. But he did as King at least try to set the new Presbyterian faith on a sounder financial basis from which it could achieve its great ambition of a school in every parish, to match the minister in every Kirk; and after eight years of negotiation, a better system of teinds to provide for both was introduced.

Unfortunately, Charles' aloof manner (especially when addressed by Scots with too much familiarity) showed him in a poor light, while his reforms upset nobles and lairds, not so much because they lost revenue as a result, but because their system of land-holding after the feuing of monastic lands had been exposed to over-close legal enquiry. At his first visit to Scotland, in 1633, the King seemed shocked by the lack of ceremony and plainness of Kirk services – in contrast to his own lavish Holyrood coronation.

How much of what followed should be blamed on his mentor, Archbishop Laud, is debateable. From the Scottish side, it seemed as if Charles' New Book of Canons 1636 was set on enforcing uniformity, in direct conflict with the radical party, who encouraged the laity to attend "private meetings," the banned conventicles under another name, to escape the regime prescribed at Perth. Even from an English perspective, Charles operated secretively, trusting only Laud, reluctant either to explain or persuade, as if fearful of direct challenge. This high-handedness fostered a reaction, a sense of Scots exceptionalism, as if the Presbyterians had a direct line to God, expressed in Old Testament language with frequent references to ancient Israel's history for justification.

As opposition grew, with demands by ministers, nobles and lairds' meetings for reform of "popeish errors," even the Catholic Traquair, now Lord Treasurer, advised caution. A riot (possibly staged) broke out in St. Giles' church in July 1637. Nobles, lairds and burgesses flocked in to Greyfriars Kirk on 28 February 1638 to reaffirm the 1581 Confession of Faith and to sign the National

Covenant – whilst still reaffirming loyalty to the Crown. The first day, the nobles and lairds signed, the second, ministers and burghs, and on the third, the people of Edinburgh. Middlemas of Lilliesleaf is said to have signed but many of the names are illegible.

In contrast to his earlier anger, Charles failed to react, leaving it to his new Commissioner the Marquis of Hamilton to handle, as the General Assembly continued to sit, before it finally abolished episcopacy altogether in December. But the King mistrusted Hamilton, sought rejection of the whole Covenant, removed central government to Dundee, and ordered his fleet to sail north. Since his English army could not be ready to invade till 1639, Traquair advised him to temporise, play for time, and exploit the intrinsic divisions among the Covenanters, and between them and lairds and nobles who would not abrogate royal authority in favour of dreams of a theocracy.

Altogether 28,000 signed the local Covenants, while the central coordinating body elected its own Commissioner,[187] so that the rest could go home and prepare to mobilise under their landowners' or burgesses' direction. At this stage they had some relative advantage over a King short of money and munitions; but Charles I was, nevertheless, correct in reading how deeply rooted were their social and political divisions. Since there had been no serious war for 60 years, it was not surprising that the Covenanters needed time: no reserve of trained soldiers existed, few possessed more than small arms to face a regular army with artillery and massed infantry.

The Commissioners appealed to Scots soldiers overseas to return, to anyone who had served in Continental armies in early stages of the 30 Year's War; and began in the autumn of 1638 to import heavy munitions from the Netherlands, while casting the small three-pounder cannon in Edinburgh itself. Their approach to military planning and supply organisation under the Committee of Estates, in the 1639 emergency, served well and became the model for the next decade –based in the southeast on the network of local lairds, clergy and church elders, who were responsible for the setting up of levies and early regiments.

Tenants, cottars and household servants as well as gentry and middle class men were drafted in response, by inducements

*Fortified houses: Westport House (above), similar to Plora; Minto Tower (below), similar to Grieston (both from Nigel Tranter:* The Fortified House in Scotland, *vol. 1)*

couched in biblical rhetoric, with ministers leading the propaganda war, each in particular districts. But inevitably, this served only in the short-term, just as Douglas levies had worked in the 15th century. In the sense of being amateur, the first Covenanting army was a popular one, with senior officers' posts reserved for men, mainly landowners with war experience. Overall, General Alexander Leslie, a former Swedish Field Marshal, took command, initially to avoid any rival claimant from the higher nobility. Appearance of a professional army came slowly, heightened by the evolution of a standard means of identification: the flat blue bonnet and the coloured ribbon or infantry sash.

But problems between clergy and lairds developed even before Charles' army approached, as the radical ministers tried, with the Act of Classes, to exclude landed officers, creating a serious military disadvantage which was reinforced after two years by pervasive war-weariness, and loss of manpower as soldiers slipped away for harvest time. Actual combat soon heightened these divisions (as it did in later revolutionary armies in the 1790s), while disease and plague in 1644-45 reduced regimental numbers, which in most cases had never reached their full allotment. Infantry regiments were intended to have 5-600 men at least; in practice, most had less. (Rather better was the ratio of pikemen to musketeers at 2 to 3, the critical factor being the supply of powder and shot, for which, in the Master of Cranston's regiment, Major Thomas Middlemas was responsible, finding himself in effect restricted to a monthly quota for both.)

Meanwhile the Covenanting leadership made offers to the English opposition, leading the king to suspect that they wanted to overthrow monarchy altogether. A last attempt at settlement having failed, in May 1639 the first Bishop's War began. Reaching Berwick on 30 May, Charles offered rewards for the assassination of 17 leading Covenanters, but his army failed to take even Kelso, and lost both Dumbarton Castle and Edinburgh, in what turned out to be a shadow war, no more than skirmishes between ill-prepared levies, glad to resume negotiation.

But while Charles' army dithered, General Leslie pulled his together through his forceful leadership and successful bluff; and induced the King in June to sign yet another treaty at Berwick, with Sir William Douglas of Cavers representing the Covenant, as Sheriff of Teviotdale. This settlement could only be temporary, embodying a transparent fiction, because the King made only verbal promises and had no intention of accepting an end to episcopacy.[188] He then withdrew to York. As vast differences emerged during the detailed negotiations, and as Charles prorogued Parliament for a year, the second Bishop's War began while the Scottish Parliament, to avoid internal rivalries, converted itself to the Committee of Estates.

This signified not only the transition to more professional warfare, but to a rising level of expenditure requiring deeper political and religious commitment. Logistically, it became impossible to keep a standing army for long quartered in the Borders; and in August, despite disquiet among the leaders, Leslie crossed into Northumberland, taking the largely undefended county, but with strict prohibition against military depredations – a "new model" indeed for a Scottish invasion of England.

In the short term, the Scots won. By the subsequent Treaty of Ripon, the King even agreed to pay for their army's daily expenses (which both sides knew would force him to raise it through his English Parliament). Their victory seems astonishing, even if all suspected that he would renege. For their own reasons, in the end the English Parliament voted to back the Covenanters, albeit with only £300,000; and in the three months it took to agree, both Laud and Strafford were committed to the Tower. But if this suggested to them the first stage of an English revolution, the Scots pushed too hard, provoking a reaction against their demands both for abolition of bishops and for a Presbyterian form of worship in the south.

They did get an Act of Oblivion, but not the longed-for access to Colonial free trade; and the more they persisted in discussion of common forms of governance for all Britain, the more the Covenanters undermined their own success, leaving it open for the King to make new offers and for his great general in the north, Montrose, to appeal for Scottish upper-class support against their fears of popular rule. As the Scots army withdrew, Charles did indeed make wider concessions, dismissed Traquair, and gave rewards to his Presbyterian enemies, in order to prepare for his greater battle against the Parliamentary opposition in what became the Long Parliament, facing up in 1642 to the Civil War.

At first the Covenanters imagined that they had succeeded, but the years 1641 to 1643 involved them in too many problems on three fronts, in Ulster, in the Highlands, and in disabling the King's party at home; which diverted resources from their chief aim, to mediate – on their terms – in the coming English conflict. The fact that they did not physically commit themselves to the English Parliamentarians raised suspicions and weakened their case there, while allowing the King to set up his administration at Oxford, secure in his belief that he could stave off the Scots till he had won what he saw as the major war of rebellion.

For all their rhetoric and, perhaps, idealism, the Covenanters were never a unified force. As part of the effort to create one, in the summer of 1643, the militant wing sought a Convention with powers to create a full alliance with the English Parliamentarians: out of which grew the Solemn League and Covenant in 1643-44. But the English were also divided between the Commons who wanted this alliance and the Lords who temporized, fearful of their own positions if such a grouping ousted their King – a concern enhanced by the louring prospect of arrival of Scots Presbyterian crusaders from Ulster.

In the end, the English leaders settled pragmatically to win the war first, then argue about religion later, a policy which increasingly excluded the Solemn League's heightened demands for closer union and the Presbytery model. But for lack of any alternative, they agreed to pay cash to finance the Ulster army.[189] Whereupon in October 1643, the Scots committed themselves to an English war against the King.

Many royalists in the Borders gave in and concurred, fearing to lose their estates. Yet the Covenanting army fell short in numbers and supplies, when they crossed the Tweed again on 25 January 1644. It still faced war at its rear, in the north against Montrose, and in Ireland, as well as in front. But however ill-prepared, it did represent, after five years, a workable compromise between the classes who had signed the Covenant, even if it was not (yet) a citizen army.

War experience being vital, most of its officers and sergeants had already seen service in the Bishops Wars. Middlemases served in two regiments: Thomas of Mangerton, brother of Lilliesleaf, in Cranston's regiment, constituted formally in spring, 1644; and James his nephew, in the Earl of Leven's Foot, one of the premier infantry regiments, commanded by General Leslie, now Lord Leven, himself.[190]

As a major, third in command to Lord Cranston and his neighbour Sir Walter Riddell, Thomas was in the first invasion, took part in the siege and storming of Newcastle in October, fought at Marston Moor, and finally at Philiphaugh in the battle where General Leslie's 6,000 battle-hardened troops eliminated Montrose. He was in fact active in three of the most decisive points of the Civil War. Acting also as supply officer, he is recorded as ordering monthly the full ration of 300 pounds of powder, 100 flintlock matches, and 100 musket balls, from 1644-47, delivered to him by the quartermaster. Numbers fluctuated, falling sharply with a plague visitation, and one-third of the regiment, possibly under his sole command, returned with Leslie to face Montrose. After Philiphaugh, recruits again poured in, bringing the regiment up to 600; but it was then disbanded entirely in February 1647 as the last Scottish soldiers returned home.

James, much younger, ranked as a cornet (Lieutenant) and enlisted also in 1644. Leven's regiment included a strong contingent from Ulster and four separate troops from each of the Border counties. The Ulstermen derived from the "plantations" made 30 years earlier, some being Catholic but most Presbyterian; and it was probably from contact with the latter, men in the old "gallowglass" Irish emigrant tradition, fresh from the attacks by Catholic Irish in 1641, that James acquired his radical views which his wife Isobel Scott also shared.[191] He may in fact have fought earlier in the Irish campaign, before a third of this regiment returned to Scotland to form the composite force of nearly a thousand men which, like Cranston's, went on to fight at both Marston Moor and Philiphaugh.

Both of these can by this stage be called professional soldiers and both signed the petition to Parliament on 23 March 1648 against the sectarians, in favour of the King's rights being restored so long as he established the Covenant. In that sense, their motivation fitted with the majority of Border lairds, for the Covenant, the

Solemn League and reform, but not opposed to monarchy itself.

Bloodied by the experience of two of the Civil War's harshest battles, they would now have looked more like the soldiery of Callot's engravings of the 30 Year's War, than the foppish officers of Rembrandt's *Night Watch* (1642) jostling for position at the well-lit centre stage. Philiphaugh accentuated an alliance of Teviot and Tweed under Scott of Harden and Kerr of Cavers, who with Scott of Buccleugh went on to oppose the sentence of death on Charles I and to support the proclamation of his son Charles II after the King's execution.

The Middlemases of Lilliesleaf thus supported the redrawn King's party in the Civil War's second stage after February 1649, up to its disastrous end at the defeat of Worcester in 1651 that sent Charles II into exile for a decade. There were few options for lairds, after all, between vestigial loyalty to a monarchy, however discredited and untrustworthy, and the profoundly radical, untried solution of a godly theocracy, close enough to a republic. (Even by the 1770s, the founding fathers of the United States had no historical model for their plans, and had to look back to Republican Rome, as interpreted by Machiavelli.) Thereafter, they appear to have joined the underground resistance to Cromwell, though it is not known whether they took part in the 1651 strike in the Borders and Lothians against his imposed administration, a time when old reiving habits revived and moss-troopers rode again.

Even if the details are obscure, the pattern of what moved them can be read in the Declaration of Remonstrance by the General Assembly to the English in 1647 "Touching the King's Majesties Royal Person and Authority, in Preservation and Defence of the True Religion and Liberties of the Kingdom...and touching the Solemn League Resolution to live and die in the same" (see illustration – repeated by the Convention of Estates to all known Scots living abroad).

These documents assumed, even as late as 1649, that their "brethren in England" would hold fast to their integrity and the Solemn League and Covenant. They formed the basis of a public, even international debate without parallel since the Declaration of Arbroath, three hundred years earlier, couched in a language appropriate to a time when at least those who fought were ready to die for a carefully-defined religious belief. Whether those who did not fight held so fast cannot be known, but the quality of the propaganda went far to ensure it.

***

From the very different English perspective, the Scottish army undoubtedly helped at Marston Moor, decisively perhaps as Leslie's lancers charged; but Montrose's threat in northern Scotland scarcely counted in the Parliamentary general strategy, focussed as that was on pinning down and finally defeating the King. It did not take part in the crucial battle of Naseby in 1645 and, in a sense, both the Self Denying Ordinance and the New Model itself, were a way of ridding the English side of "foreign" allies and their unwelcome philosophical/religious demands. (The last Scottish troops left in January 1647, just before Cranston's regiment was disbanded.)

Charles' tactical surrender to the Scots in May 1646 thus served only to undermine the residual trust Cromwellians placed in the army of the Covenant; who handed him over to them, in any case, even though they had not wished him to lose, but only to be loyal to his concessions and his word. The outcome – his trial and execution – was exactly what most Scots *did not* want: England's radicalisation in a way very different from their own godly conviction, which the English thereupon, if they had not already done so, rejected.

So the Scots bid too high in the political doctrine stakes, having been blind to the greater strength and perhaps deceptiveness of their putative allies. In retrospect, the Covenanters' peak of influence had been 1640-45. The New Model Army turned out to be Independent not Presbyterian and that made the Scots' concessions, and Cromwell's decision to try the King in January 1649, doubly hard.

At local level, the early 1640s brought not only a core of political agreement among Border and Lowland lairds (if only in opposition to the clerics) but tangible reforms in local administration and education. On the other hand, as Charles II returned briefly after his father's execution in 1649 to accept all that was asked of him in order to mobilise an army again, the third stage, with its sequential Scottish defeats at Preston, Dunbar and finally Worcester, brought Cromwell and the English army to end their game on Scottish territory. Despite General David Leslie's skilful defence in depth, his army (weakened by clerical purges) was routed at Dunbar in 1650, so that even before Worcester, a year later, the grim Commonwealth dictatorship began.

The four Border counties suffered severely, both from Leslie's scorched earth tactics and Cromwellian repression during the nine years afterwards. Dismissals and oustings ravaged the Kirk, while military purges were severe especially in the southeast and central Lowlands. Wisely, most lairds kept their heads down, and lived with it till Cromwell's death. Even then, they did little but compete locally for advantage, as the generals led by Monck cautiously re-established Scottish Parliamentary power and began to negotiate again with Charles II, before the Scottish army once more crossed the Tweed in January 1660.

After Charles' return, the Act of Recission 1661 swept away most of the previous decade's legislation and institutions: bishops and the established Church returned in full. The vicar of one southern English parish wrote simply "this day, I began again to use the Book of Common Prayer." But for Scotland it was not reversion to a clean slate, even if Charles "had learned from his travels." Episcopacy was not the people's first choice, who after 22 years wanted chiefly, peace. But if episcopacy were the price, most were prepared to accept it, if only because the Presbyterian fervour had alienated the great majority.

Cromwellian proto-union vanished, even before the Restoration, to be replaced again by two kingdoms, with Scotland once more excluded from England's colonial trade. Cromwell's high taxation of the 1650s continued, nevertheless, to pay for England's Dutch wars. If the Restoration settlement appeared unfair, after all that the Covenanters had sought to do, however, it was accepted. During the Cromwellian occupation, lairds like Lilliesleaf, where their baronial court had been abolished in 1654, were too near to the centres of his administration to show any resistance and felt particularly exposed in a bleak period with few tangible results. In that sense they might have benefited from the the Recissory Act. But the residue of conflict that outlasts any war is worst after a civil war, whether or not actual violence continues.

Some Middlemases had gone so far as to emigrate, seeking a geography of better living conditions which they had experienced in the army during the 1640s. Andrew Middlemas, youngest grandson of the last Middlemas of Middlemas in Kale Water, had established himself in Alnwick, mid Northumberland, having stayed for a time with his cousins who farmed at Old Bewick, Eglingham. He married an English wife, daughter of a long-established farming family nearby; and others found places on the land in and south of Berwick (Chapter 10). Most of these accepted communion from the Anglican church, though some stayed Presbyterian. The majority of kin however remained on the Scottish side, no doubt because it was their country, whatever Cromwell's major-generals had imposed.

Collectively, however, the Lilliesleaf family and its offshoots in Eildon, Kelso and Morebattle-Hownam, experienced a downward shift even before the Restoration. Other laird families, already owning greater acreage, added more: the division between them moved from wealth (and therefore power and influence) to social status and future aspiration. The family conformed, as it were, to the ancient Confucian rule, that each generation should lose one degree of nobility. Grieston's last echo came in 1657, when John Earl of Traquair sold his whole lands to Alexander Burnett for nearly 15,000 merks.

The war's other residue, which was not so easily abandoned or extinguished, lay in the radical experience of freedom of worship and open debate about fundamentals which, naively perhaps, Covenanters reckoned to have been their substantive contribution since 1638. Individual responsibility had been erected against state prescription; and what followed 1660 can be read as conflict between the conviction that this was the proper duty of men, represented by different factions of the Presbyterian Kirk, and renewed royal prescription. In this, certain members of the Middlemas kin-group carried conviction far beyond prudent limits into outright rebellion.

Whether they were radicalised by the war, Cromwell's dictatorship, or royal ministers' rigidity in re-imposing the old order, cannot be known. The complexities of mid-17th century affiliation are baffling enough at a general level, let alone that of individuals. But their resolution was to take them to conventicles on lonely moors, armed with swords and pistols, against a persecution as stern as anything launched by Laud and Strafford twenty-five years earlier.

Ironically, it was the Earl of Middleton, Royal Commissioner till 1663[192], who oversaw the re-establishment of royal authority within the period before the General Assembly was permitted to reconvene. Coercion came swiftly, conventicles being banned in 1662, with the perverse effect of reuniting Kirk factions. Few landowners stood out, though many tenant farmers and rural labourers did, but resistance flared in Tweeddale and the Lothians, with remoter Teviot not far behind. The Kirk itself suffered the loss of 300 ministers dismissed, out of 952 in all Scotland, while fines were imposed broadside, with Middleton taking a rake-off until his dismissal.

In response, the sacked ministers, followed by their congregations took to barns and preachings in the open fields, in opposition to the "King's curates" and the 1663 Oath of Allegiance. Resistance in Ulster as well as war against the Dutch hardened Charles' and his ministers' policy: repression and more stringent fines were exacted from lairds now held responsible for what their tenants did. There followed the Pentland Rising and a march on Edinburgh, soon dispersed by Tam Dalyell's brutal royal force accompanied by many executions.

Royal policy then switched briefly to conciliation and a release of prisoners, while the First Indulgence 1669 allowed some ministers to return. Yet in the mid 1670s, as conventicles started up in urban centres, the level of revolt and consequent repression again rose, and the preacher John Blackadder stirred up Teviotdale, while on the far fringe of zealotry, the Cameronians were outlawed and held in prison without trial, under martial law. 1678-79 brought transportations, local armed conflicts in the southwest, and murder of the Archbishop of St Andrews.

Earlier Covenanters stood aside disapprovingly. At Lilliesleaf however, the Middlemas family could not, because they lived and farmed in one of the main centres of sectarian resistance, and did not accept that those who joined the religious rebels were enemies of the state, nor even (a much later judgment) that they were "unreasonable men who prevented rapprochement between Episcopacy and Presbyterians from becoming a reality."[193] These were, after all, the same men who had signed the Solemn League and fought in the Bishops Wars.

Lilliesleaf was surrounded by moors, regularly used for conventicles, "the common and ordinary place and rendezvous of those seditious rebellious and disorderly meetings." Sir John Nisbet of Dirleton, Charles II's Advocate in Scotland, in November 1676 prosecuted Isobel Middlemas and her husband Walter Scott of Aldtoun (she being a portioner of Raperlaw) together with various Scotts, Turnbulls and Lady Riddell, all of Lilliesleaf, for attending a conventicle to hear John Welsh preach, "a declared rebel and traitor...armed with swords and pistols to fall in blood...if anyone should molest him."[194]

On the day in question, 26 November, Captain Innes arrived with his dragoons to disperse the meeting. Finding three to four hundred ready and armed, he "did send of their number

> about thretty airmed men in order forsaid upon horses to the pairtie, and the saids persones, having uttered many opprobrious and reproachfull expressions both against his Majesties persone and authoritie, did presume to show the said pairtie that they were readie and resolved to withstand and resist them, whatever the consequence might be, if the pairtie should any wayes offer to disturb or trowble them, and had the confidence to draw there swords and to show and hold out there bended (cocked) pistols in there hands, be that the said Captaine Innes, considering that they were soe numerous and desperate and that they were lyk to overpower him and that not onlie the said pairtie that cam towards him and his pairtie bot a great multitude of others that were in airmes did indeavour and were about to surround and encompass him, and he, apprehending the effusione of blood and upon assureance givin by some of the saids persones that, if he should not proceed further, the said meeting should be dissolved in peaceable manner presentlie without delay, he thought fitt to

> give them tyme to dissolve, yet nevertheless they did continow and proceed to keep the said meeting by the space of ane hour thereafter, at which tyme they dissolved and went aff in three severall bodies in a most braveing and insolent manner.

Innes should have been commended for his good sense, knowing just how long the service would continue before his troops moved in again...

But at Lilliesleaf, the rest of the family found their loyalties divided, for at least one of the younger brothers, James, formerly young officer in Leven's regiment, joined an armed resistance group which attacked Glasgow and turned back a royalist detachment. But soon after, at Bothwell Bridge, late June 1679, this poorly armed band ran into a much larger royal professional force commanded by the Duke of Monmouth and were routed.

James who was by then middle-aged and Isabella (or Isobel) his wife were fortunate to get away. Condemned to death, they went into deep hiding, escaped the trials and shipments to the colonies (many of whom, shipwrecked, drowned off Orkney) and spent the next twelve years in disguise, probably among their kin in small farms in the Kale Valley south of Morebattle, which emphasises the role of women in providing safe houses, shelter and concealment.

Under a combination of martial and judicial repression, conventicles in the end subsided; while active dissent switched focus to the Succession and Test Oath Acts 1681 of the next, potentially Catholic King (James II and VII), taking its strength from a broader-based moderate Presbyterianism.

The Middlemases remained collectively if unintentionally at the epicentre, as Major White and his royal force harried them and their neighbours across all four Southeastern Border counties, much as Grierson of Larg and Claverhouse were doing in the Southwest. The year 1682-3 brought perhaps the worst, called "the killing time," when regular use of the death penalty, often via summary justice, alternated with attempts at indulgence to buy off a new generation of conventicles. Use of the Test Act bit deep into lairds' pockets: 26 in Roxburgh alone were fined £274, 237 for non-attendance, the usual form of evasion of the oaths.[195]

Meanwhile, in October 1684, a variety of former Middlemas resisters were cited to sign the Bond of Submission at Jedburgh: Robert, George and Lancelot from Hownam, James with his wife Marion Turnbull, James and Agnes, William in Easter Grange; all refused and were put to the horn, farmers and tenants alike.

Most of them signed in the end, however, during James II's first year, who tried toleration for all as a backdoor means to restore the Catholic faith – and as a result of which terror eased. Yet this time, the Lilliesleaf family were in the minority in their own country; it was England not Scotland which ejected the last of Stewart kings, bringing in Dutch William and his wife Mary, daughter of James VI. Cautiously perhaps, this so-called Glorious Revolution was not recognized in Scotland till spring 1689 by the Convention of Estates, and Scotland got the worst of the bargain: William at first refused to abandon bishops and royal supremacy in church affairs, a settlement which the landed classes accepted. Only in retrospect, to achieve peace after so much disorder, did the new king abolish the Restoration settlement and repeal the Act of Supremacy.

The Border shires, like the Lothians and the central Lowlands, had supported the Presbyterian mainstream for 30 years since Cromwell's death and drew a final benefit with the establishment of an independent Church of Scotland – however fissiparous the dissenting tradition would prove then, and later in the 19th century. Once *their* church had purged its own members, the Kirk was free thereafter to support toleration for those who were to call themselves Episcopalian, so long as they abjured the Stuarts – on which enduring basis they were able to campaign for the Act of Union in 1707.

Historians still differ about the motivations and beliefs that clashed during and after the Civil War. These ordinary lairds and their still-small numbers of kinsmen were certainly not revolutionaries, in the sense that many of the sectarians and preachers were. None of them sought the overthrow of monarchy or establishment of a clerical regime. But they did demand, with greater or lesser fervour, a society where free individuals could hold dissenting views about the fundamental choices in their lives. In so far as that determined what they actually did, whether armed attendance at conventicles, or daily farming routine and land management, they were never far away from it, and at least four risked their lives in its defence.

*Dumbarton Castle in the 17th Century, by John Slazer*

*Cartoon of Cromwell, c. 1650*

# 10.

# Those Who Did Not Fight

By the second half of the 17th century, the extended family was going through its third transition: the first being from an Anglo-Norman military elite to Border medieval lairds, the second from that to early modern lairds or "landit men." Now they were moving from lairds not just to "bonnet lairds," but to 18th century farmers, still living on their land as owners or tenants, but adjusting – in whatever way – to modernity. If upwardly mobile, some of these looked to professional life, or to betterment migration; if downward, to skilled agricultural work or urban and industrial jobs.

This stage began after the Restoration and continued through much of the 18th century. Indeed it set the pattern for the 19th century as well. However, after the Civil War and Cromwell's occupation of southern Scotland, there were still three main kin-groups centred on land: Lilliesleaf, Eildon-Newstead-Midlem (west and south of Kelso) and southeast, Sharprig-Morebattle-Hownam (in effect the valley of Kale Water). Beyond lay the urban implants in Edinburgh, Haddington, Newcastle, and the newly industrialising Tyne (see Table 1 p.180).

It is not easy to chart these in a chronologically coherent way, not least because the increasingly accurate parish registers, while giving a far closer indication of family size, produce large numbers of individuals with similar or the same names, sometimes citing only one of the two parents. This creates confusion about who was whose son or daughter, even within the same parish. Where names are matched by land transfers (sasines) they are easier to connect, but at times, transfers or consequent litigation took place long after the event and, however valuable the printed registers of births and marriages are, the OPRS Series has not yet been extended to deaths. For that, the originals represent an almost impossible task for a single historian.

There is no choice but to tell each family group's story separately, while trying to retain a sense of their interactions, living as they did only ten or fifteen miles apart; but also their increasing differences:

Table 1. **Marriages recorded by counties**

| | 1600 –1650 | 1650 –1700 | 1700 –1750 |
|---|---|---|---|
| **Scotland** | | | |
| Berwickshire | 0 | 4 | 34 |
| East Lothian | 6 | 20 | 8 |
| Midlothian, incl. Edinburgh | 7 | 4 | 9 |
| Peebles | 0 | 0 | 1 |
| Roxburgh | 11 | 25 | 92 |
| Selkirk | 0 | 1 | 8 |
| **England** | | | |
| Cumberland and Westmoreland | 0 | 0 | 3 |
| Durham | 1 | 1 | 6 |
| Northumberland | 4 | 14 | 41 |

size of holding, type of farming, style of life, and levels of education; university having become a regular choice for lairds' sons and not just would-be priests since the Reformation.

Given the nature of 17th century records, concerned mainly with legal matters, inheritance, wills, debts incurred and sometimes paid, or crime, legal notoriety and occasionally ill-fame, this is a patchy business.While the core family in each area remained "landit men" into the 18th century, the by then numerical majority of kin names were already small farmers, tenants or husbandmen, and rural craftsmen such as shepherds and blacksmiths; if urban, they might be apprenticed to merchants and burgesses in the small town guilds, or traders themselves, artisans and workmen of many sorts (coal mining alone having seven or eight skilled categories).

The tables of ancestry in Appendix A are therefore inevitably incomplete, logical constructions intended to show continuity rather than to be wholly inclusive. Some of the connections are only implied (by dotted lines) and exclude individuals whose only known reference is birth or marriage. This is further complicated by the long change from variant spellings of the name itself, natural in a pre-literate society where only clergy and lawyers wrote habitually. By the mid-18th century, the final "t" (as in mast, most or mist) disappears, being replaced by two main variants mis (s) and mas (s), which co-exist even in the same town or parish and start a process of redefinition slowly increasing in strength, so that the 19th century censuses deal with them separately.

It was still possible for the same document to bear three different spellings for the same individual's sasine in 1733[196]; but with standardisation, the sense of identity differentiation grew, further eroding the original kin-group, and adding to the rifts created by loss of land, emigration and the opening-up of tightly-knit village communities.

***

*Lilliesleaf*

William, the younger died in 1647, having lost title to both the fortalice and the barony to the Duke of Richmond and Gordon, six years earlier, for reasons unknown. His elder son James (c. 1625-

1656) had married yet another Scott, Anna, who gave him three children, William of Lilliesleaf, Margaret and Anna. Since he died aged only 31 when these were infants, they were given tutorship by John Middlemas of Purviven in Liddesdale, an uncle who managed their affairs with a trust fund of 3000 merks,[197] accounted for yearly to the executors, two Pringles and two Scotts.

Either because the elder William had been deeply indebted earlier in the century, or had been worried before he died that James had not married, or because he still owed Thomas 5000 merks, the Lilliesleaf estate had been left to the uncle Major Thomas for his lifetime. Whatever the reason, Thomas, now released from his Civil War army career, at once renounced the inheritance to James the real heir, as soon as part of the 5000 merks debt was paid (the rest was forgone out of a sense probably of family equity).

Meanwhile Walter of Lilliesleaf Chapel, younger brother of William, became baillie *ad hoc* of Lilliesleaf in 1648, but only two years before his own death; whose elder son James, also of Lilliesleaf Chapel, son of Isobel Scott, inherited the Raperlaw lands, witnesses to the inquest being John and Robert the younger brothers. The pattern is complex, with two heads of families with the same name, married to sisters and what exactly each side inherited, or which of the two tower houses they lived in, is uncertain. But the process of estate fragmentation had begun. The Lilliesleaf Chapel marriage produced another James, of Raperlaw (c. 1650 to late 17th century) who in 1670 married Janet Turnbull. His cousin, John of Myneholme, near Kelso (c. 1650-1673) married a third Scott, Margaret; and the Raperlaw land was divided between them, first in 1660 then again in 1670. The next generation, near the century's end, William and Walter, were both styled "of Raperlaw."[198]

James of Lilliesleaf's early death, his children's tutorship, and subdivision of lands were not the only problems. Shortly before he died in 1656 he had had to borrow 5000 merks on mortgage from his brother-in-law James Scott and this debt was still outstanding after the Restoration. So in 1662, John of Myneholme, husband of Margaret Scott, paid it off in full, taking over the Aldtoun farmhouse and buildings near Hawick.[199]

John of Myneholme, originally a feuar in Kelso, was already

a wealthy man, enough to grant several loans to his neighbours, yet he in turn borrowed to finance this transaction – a common enough pattern at the time. James of Lilliesleaf Chapel was not so agile. He had incurred a second debt (in the 1650s but not recorded until 1662) to Sir Gilbert Elliot of Minto, south of Raperlaw, for £1963 plus annual interest of £98, 3 shillings at 5%, which carried on through his children and was finally called in in 1727 (see Chapter 11).

Some obscurity in these transactions, and which Middlemas married which Scott were only partly resolved when Lilliesleaf's sister Anna married Walter Scott of Aldtoun in 1670, taking with her (according to the Sasine) another 11½ husband lands of Raperlaw. This was probably one third of the original estate. It may be that all the land transactions were a means of coping with the legal vacuum created by the 1661 Act of Recission, which nullified Cromwellian legal documentation. But it does seem that, whatever the financial travails, the families of Lilliesleaf and Lilliesleaf Chapel had not suffered unduly from the war and its aftermath, in terms of social status, for these various Scotts were close relations of the Scotts of Buccleugh;[200] the bleak side being that they were already incurring mortgage debts against an estate fragmented by subdivision into three that would become a crippling burden within fifty years.[201]

***

*Eildon, Newstead, Kelso*

The descendents of Hugo Middlemas of Midlem and Thomas Middlemas of Eildon comprised at least five families by the mid-17th century. They had married Vairs, and Meins, and other local small lairds, all with lands feued in the 16th century from the Abbeys of Kelso and Melrose.[202]

John of Myneholme already owned the farm of Newstead, which after his death his widow and second wife Agnes Thompson continued to manage with their son John, a corn merchant in Kelso. John the father was farming 44 rigs in 29 separate parcels across the "great fields" (run-rig system) of Kelso in the 1650s and 60s, some of it from the Kerrs of Cessford – a hard task to do efficiently, but comparable in size to the areas managed there by Douglas of Cavers, eighth Lord and his cousin by marriage.[203]

John the corn merchant married firstly Margaret Rae in 1661 and took sasine of the lands of Myneholme in 1672. Even for him, however, the pattern of debt intruded: while he invested in various mortgages in the 1660s, he also took on a 75 year bond for £100 in Kelso, which by 1688 had risen to £182, and was only settled after much dispute by his great-nephew in 1733. The families also had to face the same sort of disputes with neighbours and kinsmen that appear to have been widespread at the time, when boundary fences were non-existent. Robert in Eildon had to contend with Meins and Slaters "who daily pasture and make inroads...and break down the timbers growing in their farmyards and dykes digged about the same."

The Eildon family at least benefited from better education. Thomas' son Peter and his grandson Patrick both took their MAs at Edinburgh University, the latter in 1699 when he married Agnes Chirnside and inherited the main Eildon farm from his grandfather.[204] The picture here is of a family retaining its roots, improving its prospects at least until the lean 1690s, while branching into the corn trade in Kelso. Yet this did not prevent at least one of John of Myneholme's children by his first wife, Thomas Middlemas and his family, emigrating to Newcastle.

***

*Kale Water*

Andrew/Dand Middlemas (c. 1609-1652) elder grandson of the last recorded Middlemas of Middlemas (Andrew David of Middlemaswalls, Easter Grubet, and Morebattle) saw out the Civil War as one of several minor lairds, in and around Grubet and Hownam. The original 1608-9 arrangement with the Rutherfords provided the basis for his farming there and in Morebattle. Of those who inherited what may, in all, have been one thousand acres in 1652, John his brother died the same year and the younger son Andrew emigrated to Alnwick in Northumberland; so that the two elder sons, William of Morebattle and George of Hindlaw took over.[205] Neither claimed the title Middlemas of Middlemas. George died twenty years later in 1672 and after a lengthy court case[206] William inherited the whole. But the state of Kale Water upland farming was such that he, having until then only farmed farther downstream on the plain, had to set up an inquiry to discover how far this bequest was encumbered by debt: should he accept and be served heir, at the risk of taking on an impossible burden of debt, or renounce it? The Kerrs of Greenhead, represented by Dorothy Kerr, proved very reluctant (presumably fearing to reopen ancient disputes) but finally produced the 1612 document signed by both Middlemas and Kerr sixty years earlier, showing that the land was properly documented.

By 1687, there were several other Middlemas families farming along the valley, [John and Robert Middlemis, James and William Middlemast, both families of Easter Hownam Grange, and George, Robert and Lancelot in Hownam itself. Note the two spellings, living side by side.]; some like William in their own right, others in Easter Hownam Grange, tenants of the Earl of Haddington. Failure to pay their teinds there, the tithe being one-tenth of the rental, indicates their level of prosperity: three families owed "a chalder (modern equivalent 2500-3500 litres) of beer, 25 bolls of oats, 5 bolls of rye, 5 bolls of pease, 4 bolls of wheat, plus fodder, with 15 stones of butter, 15 stones of cheese, and 30 lambs" all for one year. To convert this, twenty bolls of grain equalled one tonne, i.e. the crops from land between 50 and 100 acres. Multiplied by 10 (a teind being one-tenth) suggests that each farmed 500 or more acres – a fair size for the area.

But in the same year, George Middlemas, a great grandson of George of Grubet active in the 1570s, tenant in the mains farm of Kirk Yetholm downstream, right on the border of Northumberland where the army had crossed in 1638, died, leaving livestock and crops to the value of £554 against debts of £627 – a fair indication of how farming in good valley land in Roxburghshire on Bowmont Water was becoming harder and riskier, even before the bad decade began.[208] Yet these small towns were still densely populated. According to the Hearth Tax record 1691, there were 129 hearths in Hownam parish, 255 in Morebattle, 167 in Yetholm, as against 1028 in Kelso (if one multiplies by five, this gives a fair count of total population).

***

# A DECLARATION OF THE Convention of Eſtates in *Scotland*, concerning their ARMIE:

With their reaſons for continuance thereof untill March next; And in what manner the Officers and Souldiers ſhall be paid. *Dated at* Edinburgh *October* 15, 1647.

*Together with*

## An Exhortation of the Generall Aſſembly of the Kirk of *SCOTLAND*, unto the Scots Merchants and other their Country-people ſcattered in *Poland*, *Swedland*, *Denmark* and *Hungary*.

---

*EDINBURGH*,
Printed by *Evan Tylar*, Printer to the King's moſt Excellent Majeſtie. And reprinted at *London* for ROBERT BOSTOCK. M DC XLVII.

*Declaration of the Convention of Estates, 15 October, 1647*

The kin-groups which James and Isabella rejoined c. 1689, after a decade of clandestine existence in Hownam, hiding from the "killing time," had spent Charles II's rule, like their ancestors, farming their land. Apart from the two known serving officers, the Civil War passed them by and there are no Middlemases recorded in subsequent Muster and Militia roles. They were not military families; they understood and preferred the land. But it is hard to imagine that Lilliesleaf or the Kale Water families, where the dissenting spirit never died out, and who signed the national Covenant and the Solemn League, would welcome the Restoration and its consequences with anything but distaste.

Apart from those who were Covenanters until James II's diplomacy of tolerance, they seem nevertheless to have accepted a moderate Presbyterianism, without deliberately confronting the 1661 settlement. Tired of too much fervour, possibly hit by fines, they came to terms with Stuart state power and its consequence, the transfer of authority to William and Mary, even if their Toleration Act did not confer real, enduring tolerance.

But along Kale Water the Covenanting tradition hung on, even in the 18th century during the first secession from the Church of Scotland, when it remained a centre of dissent with its own meeting house. A Kirk was not built in Hownam until 1739, and until then, the official minister had to preach from a sort of makeshift tent.

At laird's level, the successors of William of Lilliesleaf still merited the old formula "one of the trusted and faithful men of the county." At the other end of the social scale, John Middlemas in Haddington in 1663 would argue against a prosecutor that he could not afford a caution "being but a simple yeoman and mailmaker (tenant) living by his handy labour"[209] – although since he was related to a young notary in this still-thriving port town, he may have been at the least economical with the truth..

But there would be no more judges of assize like William, nor judges in their own baronial courts, even for local matters though these were restored in 1660 to pre-Cromwellian status. Neither did Middlemases use their ancient seal on documents in the late 17th century, the last recorded instance being a Peebles sasine of 1618. (Slow erosion of the older traditions, exemplified by the terminal decline of Grieston, go some way to explain the curious affair discussed in Appendix B, when the up and coming Earl of Middleton appears to have misappropriated the Grieston shield of arms which the family had held for at least 300 years.)

A measure of social class differentiation was to be expected within the kin-group, if only as a result of increasing numbers, as the population rose. But the half century after 1635 was troubled, estates were being broken up or becoming unprofitable, reducing lairds' real positions (not just their status) to that of "bonnet lairds" or tenants, at least for all but their elder sons. For them, the Restoration did not restore, and the 1690s were to bring seven of the leanest years since the 16th century, worst for those whose debts were already accumulating.

Such changes can be seen both in variations of description (farm servant could be either a real servant or a laird's son doing a sort of agricultural apprenticeship), levels of crime and the way in which criminality was regarded. Many of the Middlemases had behaved badly in the early 1600s, for whatever reasons, especially at Lilliesleaf and along Kale Water. But they had either been vindicated by the courts or, if found guilty and "put to the horn," fined or even imprisoned briefly, without much stigma attached. By the late 17th century, matters were rather different: the Kirk and lay judges having established and enforced a stricter discipline and canons of behaviour.[210]

Rieving was now categorised, not as part of a Border way of life, but as theft; to be punished by judges who, as landowners themselves in the Middle Shires had a vested interest in peaceable, uninterrupted farming, maintained reciprocally on both sides of the former Border line. The same landowners and their Northumbrian equivalents were already improving and centralising their land management and turning the more marginal uplands over to sheep – a sentence of eventual death, not only for the hopelessly inefficient run-rig system but also transhumance, even "kindly tenure" and the customary order that went with them.

The quarrel with Kerr of Cavers over Sir Thomas Grey's stolen sheep in the 1590s [see Chapter 7] was one of the last episodes dealt with under March Law. Most Middlemas court cases thereafter in the 17th century (apart from the affrays described in Chapter 8) were for recovery of debts, either to or from. Once feuds had been eliminated with the assistance of the Kirk and its ministers, once lairds' own behaviour had largely been reformed, the upper social levels conformed, leaving it to criminals like Jock O'Grange to steal sheep or act as receivers.

But one case from 1695-7 displays a touch of an older style. John Middlemas, farmer and corn merchant in Kelso and a local proprietor, was accused of slander by John Lillie for calling him a "fornicator and a whore monger" and worse – charges which, given the Kirk's attitude to sexual deviance, represented a serious offence. What caused the outbreak is not known but since Lillie was a neighbour in farming, John may have suspected an affair.

In the event, John was summoned to appear in Kelso Kirk, "on his bare knees...in presence of the whole congregation" to ask God's pardon and Lillie's, and to pay a fine of £100, half to Lillie, half to the poor of the parish. John accepted the verdict but rejected the punishment. Confronted by this powerful local man, the Kirk session elders substituted a lesser penalty of excommunication "being a sufficient punishment for the slander."

John appealed to the higher court and had the money to do so, using his cousin David in Kelso as cautioner. Afraid perhaps of the consequences, in front of Edinburgh advocates, Lillie duly confessed two years later that he *had* been guilty of fornication but with another woman, Margaret Stewart; and the Lords of Council let John Middlemas off altogether on the grounds that the case was not-proven, leaving of course, as that verdict does, an element of doubt.[211]

***

It is clear from the fall in population of the whole upland region beside the Tweed from Peebles to Kale and Bowmont Waters, that disruption of an older social order by subdivision of land and recourse to debt to finance farm upkeep, were only part of a massive change which began during the Restoration years.[212] Changes in agricultural practice, forerunners of the "age of improvement" may have been as much a consequence of scarcity of labour as cause of putting agricultural workers off the land, even before the 1690s accelerated the process. Which was cause, which was effect, is hard to determine. The fact that there was no rural unrest in the century suggests that migration took its own course and landlords took advantage when leases fell in, by ending kindly tenure and by replacing agricultural labourers with many sheep, requiring few shepherds. There is really not enough evidence to support the argument that an early case of deliberate "clearances" occurred; rather, the long accumulation of individual choices made by many thousands between flight from the land and "betterment migration."

Migration however was not only part of a long-generated process; by this time, it was better documented, whether heads of households only or whole families went to neighbouring towns, or richer farming areas like the Merse and north Northumberland. In this sense, "betterment migration" might mean professional occupation – the result of a proper education, in parish schools run by the minister, usually financed by local gentry and the Kirk in tandem. Patrick, heir to Eildon, was also the son of a schoolmaster at Edinburgh High School.

James Middlemas became a notary (solicitor or in Scots, writer to the signet) in Denholme, near Edinburgh in the 1660s and thirty years later, John (probably Patrick's brother) followed him professionally in the still-thriving port town of Haddington – once one of the fastest growing towns in Scotland, comparable to Dundee, but now facing secular decline as a result of trade shifts to Edinburgh and Berwick.[213] Over 90% of the Faculty of Advocates (barristers) in the capital came from landed families, and the same was true, albeit to a lesser percentage, for notaries, some of whom lived in considerable style. John married Marion Clerk, rose in his world as Sheriff Clerk Depute 1690 and became Haddington's Town Clerk in 1696 – an important post, in such a borough. This did not, however, exempt him from litigation. After his death in 1702, his executors squabbled over who was in fact entitled, his wife claiming illiteracy as an excuse for being unable to give up the required documents – to the other executors whom she sued for the surprisingly large sum of 10,000 merks.

That case was unusual and went to the higher courts in Edinburgh. Marion may have lied: even the small farmers around

Hownam now had some degree of literacy, and only a tiny percentage needed a notary's hand to guide them when signing a contract. Both parish and borough schools served their pupils better than they had even fifty years earlier, being financed by well-meaning landowners and staffed by often well-educated ministers; who in addition undertook Poor Law duties or helped adjudicate in local boundary or other disputes. Some of the poor even enjoyed their studies free.

A smaller laird of the 1690s would have had some knowledge of history, perhaps the classics, as well as basic religion, reading and writing. But he would have hardly aspired to culture. Even in the mid-18th century, the Enlightenment remained the preserve of the elite. His culture would have reached no wider than local sports and popular music, insofar as these escaped the bleak, kill-joy injunctions of the Kirk. On the other hand, for any landed man, the standard of living was good in the 1680s, and probably for the first time in Scottish history, just as good in the towns and burghs. A notary like John in Haddington had several house servants. Whereas the diet of a rural working class dependent on subsistence farming was still monotonous, the laird or professional household enjoyed wheaten bread not oats or rye, regular meat and fish from the river or the sea.

Real hardship occurred only in the very worst years after widespread harvest failure, and as it diminished, so did criminality, though the statistical reduction in violence and executions may be explained partly by better performance of the justice ayres, partly by the informal practice of mitigating the harshest punishments: either permitting an offender to pay a fine and only hanging him if he failed, or revaluing the total of stolen goods to a level just below that set for grand larceny, which carried the automatic death penalty. To this extent, Scottish practice may have remained more humane than its English equivalent.

Trade complemented education as the great escape route. The merchant or trader sat near the top of the urban scale, well above the craftsman, although the old rigid hierarchy of status was breaking down, as crafts and trades opened up to new entrants, even in specialised market towns such as Selkirk, dependent on leather work and cloth manufacture.

John son of the Myneholme farmer, finding it almost impossible to consolidate the run-rigs his father farmed, even with the help of local officials, moved into Kelso as a corn factor before 1685 and soon accumulated house property in this thriving burgh of 3,500 people (similar to Hawick, a non-royal burgh, far ahead of Jedburgh or Melrose).[214]

But the easiest way into trade was to move further, to a growing town or better to Edinburgh itself, as an apprentice, preferably in a trade where a laird's status did not at once disappear.

Thus James Middlemas from Midlem, apprenticed to an Edinburgh armourer in 1650 became a city burgess within 25 years; William Middlemas who had started as a guild servant to Sir Patrick Murray, also became a burgess in 1670; and Walter set up as a tailor in Canongate, being a burgess of that guild by 1697, who married Margaret Lindsay, ladies maid to Lady Stewart wife of the Lord Advocate of Scotland. Highest in the social pecking order came burgesses of whatever trade, then bakers (baxters in Scots, John Middlemas a baxter in the middle 18th century being a son of William of Raperlaw), skinners or brewers. Next tailors, cordiners (shoemakers), wainers (wagon builders), and hammermen (metal workers).

Canongate held a cluster of Middlemases in the city centre. This is where Bessie Middlemas first settled and married successively a fishmonger and a cook in the 1600s. Urban life in decent style was open to any in-dweller, i.e. resident, if he paid the fee and gave proof of apprenticeship qualification; but this had its obverse, that it also offered an easy closed way for relatives of existing burgesses. The corporations of craft guilds survived into the 18th century, eased largely by connection and respectable birth.[215] Edinburgh was a city of 84,000 by 1700 – yet it still had only 20 skilled trades, a quarter of Norwich's total.

Scottish economic historians now emphasise how much was done at this time, before the "age of agricultural improvement" by individual landlords themselves, walling off their mains farms, planting trees (in pursuance of a 1661 Act) and providing better drainage. Yet their lands were still bleak and windswept, far from the richly wooded landscapes familiar from 19th century engravings. Much of the soil remained undrained and boggy (it being easier to plough the hillsides than the valley floors). Only the Merse was truly fertile and there was a steady decrease in the number of holdings in Tweed and Teviot. Of course, existing landlords bought more as it came on the market, enclosed it, and turned the Southern Uplands and the Cheviots over to sheep, creating a new landscape of permanent grassland without which the improved breeding of the 18th century would have been greatly delayed.

The cattle trade from Galloway in the southwest, and the sheep trade into Northumberland, grew rapidly as herders established drove roads in place of the old "dry marches." On the other hand, the incentive to foster depopulation also increased. Numbers of cottars fell sharply, some becoming day labourers paid in cash, others simply moving on east and northeast to more fertile farms for better paid work or, following a much older tradition overseas, into the armies of Gustavus Adolphus of Sweden or Louis XIV.

For lairds, finance proved the main determinant of whether progress could be achieved, often exemplified in the size and standards of their own houses. A large part of the Middlemases' debt problems can probably be explained by their difficulties in raising money to sustain farming at Lilliesleaf, Newstead or Bowden where they still inhabited the old pele tower-houses. A steady differentiation grew up between smaller landlords and greater ones who had better access to finance for investment, who could employ factors and baillies to manage it for them (professional estate management only arriving in the late 18th century). *Their* houses were new in the Restoration style or based on Dutch designs fashionable after the 1680s, mostly of stone (dressed not rubble) each with its policies, enclosed park and sheltering trees: what Sir Robert Sibbald in 1698 called "regular and commodious houses" surrounded by gardens of vegetables, orchards, perhaps a fish pond, and protected by dykes or dry stone walls from neighbours' roaming livestock.

Most of the recorded Middlemases had ownership or established tenure, feuars (like the Kelso families) being the lowest one with legal rights. Their size of holdings still compared well with those in Fife or the Merse (being about 400 acres for tenants on Buccleugh estates, probably over a thousand acres in Eildon, only 4-500 in

Kale Water, according to the 1718 survey of Roxburgh.) Four-hundred acres of arable included about 1200 acres of outfield, as it had at Lilliesleaf. But what mattered was fertility and that holdings were centralised. In the latter respect, the Eildon farms and Lilliesleaf had the advantage; and their little touns were set out in single or double rows of tofts, held on lifetime leases, as the sasines they signed demonstrate.

This benign picture excludes the sort of old-fashioned run-rigs with only banks not fences to keep out the neighbours' beasts, the land suitable only for the old heavy plough drawn by six oxen needing three or four men to hold it. Two Acts of 1695 attempted to assist consolidation, but this process was slow, often lacked finance, and was only completed by the mid-18th century.

On the whole, it seems fair to assume that the Middlemases of Lilliesleaf and the Eildon-Midlem area were good landlords, maintaining their tenants well-housed (the long-house of stone, clay and turf comprised barn and living quarters together, the damp kept out by lime mortar). Some tenants, but fewer overall, now lived in two or even three-story houses which matched the improvements to lairds' own houses by 1700. "Steelbow" practice encouraged sharecropping, a landlord providing seed, equipment or stock, but it also carried exploitation, mainly through thirling, tying them down to the landlord's mill, blacksmith and brewer.

In this period, what the land produced did improve a little, particularly crops destined for burgh markets rather than the subsistence economy. Yields began at last to rise, reaching fivefold on arable land (infield) but only threefold in the outfield in Minto 1690-2, next door to Lilliesleaf. Yet even before the 1690s, a large part of Border agriculture remained barely commercially viable.

So much for lairds and farmers; their wives were an integral part of the routine, but enjoyed less education and were excluded by the Kirk from parish matters; and a farmer's wife would run the domestic economy, manage the farm servants, and often as a sideline run her own small trade like brewing ale, as Agnes Middlemass did in Newstead, pursuing her dilatory customers for payment in the local courts for years on end.

Lower down the scale, outside in all weathers, the wives of cottars and labourers faced unremitting toil outside, in all weather...

and after that the cooking and the house. It is not surprising that roughly one in ten of all Scottish women fled the land in the 1690s for domestic service, shop keeping or small trades in the great cities of Edinburgh and Glasgow, Perth and Aberdeen.[216]

***

Migration had been temporarily checked in the mid-17th century by wars, military occupation and persistent uncertainty; but among Middlemases what had been evident earlier (notably in following the coal mining boom to Whickham in the 1630s) seems to have continued, as least among younger sons: such as Thomas to Newcastle and Andrew of Grubet to Alnwick in search of a future and a wife, both in the 1650s. The latter, with the farming connection brought by his wife, Margery Ditchburn, set up his own business in lime burning and supply to local farmers and the Alnwick market.

Their experience fed back to the kin-group, especially once mobility became easier after the Restoration: decline in Whickham could be remedied by going to other coal mines in Durham, or to the port city of Newcastle and along Tyneside. The agricultural moves outwards, once restricted to harvest time in the Merse (where it ended a month earlier than the Dales) spread out and became permanent, not only in Berwickshire but across all of north Northumberland. Robert Middlemas "the Hind at Ewart" in 1757 stated that he wished to be buried where his ancestors had *always* been, in the graveyard of the (lost) ancient chapel.[217]

How steady was the implementation in small Merse towns such as Semprin and Swinton, Foulden, Langton, Duns, and Coldstream (strikingly replicating the pattern of Kelso and Melrose Abbey's lands in the 1567 rent-roll) or south of Berwick and the Tweed, can be seen not only in the parish registers, but more tangibly and for the first time, on their tombstones a generation after the migration peak.

Apart from the initial choice, to stay with agriculture or go into industry, these moves depended on several subsidiary choices: who in the family to take and who to leave (inevitably, the younger ones went first and married where they settled), whether they could manage a farm tenancy or should aspire only to a better-paid job, where they could survive the still-prevalent hostility to Scots migrants (like West Indian immigrants in the 1950s and 60s). It all depended on their frame of mind, capacity to fulfil their expectations, and on their intellectual or manual skills – blacksmiths and shepherds as well as miners being in constant demand. Few ever sent remittances home, their new status becoming permanent; and loss of so many able kin further diminished prospects for those who stayed behind.

Famine in the 1690s, at its worst from 1695 to 1700, the "seven ill years," hit lairds almost as hard as cottars and labourers. Fear of starvation, and its reality in 1698, speeded up these patterns of migration, especially given the opening up of Ulster to Scots Presbyterians after the final defeat of James II at the Boyne. [Total migration to England 1600-1650 between 85,000 and 115,000; 1650-1700 78,000 to 127,000; to this should be added 50,000 to Ulster in the 1690s alone (T.M. Devine, *Scottish Immigration and Scottish Society*, 1992.)] Such a massive exodus changed Border society permanently. Yet the keynotes for choice were conservative: to go where they had some knowledge, to avoid risk as far as possible, and to decide what, on the basis of earlier experience was best for them in the long-run, since there would be no easy going back.

Edinburgh offered the advantage that it was nearby and wholly Scottish, and contained Middlemases who had been settled for a century. Equally, being open to immigration from all angles, competition was high (only 15% of burgesses came from Border counties). A skilled metal worker might prefer to join the "hammer men" of Selkirk, where two Middlemases were deacons of the guild in the 1710s, or as a weaver to go to Coldstream (where in 1667, William was prosecuted for evading the Act regulating the breadth and weaving of linen cloth).

Newcastle on the other hand, being far less cosmopolitan, but a notable port nevertheless, afforded a wider range of occupations, ranging from wharfing and shipping coal to London, to the late 17$^{th}$ century glassworks which produced some of the finest European wine goblets. Up river, the "keel trade" loaded coal from wharves and pit wagons and brought it down for transfer to ocean-going boats, either in Newcastle's own docks or later down river, in

Hartlepool, Sunderland and South Shields, where Middlemas families soon established themselves.

Newcastle city was not initially a magnet for Scottish immigrants, who in the 17th century stayed in the coal mines, Whickham and its associated pit villages Lamesley and Tanfield, or even journeyed to Yorkshire, perhaps because after the 1630 boom and bust experience and Scottish Army occupation in the Civil War, miners generally were seen locally as "a peculiarly uncouth race, little better than savage tribes."[218] Their conditions, however unpleasant and filthy, were nevertheless better than under the near-slavery which obtained in the contemporary pits of Lothian; and they were often able to return for 100 or more days a year for harvest and winter work. [The Scots went first mainly as haulers and keel men but learned on the job. Until the Civil War they tended to return home in winter (much as the Irish did on the canals or Mozambicans in the South African gold mines), but thereafter settled down, as sinkers of pits (top of the hierarchy), hewers, bearers and drainers, all highly skilled.] But by the 1700s, Newcastle like Glasgow had become more attractive to them than Edinburgh itself, and this did not change for nearly a century until it was replaced by North America.

The passage was not simple. A migrant worker travelling to England needed a testimonial, usually from his parish minister or landlord[219] though this was not required for any man of modest means. Travel had become far easier and safer for merchants or artisans, especially for smiths who were often itinerant, preferably by river or sea transport; but roads remained bad, and had not even been charted on maps before the 1660s.

He – or indeed she – needed just as much a degree of kin-group support at the destination, for initial accommodation, access to whatever job market existed, and bailing out if things went wrong. None of this would be provided to aliens by whatever was the local system of poor relief. Meanwhile their home kin, owners, portioners or tenants with secure leases, had to decide, on what they knew from the migrants' accounts, whether to follow, and take the risk or stay put.

Inheritance strategies were crucial: tenants could only very rarely buy land, so their survival depended on the landlord renewing tenure, the latter's interest increasingly being to consolidate or turn to pasture. Other interests also governed choices in towns and cities: how open or closed were the corporations and guilds, and how successful was the Kirk at carving out new model parishes for development in the larger cities, relative havens from the chaos, filth and stench of cities at the time.[220] This problem was not addressed in England until the Reform Acts of the 1830s.

None of the Middlemas immigrants left any personal record of why they chose one or other; neither do the instances of marrying kin in new localities suggest any pattern other than kindred congregating together. Clearly the Civil War's experience of large bands of soldiers moving across middle England increased the size of the marriage pool. But in fact the clusters remained rather static and local, as if the choice of place and wife initially was defined more by tradition and local knowledge than military experience.

The links between new home and the old family nexus remained strong however, consolidating over the *longue durée* into folk memory, even if they usually concerned property and assignment of goods on death. Thus it was not odd that a Tyneside heir thought it fit to attend an Edinburgh court to give evidence about a testament, since that was where his capital assets still lay. A century later, when emigration to the colonies began in earnest, those links endured, the migrant family often remembering its roots and preserving relics better than those who stayed at home in what they called "the old country."[221]

As a result therefore of a whole series of rational choices, what can best be described as clusters of often-closely related kin developed in certain towns and villages in the Merse and North Northumberland, even before the 1690s. They are set out in Table 2, 1600-1750, on the principle that some clusters were temporary (like Whickham) others permanent. There is also an obvious differentiation between marriages recorded, and marriages with consequent births, which indicated a greater degree of settlement. In both periods, infant mortality stayed very high at 170 per 1,000 – life expectancy rose slightly from 38 to 39 years in the 17th century to 40+ in the early 18th.[222]

None of the seventy-odd families of 1690 could have foreseen the lean years that started in 1692, or the consequences of seven

Table 2. **Clusters (numbers of marriages, Middlemas males, accompanied by registration of birth or christenings).**

| Scotland | 1600-1700 | 1700-1750 | England | 1600–1700 | 1700–1750 |
|---|---|---|---|---|---|
| Eildon/Melrose | 5 | 1 | (O) Newcastle | 7 | 15 |
| Kelso district | 21 | 10 | (M) Alnwick | 5 | 7 |
| Hownam | 6 | 12 | (M) Berwick | 1 | 5 |
| (O) Jedburgh | 2 | 7 | (M) Eglingham | 3 | 1 |
| (O) Morebattle/ | | | | | |
| Yetholm | 6 | 9 | (M) Hartburn | 0 | 7 |
| (O) Oxnam | 6 | 8 | (M) Morpeth/ | | |
| | | | Bellingham | 0 | 4 |
| (O) Sprouston | 6 | 4 | (M) Rothbury/ | | |
| | | | Whittingham | 0 | 11 |
| —— | | | (M) Wooler district | | |
| | | | (Glendale) | 2 | 8 |
| (O) Edinburgh | 8 | 4 | | | |
| —— | | | Durham County | | |
| (M) Coldstream | 1 | 7 | (M) South Tyne valley | 0 | 3 |
| (M) Duns | 8 | 3 | (M) Tanfield | 0 | 3 |
| (M) Fouldon | 2 | 3 | (M) Whickham | 4 | 3 |
| (M) Galashiels | 1 | 5 | | | |
| (M) Haddington | 0 | 9 | | | |
| (M) Langton | 0 | 4 | | | |
| (M) Longformacus | 0 | 5 | | | |
| (M) Polwarth | 5 | 0 | | | |
| (M) Selkirk | 1 | 4 | | | |
| (M) Semprin/ | | | | | |
| (M) Swinton | 0 | 6 | | | |

(O) = **Settlements from the 16th century;**
(M) = **Migrants from 17th century;**
**Towns with less than three not included.**

disastrous harvests in eight years. Contemporaries were aware only that the decade was the worst, even by comparison with 1622, 1636, 1642, or 1673, landmarks across what climate specialists call "the little ice age." Poverty and misery turned to sheer starvation of the Border population, comparable to the Irish famine of the 1840s. And in some cases, like Chirnside, a Covenanting centre, families were too poor even to pay for their coffins.

Dearth, if not actual death, hit the landed families and tenants in different ways, as most borrowed frantically to help tide over, or reneged on existing debts and mortgages. There had been earlier debt crises, at Grieston in the 1490s, Lilliesleaf in the 1610s; but these had been resolved out of the estate income or by sales of small plots of land. In this case, it was made worse by fragmentation and portioning, and the lands still held were put at risk in a more fundamental sense, usually indebted to greater men who, being at severe risk themselves, were disinclined then or later towards generosity.

This explains quite simply why no Middlemas invested in the inflated hopes of the Darien Scheme for trade with Central America to evade the English Navigation Acts, where many of their related families suffered severe if not catastrophic losses.[223] [Darien had its origins in Scotland's exclusion from English colonial trade. Subsequent mercantilist or import substitution policies led only to English trade retaliation, and although the 1680s were on the whole good years for Scottish textiles, with big new mills built at Haddington, extensive smuggling as well as bad harvests undermined prosperity in the next decade. The Company of Scotland Trading into Africa and the Indies did provide some outlet for Scottish capital to compete with the East India Company, without the head-on confrontation in North America via Darien; but was wound up in 1706 as a preliminary to the Act of Union.]

By the 1700s the various family branches displayed elements of a class in severe decline, yet maintaining their social contacts and friendships, especially with other former Covenanters such as the Riddells, and marrying Scotts and Turnbulls, albeit only from cadet branches. But they were not able to compete with Sir Walter Riddell's grand new house outside Lilliesleaf; while their own ancient pele tower at Chapel became desolate, lived in eventually, according to local legend, by a witch.[224] The diaspora accelerated after the 1690s, despite the residual ties of kinship, in which there were already rifts growing (Middlemass being retained by landit men, Middlemiss on the whole by migrants to industrial occupations).

Nevertheless, the kin-group seems, like certain trees, to have been able to regenerate itself even after the lead branches had been cut down. They survived the half-century of adversity after 1690; albeit from lower rungs on the social ladder by the early 19th century.

To adopt the metaphor of Raeburn's famous painting c. 1795 of the Reverend Dr. Walker skating on Duddington Loch, the ice on which the family had glided, if not as elegantly but as effectively, through more than four hundred years, cracked. Some fell through it in the 1690s. As one modern commentator puts it "his efforts and risks involved in keeping up appearances...his brief and serene performance is founded on perilous skill and hard physical exertion – it's almost a tragic image."[225]The rest struggled towards the shore, surviving for a few decades more. But the battle for survival as lairds was almost over before the Act of Union passed the Scottish Parliament.

***

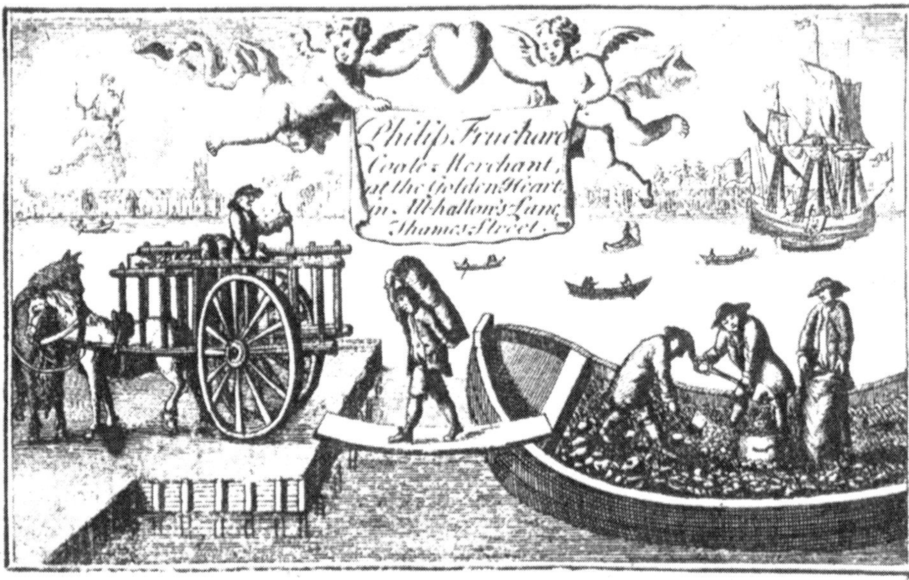


*Coal mining and transport*

*Coal wagon and wagonway*

# 11.

# Reckoning 1700 – 1750

The Union, which a recalcitrant English Parliament had denied to James VI/I in 1607, came about a century later, at the instigation of another English parliament; and in 1707 it at last coincided with what the majority of Scotland's political and landed elite desired. Francis Bacon's judgment, that "the realm of Scotland is now as an ancient and noble realm of itself substantial, but when this island shall be made Britain, then Scotland is no more to be considered Scotland but as a part of Britain, no more than England is to be considered England but as a part likewise of Britain; and consequently neither of these are to be considered as things entire of themselves, but in the proportion that they bring to the whole," stood – even if many Scots did not share it, and many English accepted it only out of strategic necessity.

England's reasons were rational, if selfish and variable. Having legislated in 1701 for a Protestant successor to the ailing Queen Anne, without any consultation, English legislators professed themselves surprised when the Scots refused to accept this Hanoverian arrangement. They broke off union negotiations. But the threats which had inspired both a renewal of the idea of union, and determined the choice of a Protestant future, remained: England faced huge continental dangers, possible war with France (where Louis XIV championed the Stuart claimants and a Catholic revanche) and a rapidly growing national debt which put at risk her capacity to fight another European war.

Reversing its stance, Queen Anne's government in 1704 offered the Scottish Parliament a deal: reparations for the Darien disaster – for which they were partly responsible – and guaranteed access to their colonial trade. This was backed up by political machination, much use of leverage and subsidies to Scottish nobles and parliamentarians; but also with threats to stop all trade between the two kingdoms and deprive individual landowners of their lands held south of the Border.

The Scottish magnates had few reservations. Apart from the threats to their revenue, which could have affected all the great

Border estates, Buccleugh, Roxburgh (both soon to become Dukes) and Hume and March, they were very aware that, once ensconced in the Westminster legislature, they could vote together as a block, providing support, often venial if not actually corrupt, for whatever administration ruled in London, thus ensuring suitable treatment for their country and themselves.

That this perpetuated the old unreformed order of patronage only later became a political criticism. More immediately, it ensured defeat of both Old and Young Pretenders in 1715 and 1745 – though the latter turned out to be a close-run thing. Opposition came from those who saw union as a betrayal of the Scottish nation and its distinctive Presbyterian culture, even though the Kirk and the legal/educational system were to remain intact. Evidence of corruption was filtered out to a volatile and hostile Edinburgh public.[226]

Supporters however argued that the recent past, the extravagant Darien failure, and the economic nightmare of the 1690s made futile any dream of a Scottish empire run by a nation one-fifth the size of its hostile neighbour. Common sense dictated that it would be better to trade by land or sea with England, its European markets and its colonies, freely and uninterrupted.

For the Edinburgh elite, members of the Faculty of Advocates, the College of Physicians (both established in the 1680s) and their professional or academic counterparts, scientists, mathematicians, doctors, botanists who were, within fifty years, to inspire the Scottish Enlightenment, the arguments appeared self-evident: Scotland would retain its institutional identity and benefit from commercial and intellectual access to the wider world. Ambitions and greed matched careful calculation; and modern historians tend to argue that Scotland did actually win a confederal solution in civil life, not dissimilar from what James VI/I had originally sought.[227]

Minor Border lairds took no part in this debate, though former Middlemas associates and kin by marriage such as Douglas of Cavers and Murray of Philliphaugh did, as hereditary sheriffs of Roxburgh and Selkirk. Neither did the Middlemases support Pretender rebellions. They had had no reason since 1638 to love the house of Stuart, even when the Old Pretender raised his standard in Kelso in October 1715. If they read Andrew Fletcher of Saltoun's diatribes against Union, there is no record. Saltoun's arguments were soon vitiated by experience (and not revived until the 20th century, first by Marxists and then by Nationalists); and they no doubt agreed that there was no other future for Scotland – like Ireland – on the British periphery.

Thus they acquiesced not only in the Treaty of Union but its consequences: a future where emigration would become as much a national experience as early, fierce industrialisation of the central Lowlands; and in which the interpretation of a unique Scottish history, for which their ancestors had fought, would slowly be eroded, so although the religious element survived until and beyond the 19th century, much of the rest, like their ancient pele towers and the kin-group pattern of life, was first ignored, in the flowering of an urban, proto-European culture, then relegated as if it were a relic of barbarism.

Like Jacobitism but for other reasons, this was what the Enlightenment luminaries and the landed elite wished to avoid by a flight from the past – evident in their neo-classical houses, designed and built by the Adam brothers and fitted out and furnished in their Edinburgh workshops, in what became a common British aristocratic style. Much later, in 1828, Thomas Carlyle would judge that the Scottish Enlightenment had "no patriotic and not much human affection" and that David Hume, Adam Ferguson and William Robertson had substituted for the real past a "conjectural past," a foretaste of Walter Scott and antiquarianism, which ignored the real past as it had existed up to the 1690s.

In terms of their history, aspirations and achievements, the Middlemas family, since the early 15th century or before, *were* that rejected past, and their resulting dilemmas exemplified how rapidly they were to become marginal or subordinate – with only a few individual exceptions. Against a background of steady depopulation of the upland valleys, continued migration, and the descent of middling lairds into tenant farming status, their story becomes more fragmented as its elements diverged. Even their commitment to reformed religious faith fell away, as it tends always to do in periods of migration; the act of leaving freed them from the bonds of religion as well as politics and deference to Presbytery and shire synod, so that they conformed easily enough to the Anglican Communion where they settled. What they themselves remembered about the lost past cannot be known. Folk memory rarely survives more than two or three generations and none of the legal documents elicited by 18$^{th}$ and 19$^{th}$ century processes or searches goes back before 1700.

***

The loss of Raperlaw and most of the Lilliesleaf inheritance provides a mordant example of how old-fashioned smaller lairds diverged from great landowners, hanging on as they did to agricultural practices which were already outdated in comparison to the now-vast Buccleugh or Cessford estates. The 1690s had exposed the weaknesses of Border livestock and arable husbandry (lack of capital, overstocking, lack of winter fodder, low returns) leading to farms being abandoned by starving tenants. Perennially short of ready money, they had to defer payments, and this became a way of life.

"The system of recording arrears in kind after bad years at a money equivalent based on the high market prices then prevailing, could leave tenants a burden of debt...bankruptcy often followed several years later." This sums up the Lilliesleaf story. What had begun as a manageable loan from a close neighbour, Sir Gilbert Elliot of Minto, taken on at 5% in the late 1660s, had risen by 1724 from £1963 to over £4000. When Elliot finally called it in, the total (including accrued interest, tailzies – tithes – and expenses) came to £5050.

By then, three portioners held Raperlaw, the senior member, William of Lilliesleaf (once tutored in the Civil War), William (son of James Middlemas and Janet Turnbull) and his wife Margaret Leithead, (whose son was the master baker in Edinburgh), and Francis Scott of Aldtoun (son of Anna Middlemas and Walter Scott). It was the Lilliesleaf William's death in 1723, followed by the exceptionally severe winter and dearth of 1724 that set off the process of liquidation by the feudal superior, whose legal duty it was, the Marquess of Lothian, Kerr of Newbattle.[229] Francis Scott was no more able to pay than his co-heirs and became the last to go through the formal process of infeftment, so that the legal transfer could proceed. Everything went to Elliot in 1727.

***

The families in Kelso and Eildon did rather better in the first half of the 18th century, though they too had debt problems. When John of Melrose's original 75-year bond fell due in 1688, it took another fifty years before it was settled by his great-grandchildren, after his grandson David's death. More serious, David's son David himself had to pay off similar bonds to local lairds and Kelso merchants, amounting in all to £2000 before 1703; and this latter debt demand in 1708 set off a dispute between his brother, Andrew the cordiner, who still owned the Myneholme land with eight acres of building land in Kelso, and his brother Thomas, who had already emigrated to Newcastle but returned for the final hearing in 1733.

Other relatives continued to farm as before. William, another grandson of Myneholme, wealthy enough to own land, houses and tenements in Kelso, and a corn merchant like his father, married Mary Trotter from a well-to-do burgess family which included skinners, maltmen, coopers, and in one notable case, cordwainers (cordiners or boot makers). But Nathaniel Middlemast, farming at Stichel lost his crops and household furniture in 1750, sequestrated by Sir Robert Pringle for arrears of rent, "legal formalities having been observed."[230]

Change in Kale Water was more radical: Hownam's population dwindled from 632 in 1755 to 365 in 1791. By the 1800s, Grubet had vanished altogether bar a simple shepherd's cottage and a byre, while Hownam Grange was empty, with but a single tenant. Apart from the valley floor, the land had never been good and was now wholly given over to sheep. What had been a centre of the "anti-burghers" (the first secession movement from the Kirk) held only a tiny school and two ale-houses. Both pele towers lay in ruins. All Middlemases had emigrated, leaving forever the site of the eleven prehistoric standing stones, once known locally as "eleven sheep shearers turned to stone for reaping corn on the Sabbath..."

***

This half century saw the end of Middlemas lairdship in the traditional sense, although the farmers in Eildon and the burgesses in Kelso retained what should be called middle class prosperity. But it also produced individuals with different abilities, notably "Luckie" Middlemas (below page ) and John, a master mariner in Dunbar, who by the 1740s was commanding merchant ships engaged in European trade. In January 1751, his command, *Cumberland* of Dunbar, is recorded as docking at Peterhead after a rough passage from Lisbon across the Bay of Biscay.

John died abroad in 1758, his executor being his brother, also a mariner, and two sisters all living in the port. John the baxter (baker) born in Lilliesleaf succeeded well enough to become an Edinburgh burgess in the 1750s – but the inventory after his death in 1763 came to only £372 (or £32 English money), a smallish sum which indicates as much about the problem of saving money as it does entrepreneurial ability. It may be that Lilliesleaf emigrants were less commercially acute than their Kelso kin; certainly David's son Andrew in Kelso seems to have known how to combine local politics successfully with the corn trade.

Andrew, a leading cordiner, a bootmaker, aimed to become deacon (president) of his guild. The story starts in March 1738 with James Purvis, convener of the town trades' guilds, seeking to make the appointment himself to Alexander Milne, "the trade all being divided," after a contest that came to "a pitch of confusion over the voting and a tumult because the deciding vote (in favour of Andrew against his rival) was that of a notorious madman," or so said Purvis, who called an adjournment.[231]

According to Purvis' later account to the court, Andrew "who now pretends to be deacon, and his adherents, thought proper to return to the council house without warning, and without requiring him to warn the trade. And there, in a most unprecedented manner, thought it proper to get himself elected deacon...and gave a petition to the Baillie of Kelso setting forth several falsehoods and craving that his lordship would find him duly elected."

The Baillie, Gilbert Ramsay went through the voters' lists, with Alexander Oliphant the town clerk, judged Purvis' adjournment *ultra vires*, and sustained Andrew's election. Protests continued, focusing first on "the voice of the madman," whose vote the Milne faction claimed should have been denied, second on the fact "that after the adjournment, all the trade left the Townhouse and the door thereof was locked up...(but) thereafter Richard Gillespie got the key; and the said Andrew Middlemas and his adherents by ways and means got possession...and thought proper to return and choose the said Andrew as deacon; which the comptroller takes to have been a most illegal and unwarrantable thing...unfair and contrary to the uniform practice and custom of elections among the trades of Kelso."

The judge, Lord Balfour, kept to the original finding that Andrew had won; but Purvis appealed it to the High Court in Edinburgh, where the Lords of Council and Session confirmed Balfour's judgement. The case reverted to the Baillie of Kelso and Purvis was ordered to pay Andrew's costs of £15 Scots. Yet it went on, revived after Purvis' death by his wife, so that in spring 1744 it reached Lord Balmerino, judge of appeal in Edinburgh: where in December, after "great avisendum" (taking time to consider judgement), Andrew's status was upheld.

Much more than local jealousy hung on the case which had been long, expensive and divisive – in fact a feud by non-violent means. Andrew joined the small, vigorous but litigious cabal that ran the town of now nearly 4,000 people; and it is fair to judge the case on a par with the phenomenon later known south of the Border as an "Eatanswill election."

Kelso was at its peak, like Hawick, well ahead of its former competitors Jedburgh and Melrose, and it is scarcely surprising that it rates second in numbers of the Middlemas kin-group. It remained a centre of old affiliation, as Newcastle and the Tyne Valley were ones of the new migration. The others are set out in Table 2 (p. 199), old and new in Scotland and northern England.

The broad pattern of change is quite clear, showing those who stayed, those who moved to the agricultural jobs in Merse villages and towns, or north Northumberland; those who joined the commercially-based clusters in Edinburgh, Newcastle, Berwick, Alnwick; or, having abandoned Whickham after the boom, other coal-mining areas of County Durham. What was established by 1750 was to govern the pattern of migration down at least to the 1840s, suggesting that for a family that had been neither military in orientation, nor Atlantic colonial-minded, migration was determined as much by kin-group knowledge, tradition and affinity, as by skills or economic opportunity.

Some of these small towns were in serious decline, as comparison of the *Statistical Account of Scotland* (Eastern Borders) 1791 with the 1755 figures given by Doctor Webster, suggests. Chirnside, a centre for sheep, black cattle and horses, fell in population from 609 to 352; Greenlaw, mainly occupied with agriculture, from 1210 to 895; Hownam, after turning to sheep, from 632 to 365. Conversely, some thrived: Coldstream, a weaving centre, rose from 1493 to 2017; Duns, despite a smallpox outbreak in 1782, reached 2324 and its neighbour Langton rose from 290 to 435.

Many different reasons were given by the *Surveys*' authors. In Polwarth, tenants had more rights, better sustained by a good landowner; Swinton and Semprin (up from 494 to 898) enjoyed good access to coal, local stone quarries and the Berwick town market; those of Ancrum were said to be "a healthy robust people," while those of Bowden were sober, industrious and benefited from good roads and early threshing mills – as opposed to Longformacus "an idle place," fit only for black-faced sheep.

Bad roads, few bridges, lack of schooling, poor access to markets – and their obverse – set the tone.[232] Kelso itself, up from 2781 to 4324 by 1750, was depicted as a sort of metropolis, its five-span elliptical bridge designed by Rennie being the model for London's Waterloo Bridge, while the agricultural produce from Oxnam (still a Middlemas cluster) reached both Edinburgh and Berwick. Sprouston had its salmon from the Tweed, Stitchel, a heavier breed of cattle and Dutch bulbs; Selkirk enjoyed a revival in the woollen trade throughout the 18th century; and Yetholm had become the passage to England, literally, in the whisky-smuggling trade. One cousin farming in Eildon, Thomas Mein at Newstead, even introduced tobacco cultivation into Scotland in 1778.[233]

Across the Border, the distinction between types of cluster sharpened. Unlike the complex city economy of Edinburgh, most Middlemas occupations along the Tyne and in County Durham came from coal: hewers and sinkers, drainers and keelmen. For agricultural supply of lime and coal for the local towns, and related metalwork, wagon-builders or wheelwrights, they went to the other half of the county, north of Morpeth, in particular the areas around Alnwick, Rothbury, Whittingham, Wooler (Glendale), and Berwick, including Norham and Carham up river from Berwick.

In the half century after the Act of Union, Scotland's smaller size compared to England, the backward state of its agriculture and transport, and the slow, persistent increase in population, made migration an economic and social necessity, fifty years before Dr Johnson's celebrated witticism that the best sight a Scotchman ever saw was the high road to England. Yet in an apparent contradiction, the mid-18th century provided the turning point, when Scotland became recognised in France, the German states and all across northern Europe as economically vital, culturally enlightened and only in strict geography, peripheral.

To Voltaire or Kant, the universities of Glasgow and Edinburgh were hotbeds of talent, in a pan-European mainstream from which the sleepier spires of Oxford and Cambridge were absent, unreformed. Scotland's legal system, based on Roman law, the intellectual legacies of Calvinism (shorn of the harsh discipline), the sheer brilliance of output from its learned societies and clubs, put it for half a century at the Continent's leading edge; not like Sicily or Rome by earlier tradition, but by its advances in science, philosophy, medicine, economics, arts and letters.

The illusion is that this represented all-Scotland; but it was in fact restricted to the great cities of Glasgow, Edinburgh, Aberdeen, and the Lowlands. The Borders and the Highlands and Islands, and their populations, bar a few landowners, had little to do with that reputation, as Boswell and Johnson discovered on their tour in 1773. Border towns, as Kelso demonstrated, remained oligarchic, run by merchant-traders squabbling with craft guilds; while enclosure turned the land either to sheep or cattle, [40-50,000 cattle were exported annually to northern England by the early 18th century. The southeastern grain areas supplied Edinburgh and beyond by river, and out of the ports of Eyemouth and Dunbar; in which trade in coastal vessels Christopher Middlemas was to make his fortune in the 1820s] or to new more profitable crops. "Luckie" Middlemas is known to have kept a famous oyster-house in Edinburgh during the peak of the Enlightenment; but while many of the great thinkers and their clubs supped and drank there, it is unlikely that the owner took part in the discussions between Lord Kames, David Hume, Adam Smith, Alan Ramsay, or James Ferguson and Robert Adam, founders of the Oyster Club and the Select Society, which sometimes met there in the 1760s.[234]

What changed least was the role of women in farming society: milking, feeding livestock and poultry, gleaning, shearing, spinning, carrying hay and peats, muck spreading, clearing yards and stables; or carrying the coals that their pitmen husbands hacked out underground; followed by all the household tasks and upbringing of children, often six or eight to a family, as diet improved a little and the age of marriage fell slightly. It is hardly surprising that for many, early industrial factories offered by comparison a better life, better housing (until it decayed in the 19th century) and higher wages – if still only a fraction of those earned by men.

Only middle class women knew what leisure was; only the wealthy ever saw high society in Edinburgh. But for farmers and merchants' wives, there might be extra income for them to manage, from brewing and selling ale, running small shops and minor businesses. Migration for unmarried women meant service – domestic, shop or farm. Education did exist for women but in the manner described in Flora Thomson's *Larkrise to Candleford*: hardly even the three Rs; but enough, as Adam Smith pointed out, for service and dependence. By the mid-18th century, roughly 35% of women were literate as against 65% of men.

At least, unlike the Highlands a century later, these transitions took place peaceably, partly because of the mixed nature of Border society, quite different from the clan system, partly because of the well-established links that fostered their emigration; partly perhaps because some elements of the older, patriarchal system of "kindly tenure" survived, for example on the Buccleugh estates – that is, until professional factors intruded, aided by harsh enforcers in the mid-19th century.

Border migrants also found it easier, speaking good English, than the Gaelic-speaker; and they remained close to their roots, no

18th century Middlemas cluster being more than 80 miles by road from Kelso. Yet they had to survive virtually without a Poor Law recourse: even lairds' sons were found in the 1690s famine among the wandering crowds of beggars in Lothian and Tweeddale. Kirk and gentry ensured that the Merse and Teviot were among the best administered localities by the 1740s but, even there, assistance was often haphazard, short-lived, and subject to reduction using evidence of what was being paid out in northern England.

Without trying to assess or aggregate the journeys of upwards of a hundred separate families, measured by the marriage figures in Table 3, p. 214 (1700-1750) for counties outside the old Middlemas implantations in Roxburgh, Selkirk and Peebles, it is clear that a culture of mobility had developed, rather different from the later waterborne migrations of poor peasantry from 19th century Ireland or southern Italy and Sicily. The flows looked more like those from Slovakia into Hapsburg Bohemia, or Catalonia into mainland Spain. They relied on local knowledge, transmitted through a kin-system by word of mouth, usually via temporary migrants returning "home." Vestiges of the system can still be seen in the question "where born" on the 1841 and 1851 censuses. Youngest kin are found being dispatched to join established families, either to stay and survive on their own, or to return with added skills, shepherd, blacksmith, roofer, pit-drainer. [The evidence fits the argument made by Gregory Clark in *A Farewell to Alms* (2006) that downward mobility leads to the creation of a society favourable to rapid economic change. As lairds' sons become merchants, their sons small traders, theirs craftsmen, so the attributes of patience, hard work, self-discipline, and capacity to adjust, spread throughout society, and the regions where migrants settled. Even if higher population, via the Malthusian trap, brought lower wages and living standards, the 18th and 19th century economic revolution redressed the balance in the end.]

Most in fact stayed, especially once they married and had children. Some, but only a small proportion, moved out only after producing a family first. None had yet crossed the Atlantic – that was for the 19th century. For the rest, and for the old laird class, "their names are extinguished and their mansions confounded in the dust," as the *Old Statistical Survey* put it, analysing Hownam and lamenting the replacement of ancient families to make way

Table 3.

**Marriages recorded by counties**

| **Scotland** | 1700–1750 | 1750–1800 | 1800–1850 |
|---|---|---|---|
| Berwickshire | (34) | 62 | 90 |
| East Lothian | (8) | 6 | 17 |
| Midlothian, incl. | | | |
| Edinburgh | (9) | 8 | 70 |
| Peebles | (1) | 1 | 4 |
| Roxburgh | (92) | 33 | 53 |
| Selkirk | (8) | 4 | **2** |
| **England** | | | |
| Cumberland and | | | |
| Westmoreland | (3) | 11 | 9 |
| Durham | (6) | 40 | 44 |
| Northumberland | (41) | 79 | **67** |

for sheep and new capital-intensive farmers, while surviving lairds became great noble landlords, far distant from their tenants.[235]

The old laird's pride, according to the *Survey*, had been "to have his tenants, retainers, and even domesticks, of his own surname, many of them his near relations, and he commonly treated them as such..."[236] Maybe, even for a writer in 1791, this was an example of the golden age always being in the past. But from the perspective of any Middlemas after 1750, having seen the holdings of 300 years dispersed in thirty, it represented the simple truth.

*Cartoon Map of Scotland, 1794*

# 12.

# The Long Diaspora

Beyond the mid-18th century, it is impossible to do more than sketch out the multiple strands of kin-group branches, in their original four counties and across northeast England, where their expatriate descendants were to become a numerical minority of Middlemases – demonstrated in the 1841 British census, the first to give names, locations, occupations, family, and (helpful in charting the continuing process of migration) their places of birth.

Using the census and the more reliable 19th century records, however, it can be shown how the formation of clusters – either temporary or permanent – developed in the late 18th and early 19th centuries, including the new dimension of irreversible migration to North America, even Australia and New Zealand. (Few if any Middlemases settled elsewhere before 1900); and how both those who left Scotland and those who stayed became part of a north-eastern *British* economy and society, even if they had not by then taken on a British rather than a Scots or English identity.

Nevertheless the century from the 1750s to the 1841 and 1851 censuses is a long period to capture in a single chapter. One reason for doing so is that the material is necessarily more general, there being few outstanding or influential individuals to point up; another being is that there is no set of obvious events to break off or divide the narrative. The various family elements in the kin-group, being of little economic or political significance, were steadily amalgamated in any case in a wider, British history, losing their individual, local or regional significance, absorbed by longer term social and economic trends which flowed through their lives to an unprecedented extent.

This chapter is, then, set out in terms of trends, including demographic patterns of migration, as they were caught up in the population expansion, the occupations newly available to them, together with short notices of a few individuals about whom something more detailed can be said.

***

There were to be no more Middlemas lairds after the loss of the last part of their earlier estates in 1732. No Middlemas is recorded in the 1770 Directory of Land Ownership in Scotland as being a "landit man."[237] On the other hand, there were prosperous farmers, of whom at least four are well-recorded in the 1800s. Though a few, mainly in Eildon and Kale Water, held 40/- freeholds and therefore could vote in general elections for the London Parliament, before the franchise reforms of 1832 and 1867, the kin-group was politically insignificant: none had been wealthy enough or interested to take an active part in party politics, none was until Robert Middlemas, solicitor of Alnwick, became Conservative agent for the whole of north Northumberland, a predominantly Liberal area, in the later 19th century. And none emulated their neighbour James Hogg "the Ettrick Shepherd," in memorialising the Borders in poetry and print.

Two great changes in this century transformed the kin-group's way of life: the downward drift into tenant farming or agricultural labour on great estates, once smaller land owners had sold up to the capitalist-improvers; and the lateral movement of perhaps one-third of the total into small-town trading and professions, or the industrial working-class. This took place in the century which witnessed the peak of prosperity for the largest landowners on both sides of the Border, above all the three Dukes, Buccleugh (over 460.000 acres with an income of £ 217.000, roughly £20 million today),[238] Roxburgh and Northumberland, (roughly 250.000 acres), together with the earls of Hume and March.

Whether their heads of families are counted as AgLab in the censuses, which did not indicate the real level or nature of skills that agricultural workers possessed, or became miners, chemical workers, etc., the group's *numerical* majority can be described in the format chosen by Marx and Engels in the 1840s, as working-class, a designation from which upward mobility was only possible through education and professional aspirations. Yet the power now vested in the landed class, maturing since the 1680s, did not necessarily mean that agricultural workers were subjected to the immiseration Marx and his colleague observed in the industrial cities–even if all these great estates were managed by tough professional trained factors/managers by the 1860s. Already the Percies had accepted

*Grain harvesting (*Scotland Illustrated, *William Beatty, 1838)*

*Quarry near Melrose Abbey (National Museum of Scotland)*

automatic continuity of tenure, and Arthur Young observed on his travels in the 1760s and 70s that the third Duke, having watched trials of an early reaper-binder, ruled against its adoption on the grounds that it would increase rural unemployment. Some lairds provided hand-operated corn mills to free poor cottars from reliance on the landlords' mills, and all three Dukes authorised forbearance of rents during the bad harvests of 1816-20.

North-eastern agriculture may have been kinder on the agricultural workers than much of the English south and midlands, at least until the 1832 Poor Law regime of Guardians and its 1845 Scottish counterpart, the Parochial Boards, came into operation. But this made little difference during the serious harvest failures 1782, 1795-97, above all 1816-20. A hard life, worn out by 50, living in virtual hovels, marked the labourer; it was demonstrably better for those with some rural skills, blacksmiths, wheelrights, waggoners, and on hilly land shepherds.

Unlike the Highlands, with its clearances of rural communities which stood in the way of sheep farming, often inspired by the clan heads themselves, a relatively peaceful transition took place on the Borders, partly because of its mixed society and the existence of alternatives, partly because of its relatively specialised economy and trading links, north to the Lowland city-markets and south to England. The main process, which did provoke rural radicalism in the century before the great agricultural depression of the 1870s, was landlords' increasing control over their tenants and the higher rents imposed, mainly to pay for the owners' own improvements, mains farms, and for better roads.

Larger farming units developed, of three to five-hundred acres arable,[239] plus a thousand acres of outfield; three Middlemases with such acreages are described below. On these holdings, even in Scotland, capital investment could take place and did, in the 19th century. Sub-tenants and cottars on the other hand suffered the consequences and had very largely disappeared, becoming labourers by the 1850s in the Merse and north Northumberland. [Wages were higher in Northumberland than the Merse in this period, partly because the land was generally more productive, partly to limit the counter-attractions of the Durham coal mines and the Tyne industrial belt.] Improvements, dikes, walls, roads,

*Cheviot ewe and lamb (National Museum of Scotland)*

*Women bondagers, 19th century (National Museum of Scotland)*

drainage, did of course require much labour, even if less was needed in producing and harvesting crops – labour paid in cash, fixed in a hierarchy below specialised skills, there being no chance of rising from farm servant to tenant. The hind became typical after the 1750s, with his small plot, a fraction of an acre, enough for vegetables, a cow, pigs and poultry, who lived in a rented cottage, usually with his female servant for the most menial jobs; a secure, relatively comfortable, conservative position; while the farmer enjoyed privacy, in a big farmhouse, whose rebuilding came in the 1820s, preceding improvements in the cottage by quarter of a century.

By the end of the Napoleonic War, farmers faced the market directly, their tenure being set by 19-year terms. Most benefited from consolidated holdings, once the run-rig system disappeared, and they traded now with local towns. Their workers lived, not in the almost-vanished chaotic touns, but in well-laid out villages of two rows, like Midlem, Sprouston, Lilliesleaf, and their Northumbrian equivalents. In the Merse towns, where Middlemases clustered, Stichil, Duns, Edrom, Eccles, as in Oxnam or around Kelso, farmers worked one-third arable, two-thirds outfield-pasture, with livestock grazing the stubble after harvest. Break point, in terms of the leap from subsistence to profit, was about a hundred to two-hundred arable acres.

Improvements after the 1760s affected all rural inhabitants: crop rotation, planted woods, sown grassland, use of turnips and potatoes, breeding of livestock, sheep of Cheviot stock, cattle with short horns and better breeds such as Aberdeen Angus; replacement of the ox-plough with a lighter horse-drawn one; drilling, sowing, reaping and threshing machines; and of course a commercial orientation of which Christopher Middlemas (below) was an embodiment after 1809.[240]

As James Robertson, following Arthur Young, noted in 1799, "An astonishing change has taken place...about half a century ago, the farmer went on foot to market. Now he rides, well-dressed and mounted. Formerly, he ate his food off his knees–it consisted of meal, vegetables and milk. Now his table is covered, his knife and fork are laid down before him, to dine on meat."[241]

But there were fewer tenancies as a result, so that while elder brothers lived better, younger siblings had no choice but to work for them as farm servants or to leave. Not all towns where Middlemas rural workers lived did equally well: comparison of the 1791 Statistical Account of Scotland with Dr Webster's compilation of 1755, shows that Eildon and Fogo declined. Worst of all, Hownam fell from 632 inhabitants to 365. Polwarth remained stable, Duns, Lilliesleaf, Melrose, and Sprouston increased, Swinton and Semprin from 494 to 894. Meanwhile Selkirk with its shoemakers and woollen goods, Coldstream the weaving town, Langton and Kelso all rose on the back of demand for their craft manufactures.

Kelso, origin of the Middlemas family, can be compared with Alnwick in Northumberland, not only because both had dukes as patron-occupiers and were roughly similar in size though Alnwick was politically far more important. For the former, Rennie constructed a fine five arch bridge (model for Westminster Bridge in London) at a cost of £17.800 after the flood of 1797 swept the old one away. Kelso was the first town in Scotland lit by gas, in 1818, and possessed a lending library, a dispensary, public baths, and by 1834 a high school and a museum, to say nothing of the "neat and spacious poorhouse" for its hundred paupers out of a population of 4.500. In all this, it was similar to Alnwick, though the latter had more schools. Its racecourse was laid out formally in 1822, while cricket, bowling, curling, livestock shows, and auctions had become regular calendar features. Like Alnwick, it was a centre of printing from the late 18th century; but unlike it, two newspapers flourished in Kelso, one Tory, one Liberal.

If that was the elegant best of early 19th century town life, other smaller towns where Middlemases had been lairds lagged behind: Lilliesleaf remained small, the old towers in ruins, ruled by four landowners, haunted by its Covenanting past. Morebattle spawned the first Secession Kirk in 1739, drained its mere in the 1830s and "afforded a comfortable asylum to several farmers and cottagers who were forced to abandon the abodes of their forefathers (when) the accumulation of small into large farms took place."[242] What that meant for a labourer was piecework, for his wife, spinning yarn or managing a small dairy producing butter and cheese.

Yetholm on the other hand, profited greatly from the whisky smuggling trade (worth perhaps £20.000 a year) and one of the early 18th century turnpikes, carrying coaches three times a week to Kelso, and a postal service delivered by an old woman on a donkey. It also remained a centre for Scottish gypsies, whose forerunner had been Johnny Faa "lord of little Egypt" in 1540 (origin of the character in *His Dark Materials*).

This much relates to rural life, because of the fact that the Middlemases (however they spelt the kin-name) who stayed behind, in spite of the 1870s depression and the harvest failures of 1879, 1888 and 1895, became a majority of the group by 1900.[243] As the Middlemases of Lilliesleaf found in the 1690s, bad harvests accompanied by lack of capital brought disaster for lairds: their small farm successors, on short leases, faced essentially the same problems, and there was virtually no safety net except eventually the harsh 1834 Poor Law for Northumberland and its 1845 Scottish equivalent, which may have improved administration of an essentially 16th century system, but were interpreted with a harshness that made recovery and a return into normal life almost impossible.

So for those who left, using the network of turnpike roads begun in the 1780s,[244] the accumulating northeast Industrial Revolution offered an alternative for the population which was expanding at the same time on the back of newly-generated productivity, unforeseen by Malthus' gloomy prognosis. But which to choose: the general mixed economies of cities such as Edinburgh, Newcastle and later Glasgow; or the pit villages of Durham which employed over half of the local male population?

Middlemases had, briefly, tried Whickham in the 1630s boom years and this mining tradition clearly lived on far into the 18th century in their collective memory, leading them even to the small pits on the seams between Berwick and Alnwick. Yet this was not only an exceptionally hard, dangerous life, albeit with higher wages than agriculture: it grew steadily more circumscribed in the mining villages, whose inhabitants saw relative wages and the size of their tied cottages fall in the early 19th century, accompanied by an increasing poverty which justified Marx's analysis of immiseration. Cut off by a much more acute social gulf than agricultural labourers knew from the smaller and more autocratic number of mine owners and managers, mining communities had become

*Lilliesleaf street, 19th century (National Museum of Scotland)*

*Grain harvest, 19th century, (National Museum of Scotland)*

isolated from their rural surroundings, long before the bitter strikes culminated in 1844, led by the Durham Miners' Union.

As pits were dug deeper, down to and beyond a hundred fathoms to fuel the export of two million tonnes a year to London by 1828, frequent explosions and large numbers of deaths (comparable to China and India today) made it a dangerous choice to follow a father down the mine;[245] yet the leap back into industrial occupation was also hard, given competition from other migrants – one reason for the remarkable degree of self-help among mining villages and the focus on education as a way to escape this sort of marginalisation.

Most Middlemases living in Durham recorded in 1841 were pitmen; but the Tyne Valley as a whole offered a wide range in the second half of the 18th century, from steel manufacture using imported Swedish iron (until the rise of Sheffield), salt extraction from pans at the river mouth (till overtaken by Cheshire), ship building, glass manufacture (centred on Sunderland and South Shields) which supplied the 1851 Crystal Palace, chemicals, mainly alkalis from brine (half of all British production), and rough, serviceable pottery.[246]

If they chose not factory but a craft occupation, there were the metal trades, with small workshops for hand tools, supplying all manual occupations from farriers to blacksmiths. The firm of Poor and Fawcus grew out of such agricultural ironwork to make massive chains and anchors for the local ship builders, all on the back of a peak in the northeast coal field which in turn sucked in an entire new rural population (12.000 in 1804, over 40.000 by 1850). It is not surprising that some Middlemases became merchant seamen, nor that the table of occupation in the 1841 census shows Middlemases living as far away as Middlesex and Surrey, Gloucestershire and Sussex.

Yet this century-long diaspora was not a simple choice between industry and agriculture. Whether or not, after centuries of rural occupation, the Middlemases maintained a deeply conservative affinity with agriculture, the majority of occupations on both sides of the Border was at least connected to rural skills. That may be explained by the fact that their clusters extended in certain towns with a rural hinterland, particularly Kelso and Berwick, and the cities of Edinburgh and Newcastle, from the 17th to the 20th century, probably on the basis of information circulating inside the kin-group, with its assessments of whom could be trusted, who might help or give shelter, circulated by Middlemases going back and forth, influencing the crucial choice of whether to migrate as an entire family, with children, or before children, or as a youth, male or female, looking to farm or domestic service temporarily, while deciding whether to stay or even marry locally.

Beyond the complexities of factors known to them like expected wages, housing and conditions of work, the final determinant as for any emigrant was an inner quality, present all through the long diaspora, of imagination and possibly even entrepreneurship. Yet it is self-evident that what they found was often not what they had expected: social stratification turned out to be better-defined and enforced in the south than in Scotland (and worse in Northumberland than industrial Durham, the gap between tenants and landlords being especially wide); prejudice against the Scots had not disappeared with the Act of Union, and it was hard for Andrew Middlemas to maintain his social status in Alnwick, despite his in-laws' prosperity; after his son's very early death, they too fell in the social scale.

Nor did this improve. The 1861 census showed that one-third of all those listed as "born in Scotland" i.e., the most recent arrivals, were living in one room: gross overcrowding with all its health and moral consequences grew worse at the Industrial Revolution's peak, until reform and new building began to take hold. Yet as one Canadian emigrant remembered, her father found urban life hard but not isolated – it provided friends, jokes, companionship, and refuge from rural poverty.[247] The costs of migration fell sharply after 1790, given better transport. Equally, migrants brought no capital with them, could buy no land, nor education, and even if they were able to establish themselves as tenant farmers (very unlikely), the majority of their children would have to move on, as Border shepherds did, to the Highlands, to establish sheep-farming after the clearances, or go overseas to North America and the Antipodes.

***

The 1841 census is the first to give reasonable accuracy to names and their spellings, positions within the family (head, wife, children), occupation, date of birth and where born. From this, supplemented by the greater detail of 1851, one can get a fair picture of the whole kin-group, its numbers, location, size of family, work pattern, even its education, "scholar" meaning a child in formal education.

Establishment of clusters has to be measured in the context of population growth. The total population of Scotland rose steadily in the later 18th century, mainly because of a fall in mortality caused by better diet and better housing,[248] which took place before the rise in fertility that produced the genuine population explosion of the 19th century. This pattern resembles that in France, but applies to southern Scotland rather than the increasingly depopulated Highlands. It fuelled the almost inexhaustible demands for labour from Lowlands industry and is at the root of all 19th century migration.

In 1755, Berwickshire held 24.000 people, Roxburghshire 35.000, Selkirk and Peebles each 13.000, sparse indeed, as they remained through the 19th century. In comparison, the town of Kelso reached 4324 in 1790, Duns 2324, Jedburgh roughly 2000, Melrose 1500, and Coldstream 1160. Despite the prosperity of its cloth industry, Selkirk held only 1000, Yetholm 862, compared with Edinburgh 84.816.

Setting the Middlemas kin in that context, the first accurate total of individuals derives from the 1841 census which, if all children are included, gives 334 for Scotland, 462 in England. Working in reverse, taking into account what is known about population increase and the live birth rate between 1650 and 1850, approximate totals for the size of the kin-group at earlier dates are:

| | *1800* | *1750* | *1700* | *1650* |
|---|---|---|---|---|
| Scotland | 270 | 210 | 150 | 100 |
| England | 260 | 120 | 50 | 15 |

The latter column is roughly confirmed by existing parish records in the OPRS Series. In the mid-16th century the total (all being in Scotland) would have been between 40 and 60. The total number of families in 1841 comes to 120: 49 in Scotland and 71 in England. The pattern of clusters set out in Table 4. (page 230-1) shows changes from Table 2, sometimes quite dramatic ones. Edinburgh remained a city of choice on the Scottish side, with one Glasgow parish coming into focus, while among small towns, Jedburgh and Peebles reappear: both cases being less than Kelso, the original settlement. Out in the Merse, there were extensions: Swinton and Semprin close to the Northumberland border, Coldingham and Edrom, and some new small towns such as Hutton, Gordon and Whitsome.

On the English side, at least in Northumberland, the old division remains between those in agriculture and its crafts, concentrated in Glendale, and what until 1843 remained the administrative part of County Durham – that is, Norham and Islandshire, south and east of Berwick on Tweed.

On the southern side of the Border, the parish of Lowick contained three substantial farmers and a mini-cluster of mining families engaged in the closely related mining of coal and limestone, along the geologically rich seams from Spittal by Berwick, through Scremerston, Bowsden and Lowick, to Alnwick. Further south, as in the century before 1750, is the Tyne valley with Newcastle as its centre and Middlemas families along both sides of the river, in Gateshead, Sunderland, North and South Shields, and the port of Tynemouth.[249]

Of the 462 recorded mainly in northern England, 36 mature individuals (i.e. aged over 17) declared their birthplace to have been in Scotland. Naturally, these were concentrated in the Berwick area or Glendale and the Tyne Valley. Some were very recent migrants, being farm servants in Rothbury, or Alnwick. Four of the women had married Middlemases born south of the Border; and 13 had come south as part of two large families together.

***

It is clear that, from the kin's origin in Middlemast-Middleton, and during its late medieval history (confirmed by the two extant seals of 1296 and 1435) that the family name always ended in "t",

Table 4.

## Clusters

| **Scotland** | (1700-1750) | 1750-1800 | 1800-1850 |
|---|---|---|---|
| (O) Eildon/Melrose | (1) | 0 | 0 |
| (O) Kelso and district | (10) | 4 | 11 |
| (O) Hownam | (12) | 1 | 1 |
| (O) Jedburgh | (7) | 3 | 5 |
| (O) Morebattle/Yetholm | (9) | 3/3 | 3/2 |
| (O) Oxnam (8) | 7 | 0 | |
| (O) Sprouston | (4) | 2 | 1 |
| —— | | | |
| (O) Edinburgh | (4) | 13 | 31 |
| —— | | | |
| (M) Coldstream | (7) | 10 | 2 |
| (M) Duns | (3) | 3 | 2 |
| (M) Eccles | (1) | 3 | 2 |
| (M) Edrom | (0) | 3 | 8 |
| (M) Haddington | (9) | 4 | 3 |
| (M) Langton | (4) | 3 | 3 |
| (M) Peebles | (0) | 1 | 4 |
| (M) Selkirk | (4) | 1 | 1 |
| (M) Semprin/Swinton | (6) | 5 | 9 |
| (M) Stichel | (3) | 12 | 2 |

Others in Scotland: Coldingham, Chirnside, Eyemouth, Greenlaw, Westruther.

| **England** | (1700-1750) | 1750-1800 | 1800-1850 |
|---|---|---|---|
| Northumberland Newcastle | (15) | 29 | 37 |
| (O) Alnwick | (7) | 17 | 6 |
| (O) Berwick/Tweedmouth | (6) | 8 | 12 |
| (O) Belford | (4) | 5 | 2 |
| (M) Ellingham | (3) | 3 | 2 |
| (M) Hartburn | (7) | 6 | 1 |
| (M) Morpeth/Bellingham | (4) | 5 | 3 |
| (M) Norham/Carham | (5) | 9 | 8 |
| (M) Rothbury/Whittingham | (11) | 11 | 3 |
| (M) Wooler district (Glendale) | (8) | 15 | 15 |
| (M) Corbridge | (0) | 7 | 0 |
| Durham County | | | |
| (M) S. Tyne Valley, incl. Gateshead | (1) | 10 | 11 |
| (M) Tanfield | (3) | 10 | 2 |
| (M) Whickham | (3) | 4 | 2 |
| (M) Auckland | (1) | 4 | 0 |
| (M) Chester le-Street | (1) | 8 | 3 |
| (M) Sunderland | (0) | 4 | 9 |
| (M) Sedgefield | (0) | 9 | 2 |

Others in Durham: Bishop Auckland, Durham, Howarth, Lamesley, Monkwearmouth, Medomsley, Ryton, Stockton, Washington.

and that this consonant distinguished it from its ancient neighbours and possible rivals, the various families of Middletons. The last vowel in these three centuries varied widely, partly because of eccentric orthography (giving different versions in the same document or on the same tombstone until the late 18th century), but mainly because, in a predominantly oral culture, the clerk or scribe simply followed the local accent/dialect. It appears as mast, most, mist, or even maist, and this explains the origin of permanent variations shown in Table 5. But for simplicity's sake, I have kept a single version Middlemas throughout this book, until the present chapter.

From the later 17th century however, the final t began to disappear, though it still surfaced in the mid-18th century, probably because it had become silent, being no longer pronounced.[250] Variants then began to acquire a more permanent usage, though not at first in any definitive way. What was initially a random process began to stabilise, conveying its own sort of legitimacy which, by the late 18th century, had settled into three main stereotypes: mas/mass/mis(s). Moss was clearly on the way out, and although a handful still appear in the 1841 census, it had disappeared entirely by 1901 (see Table 6).

Table 5

**Spellings by nation 1841-1901**

| | mas | mass | miss | moss |
|---|---|---|---|---|
| Scotland 1841 | 132 | 57 | 144 | 5 |
| Scotland 1901 | 228 | 189 | 233 | 0 |
| England 1841 | 200 | 55 | 198 | 11 |
| England 1901 | 164 | 35 | 398 | 0 |

Table 6

**Spellings by counties, 1841**

| Scotland | Berwick | Peebles | Selkirk | Roxburgh | Mid Lothian | East Lothian | Glasgow | Edinburgh | West Lothian | Fife | Perth | Ayr | Argyll |
|---|---|---|---|---|---|---|---|---|---|---|---|---|---|
| mas | 9 | 0 | 4 | 44 | 7 | 18 | 4 | 17 | 17 | 1 | 0 | 0 | 0 |
| mass | 12 | 10 | 0 | 1 | 7 | 3 | 10 | 9 | 0 | 0 | 1 | 0 | 0 |
| miss | 103 | 0 | 0 | 18 | 0 | 0 | 0 | 6 | 0 | 2 | 9 | 3 | 1 |
| moss | 0 | 0 | 0 | 4 | 0 | 0 | 0 | 1 | 0 | 0 | 0 | 0 | 0 |

| England | Northumberland | Durham | Lancashire | Yorkshire | Westmoreland | Middlesex | Shropshire | Sussex | Surrey | Gloucestershire |
|---|---|---|---|---|---|---|---|---|---|---|
| mas | 42 | 20 | 2 | 4 | 0 | 2 | 1 | 1 | 0 | 0 |
| mass | 24 | 11 | 0 | 0 | 0 | 0 | 0 | 0 | 4 | 0 |
| miss | 84 | 62 | 0 | 34 | 1 | 13 | 0 | 2 | 2 | 3 |
| moss | 5 | 6 | 0 | 0 | 0 | 0 | 0 | 0 | 0 | 0 |

There is no doubt that these variants all had a common origin, starting with the single Anglo-Norman incomer to Kelso. But as the spelling separated, so did the kin-group itself, even if this process is hard to infer, let alone document. Co-existence side by side in small towns or city parishes, agricultural communities or mining villages evidently continued, in a long overlap. Once the process had started, however, separate patterns show up but with no particular logic except to demonstrate how the in-groups' flow of information attracted the variants towards certain clusters to live.

What appears certain is that, once fixed (mainly in parish registers) the spelt variants had a long continuing effect, becoming defined by family tradition and formalised by relations to church or Kirk or local authority. Subordination of the sense in folk memory of an original kin-group, in the diversity of subgroups, had a corrosive effect on earlier kin identity and loyalties, which seem to have been lost, even in original towns like Kelso, within the century 1750 to 1850. Yet this does not appear to have had any effect on the pattern of occupations or education, only on where they chose to live. The sole rough correlation is that "mass" prevailed in the old heartlands and "miss" among migrants, especially in industry and large towns.

***

The age at which they married conforms to the general pattern of the northeast. Most of them had married by age 25 or 26 unless it was a second marriage caused, only too frequently, by the death of the first wife – usually in childbirth. Marriage occurred slightly earlier on average in towns and was delayed generally in the Borders after the 1840s, possibly because of the falling rates of return in agriculture. For lack of available contraception, birth rates remained as high as in the early modern period, up to the later 19th century.

As to the choice of whom to marry, this too remained restricted to a given distance from the suitor's house – in the Merse, between five and ten miles, a circle rather wider than in England, because of the sparseness of population and the smaller size of country towns.[251]

This does not, of course, apply where particular occupations such as shepherd or blacksmith required travel over greater distances, sometimes – as in the small pits of north Northumberland – for periods of several years.[252]

Children surged around their small usually two-room cottages or the large stone farmhouses where the better off Middlemas tenants lived. Those aged under 15 equalled those over, a balance known today only in the third world. To be old meant 50 (or for a worn-out agricultural labourer or pitman 40): life expectancy varied according to profession, but rarely exceeded the early 60s for tradesmen or labourers. Only a very few in the 1841 and 1851 censuses were over 70.

Given that the total of households came to roughly 120, and subtracting husband and wife from the total 796 of 1841, children then numbered 516 – an average of 3.5 per household. Allowing for those where there were none, and a few that were as high as 8, the average is 4.2. Infant death rates remained high for another 40 or 50 years (so high that the early modern practice of baptising new children with the same forenames as earlier, dead ones survived, perhaps as a token of affection for what had been lost, perhaps simply as a form of replacement). But the birth rate started to fall in northeast England after the 1850s in a climate of increasing prosperity, so that by 1900 the Scottish kin regained the majority.

This in turn can be connected with what some historians claim to be a sort of Darwinian selection process, in that migrant families proved to be more successful not only at reproducing themselves but at passing on to their children attitudes towards hard work, initiative and (if the possibility existed) deferred consumption, thus aiding their economic survival, and forming part of the genesis of modern economic growth.[253]

A glance at their 1841 occupations reveals a huge diversity of choice, one much greater however in England, because of the progress of mid-19$^{th}$ century economic growth. Still, the numerical majority of jobs were unsurprisingly in or connected to agriculture. Out of heads of households, this sector included 79 or 55%, among them 8 farmers, 2 cattle dealers, 6 blacksmiths, and 57 registered simply as “AgLab,” which of course says nothing about their individual skills, say as ploughman, hedger or cattleman.

Beyond that category, the next cohort can best be described as artisans or craft workers, whether rural or urban (coal miners being a section apart); followed by those trading in the markets, farmers again, corn and cattle dealers; and finally those who, by the standards of the time, should be called professionals. The results of two centuries of migration can be read in Table 7, (p.238-9), illustrating the surge towards urban living and the flourishing of small shops and small traders.

One other outcome demonstrates the traditional Scottish concern with good education as a correlative to hard work. Long effects of Kirk practice in the Borders and Lowlands combined with the late 18th century burgeoning of Enlightenment culture, and the results appear in the 1841 designation of a child in education as a "scholar." Taking only Northumberland, and assuming that the children who might benefit were more than six years old but under twelve, the total pool of eligible ones among 71 families living in the county (of whom 42 had children resident at home) was: eligibles 45 (of whom 4 had been born in Scotland); scholars 36, plus 3 older ones of 14-16.

This is a remarkably high percentage, some 30 years before the 1870 Education Act made primary schooling compulsory, yet it was exceeded north of the Border, notably by Middlemases in Kelso. In any case, the 1870 Act needed another decade to become truly universal. But provision scarcely supplied demand. Privately funded church or charitable education for working class children, though increasing slowly and controversially (who should pay and for what curriculum?) in the half century before 1841 still lagged behind Scotland, confined as it was to certain areas in and around Berwick, Wooler, Warkworth, and Alnwick in north Northumberland.

Blyth, though a thriving port, had no school at all until 1858. Even Alnwick, though well-served by the Duke's School for 9 to 14 year old boys after 1810 and the Duchess's, teaching domestic crafts for girls, only set up a Ragged School for children of the destitute in 1848, and a national Church of England one year later. The ancient grammar school had been updated to teach the three Rs in 1790 – perhaps a century after Scotland, then, northern England had at last repaired the ravages caused by the Reformation. Certainly Middlemases living there were at least as literate as their laird ancestors had been in the 16th and 17th centuries.

Yet few if any benefited from higher education and the stimulus to intellectual adventure emanating from the Scottish Enlightenment, which of course was limited largely to Edinburgh, Glasgow and Aberdeen. A few literate farmers may have benefited at one remove from the wave of agricultural improvement stemming originally from *Defoe's Review* (1706-13) and the Select Society's discussions over succeeding decades. But no Middlemas attended university after Patrick in the 1680s. In fact the first exemplar may have been Robert Middlemas, son of a skilled miner, born in 1831, who became a High Court solicitor in 1859 and Treasurer for 25 years of the Berwickshire Naturalists Society, one of the last flowerings of Edinburgh debating and scientific societies and clubs.

In due course, the question of who would pay was answered by county notables and landowners in tacit alliance with the Anglican church, just as the Presbyterian synods and lairds together had funded basic education as a means towards godly discipline and social conformity. Indeed, Presbyterian chapels were built across the region to accommodate the needs of Scots migrants, especially under the auspices of the Northumberland Presbytery, although education provision suffered from the three great Disruptions of the Kirk in 1733, 1761 and 1843.

***

The question whether migrants brought their Presbyterian faith with them, or delayed migration until provision existed (as seems the case in Wooler and Alnwick) or turned to the Anglican one, can only be answered in individual cases. There is evidence of switching between the two over the centuries. Andrew Middlemas lately of Morebattle, arriving in the 1650s, simply conformed to the Anglican practice he found in Alnwick, married a local girl in St. Michael's church, and was buried there in 1683. None of his descendents reverted to the Kirk.

But from the 1790s, chapels in Berwick, Carham and Wooler witnessed regular baptisms and marriages, and at a guess, the Kirk

Table 7.

**Occupations (1841 Census)**

A= Manual; B= Craft/Artisan; C= Trader; D= Professional

| **Scotland** | | | | | | |
|---|---|---|---|---|---|---|
| A. | Agricultural labourer | 14 | B. | Joiner | 7 | |
| | Hand loom weaver | 1 | | Blacksmith | 1 | |
| | Merchant seaman | 2 | | Brass founder | 1 | |
| | Hedger | 1 | | Wool factory foreman | 1 | |
| | Building developer | 2 | | | | |
| C. | Farmer | 2 | | | | |
| | Cattle dealer | 2 | D. | Shipping entrepreneur | 1 | |
| | Grocer | 1 | | Clerk to spirits dealer | 1 | |
| | Tailor | 1 | | Bottled water entrepreneur | 1 | |
| | Brewer | 1 | | Surgeon | 2 | |
| **England** | | | | | | |
| A1. | Agricultural labourer | 43 | B1. | Joiner | 2 | Agriculture-related |
| | Gardener | 2 | | Blacksmith | 4 | |
| | Railway porter | 1 | | Saddler | 1 | |
| | Merchant seaman | 3 | | Bootmaker | 1 | |
| A2. | Miner/pitman (unspecified) | 9 | | Shepherd | 2 | |
| | | | | Gamekeeper | 1 | |
| | | | | Sawyer | 2 | |

| | | | | | | |
|---|---|---|---|---|---|---|
| C. | Cattle dealer | 1 | B2. | Iron founder | 1 | Industrial |
| | Grocer | 3 | | Shipwright | 1 | |
| | Farmer | 6 | | Alkali worker | 1 | |
| | Tailor | 4 | | Roper | 1 | |
| | Baker | 3 | | Mason | 4 | |
| | Confectioner | 1 | | Builder | 1 | |
| | Miller | 1 | | Plumber/Glazier | 1 | |
| | Butcher | 6 | B3. | Dressmaker | 4 | Female |
| | Commercial traveller | 1 | | Straw bonnet maker | 1 | |
| D. | Farm steward | 1 | | Housekeeper | 1 | |
| | Auctioneer/Surveyor | 1 | | Lodging house keeper | 1 | |
| | Teacher | 1 | B4. | Colliery engineer | 2 | Mining (skilled) |
| | Attorney's clerk | 1 | | Boiler builder | 1 | Other skilled |
| | | | | Railway guard | 1 | |
| | | | | Fisherman | 1 | |
| | Sub-postmaster | 1 | | Mine drainer | 1 | |
| | | | | Coast guard | 1 | |
| | | | B5. | Dray man | 1 | |

Notes: 1. Close linkages in agriculture, including shepherds, corn or cattle dealers, butchers.

2. Range of occupations much larger south of the Border, grows more diverse in Yorkshire, the Midlands and the South, and London.

3. Largest farms, 300 acres in Scotland, 452 and 431 acres Northern England.

held the loyalty of a quarter of the migrant families of 1841. For their other educational needs, the Middlemas diaspora benefited increasingly from late Enlightenment philanthropy and patronage; Newcastle following Edinburgh, just as Berwick and Alnwick raced to keep up with Kelso in providing public libraries and institutes.

Unacknowledged cooperation between church and landowners on both sides applied not only to attendance at church or kirk, but to work and leisure – despite the growth of rational scepticism among those who actually enjoyed leisure. In work and at play this lasted well into the later 19th century and served to delay labour movements, though not in the coal mines where the gulf between pitmen and owners had been much more sharply defined even in the 17th century. There, political activity and labour ideology flourished, as the early Chartist enthusiasm shows and the great Durham miners strikes of 1844 demonstrated.

Yet underneath, even after the Kirk's prohibitions ended medieval carnivals with their days of turning the world upside down, vestiges of an older anarchy survived, albeit confined largely to sporting events which the minister or parson usually avoided, where aristocracy, gentry and ordinary folk let their hair down together, sometimes with extreme violence.[254] Sport might vary from rural to urban areas, where throwing, quoits and bowling alleys thrived, but what categorised football or bare-knuckle boxing, wrestling or cock-fighting was the sheer variety of local rules and local champions, and the backing of individuals making extraordinarily high wagers. So too were the carters' races and horseshows on the moors above Hawick or Rothbury, Jedburgh or Wooler. Cock-fighting in pit villages, though long illegal, survived into the 1940s, as this author can remember.

More sophisticated, organised games governed by national rules came later, as did sports for women such as gymnastics, lawn tennis or toxophily. But in the 1800s, restrained only by a collective understanding about the limits of disorder, most games were played by a social mixture, even if for golf the gentry used hand-crafted clubs and feather balls, while commoners held shaped sticks and wooden balls.[255] Only in the Victorian era did decorum modify competitive anarchy, and even then the traditional holidays continued, barely Christian at all: Yuletide, New Year, Candlemas, Beltane, Halloween.

But the lasting effects of the Puritan ethic affected another aspect of life altogether, migration itself. Middlemases had not actually gone permanently overseas, other than to Ulster in the late 17th century,[256] nor to Continental Europe, nor to England's colonies as they had grown up in the 18th century. But at the start of the 19th century, they did, particularly after the bad harvests of the early 1820s. Several reached Canada, settling mainly in the undeveloped parts of Ontario, which were allotted free to immigrants to farm. Among them, in 1837, went six of eight members of James Wightman's family, a former postmaster of Wooler (1786-1864) and father of my great-grandfather's second wife. A moving account of the Laidlaw family's similar experiences, coming directly from Tweed Valley to clear the land in Huron County in the 1830s, is given by Alice Munro in *The View from Castle Rock*[257] when they soon came to rely, like Scots anywhere, on the public library for education and pleasure; and where the choice between Kirk and church was an individual, not even a family matter. There, as in the Appalachian Mountains in Virginia, ancient Border ballads like "Lord Randall My Son" lived on, but as the American musicologist Childs annotated them, with different words to the same tunes.

Such emigration was the only choice for the truly dispossessed, other than the workhouse, for the Middlemas who was a handloom weaver in Glasgow or Selkirk, a craft utterly overtaken by the machine in the 1840s. It was made easier by the start of assisted passages to North America also in the 1820s; and increased thereafter, thanks to the efforts of the Colonial Land and Emigration Commission, once the government in London had switched from opposing the loss of skilled labour, first to neutrality, then to full support.

But "the typical emigrant emerges as a person of some means, independent in thought and action, with the members of his family fleeing from social degradation and strict control at home. From upper Canada, in particular Ontario, New Zealand and Australia, they would write home, extolling the virtues of independence supported by good wages."[258]

Unlike the 17th century immigrants who had gone, mostly as individuals, to make money in the Virginia plantations, those in the early 19th went as families or part-families to New England and Eastern Canada. Their correspondence home reveals both the magnitude of their transplantation and the advantages they could recommend to those still at home.

James Middlemas, son of William and his wife Jane Stewart, settled in Grantown, in this first wave, going in 1821. Possessing some capital, he emerged as a plantation (and therefore slave) owner in St. Vincent, Leeward islands; closely followed in 1825 by a Presbyterian minister Jasper Middlemas fromYetholm, and his son Joseph a divinity student, both aiming to serve the existing Scots communities on the U.S. East coast. Jasper was soon appointed minister at Bethlem, Albany County, later the centre of a vast steel works, and it is just possible that the young emigrant Andrew Carnegie may have heard him preach.

Francis Middlemas and his wife, immigrants from Swinton also sailed to the U.S. in 1833. Then there was a gap till 1870 when Andrew, son of Robert Bell Middlemas (1818-1887) landed at Dunedin, New Zealand, to be joined once he had established himself, by his parents, his grown up son and daughter and three grandchildren, who debarked from the *MS Trevelyan* after a 90-day voyage. All farmers, they stayed, produced many grandchildren and their descendents live there still. Ontario however remained the first choice, reinforcing the earlier argument that migration choice depended very largely on kin-group fellowship cooperation, information and innate caution, as had always been the case in northern England.

"The person of some means, independent in thought and action" characterised those Middlemases who emerged as entrepreneurs in the first half of the 19th century, among them Andrew Middlemass who in 1847 set up a cork-cutting and beer-bottling factory in Kelso, which later expanded into soft drinks production, to become Middlemass Aerated Waters. Run by the same family, father to son for six generations, it was finally taken over in 1985.

At the same time, William Middlemiss was appointed as resident engineer in charge of building the North Esk Reservoir, a water 24 kilometres long, held back by an earth dam faced in stone designed by D & T Stevenson (not the railway contractors). The seven year project ran from 1843-50 and replaced the old sluices and conduits for all the factories along the river Esk.

Nothing more is known about Martin Middlemiss and his wife Dorothy except that they ran the Doncaster Union Workhouse in the 1840s, he as Resident Master, she as Matron. They may have been genial in a rough place, or they may have been archetypes for Dickens to use in *Nicholas Nickleby*.

Farmers too should be counted as entrepreneurs, at least on the scale of Mark Middlemass, born Tweedmouth 1811 and a farmer's son, who was tenant of the 452 acre Woodside Farm near Lowick in 1851, and Thomas Middlemiss, also of Tweedmouth, farming Bowsden Moor Farm 432 acres in the same years, aided by nine farm labourers. Others included John Middlemiss born 1790 and his wife Agnes, tenants of the 300 acre Crookston Farm at Traquair (part of the original Grieston estate) with a household of eight farm servants, several of them his own sons by two marriages. James Middlemiss had a slightly smaller farm near Berwick, and John Middlemiss, possibly his uncle, another one in Lowick. *His* son, William died in 1869 leaving the sizable sum of £5000 in cash.

Others included John Middlemas from Kirknewton, retired from farming and living near Alnwick, as the 1871 census records "of independent means" (whatever farmer did not?) and a neighbour John Middlemiss, holding the Town Moor farm but living at Denwick. Strangest of all, Alexander Middlemiss, born in Scotland in 1791 was by 1841 farming in Finchley, then a small village northwest of London, now part of that vast conurbation.

Many more farmed small holdings of 50 or 70 acres. None came near to Christopher Middlemas of Dunbar as an agricultural entrepreneur. Born in 1787 to a family established in the town for at least a century,[259] he married Janet Hume, daughter of the Provost of Dunbar, a distant relative of Lord Hume (the Earl whose 16th century dowry had brought Raperlaw to the Lilliesleaf family) and they had six children. He does not appear to have inherited land but in 1809, practising as a corn merchant, he bought the West Barns farm southwest of Dunbar, next to the Great North Road, a hundred and eight acres and three great fields with three acres of houses in the town and the parish teinds, from an Edinburgh banker, Thomas Allen, for £17.347.

This was an enormous price, but it included much potential building land and a new distillery, established by a neighbour James Taylor. Christopher paid off the debt in a mere six years, just in time before the onset of bad harvests after Waterloo. Trading as a corn merchant, initially for local farmers, he was also dealing in houses built on the edge of an expanding town. Property speculation in the early 19th century could be risky: some land he had bought earlier, in 1808, with houses already constructed, he sold back to the original owner 10 years later and only just covered his costs.[260]

But from then on, he prospered, particularly as a grain dealer and shipper on a much wider scale. He kept a diary and letter book from 1815-24 and though confined to business, these letters give an idea of the range of his transactions. Farming in Dunbar, engaged in distilling (he put his eldest son Christopher in with Taylor as a partner in 1824), trading and shipping cereals 200-400 bolls at a time by various packet boats to Grangemouth, the port for Stirling and the long-established Carron Ironworks, casting among other things cannon for the 19th century wars, and terminal for the Forth-Clyde canal. He also shipped to Inverness and the Low Countries and dealt in grain futures on commission for several of his friends and clients, as well as shipping coal and timber from Tyneside to Glasgow, Govan and Maybole, and iron anchor chains, 60 cwt at a time, from Leith to Glasgow. All this at a time before the Caledonian Canal opened in 1822.

Acting as what today would be called a financial services advisor, broker and shipper, when the postal service (before the Penny Post was introduced) was still primitive and dependent on a post-chaise, and before steam vessels freed marine transport from reliance on sail, turned out to be both adventurous and highly risky, subject to storms, human incompetence, misapprehension, and fraud. He recorded disputes with dissatisfied corn merchants, angry at delays in cargoes for Glasgow, problems with intermediaries, and his own difficulties in establishing a decent profit margin with farmers whose market awareness was nearly as keen as his own.[261]

One bad case occurred just after his eldest son's death in 1833. The father had been investment advisor to Catherine Neilson, widow of a Dunbar ship master, and he had already acted for her after the death of her son, a Lieutenant with the East India Company and a friend of his own two younger boys. Early in 1827 he had invested £2700 for her, in housing development in Spott, against the security of his own West Barns estate, a deed witnessed by Dunbar's Town Clerk. At the time Catherine had fully approved this, but she may not have agreed a loan of £750 from her fund to Christopher's son, when he became partner in the distillery. After the younger Christopher's death, and the bankruptcy of the senior distillery partner, Taylor, Mrs Neilson sued for a return of the loan. The case was never resolved in court although there was talk of a special jury, because of its complexities, and it dragged on till the 1840s. It is hard, for lack of records, to know who was right or what was the outcome. The affair seems a bit incestuous, perhaps not surprising in a middling-sized town, misguided, but scarcely fraudulent.

But Christopher's death left the father to sort out the distillery's future with his second son Robert Hume Middlemas, since 1829 a trustee of the now extensive West Barns estate. Only a year later, in 1839, Christopher was again sued in the Court of Session by Henry Morton, corn merchant of Wisbech (so widely did his operations reach) and two corn factors in Leith: at issue was the full payment for 250 quarters of wheat and 500 quarters of beans, which, when delivered, fell short both in quality and quantity, so that Christopher deducted £380 from the bill of £2085.

This was enough for the dealers to go to court. Christopher argued that the dealers had first tried to sell him more than he wanted, then shipped it to Rainsford, up the canal from Grangemouth, and failed because the ship *Royal William* was too large for the locks, despite his explicit instructions, so that the cargo had to be transferred to lighters at much expense, and with a month's delay which cost him his market. Nevertheless, he lost the case and agreed to pay.

Only the hard cases came to be recorded. Overall, he did well and could have served as a model for Hardy's *Mayor of Casterbridge*, becoming lay Chief Magistrate of Dunbar in the 1850s. He died October 1858. By then he was styled Middlemas of Underidge and West Barns, while his third son qualified in Edinburgh as a surgeon for the East India Company, and the youngest, John, who joined the same company as assistant surgeon in 1835, both being posted to Madras.

All these were well settled, partners in the family Trust from 1848, and locally well-connected, a move upwards into the gentry (the term laird being less appropriate) achieved in one generation. But a century and a half later, it is the scope and diversity of Christopher's entrepreneurship and ability to take high risks which catches the imagination. On his death, Robert Hume Middlemas, then living in London, inherited both the West Barns estate and the distillery – left to him by his long-dead elder brother.

One final note: the map exists detailing how the new North British Railway was to run through West Barns – a symptom of economic modernity from which his business dealings had never had the luck to benefit. No testament or will exists and the Trust records are lost. But three testaments from this period do exist and are worth setting out, again for their diversity.

- John Middlemiss, master mason of Gavinton, died 1832, leaving various small plots of land in Duns.
- George Middlemost, farmer of Jedburgh, died 1805, farm inventory £134 6/8.
- The widow of Thomas Middlemiss, Edinburgh mason, died 1809, leaving £360; "and to my dear friend Robert Middlemiss the sum of £5 sterling for the purchase of a ring as remembrance and 25 shillings to his daughter to buy a black gown; to his son "Boston's Works" in one volume."

***

There can be no easy summing up for a chapter where, in any case, there is no cut-off point, not until the long downturn in northeastern agriculture after 1870. Farmers on the Border had survived Peel's repeal of the Corn Laws in 1846, to re-establish themselves in a British market irrevocably committed to free trade, unlike France or the German states. But then in the 1870s they encountered sustained imports of American grain, shipped in steam vessels, acting to the long-lasting detriment of British corn growers. This hit worst the cooler, wetter arable lands in Tweed and Teviot valleys as well as Northumberland.

Even so, agriculture was still the largest single occupation in Britain in 1900. But industrial demand, spectacularly demonstrated by the rise of Glasgow and Lanark had taken over the labour market. At the same time, because of higher living standards, better housing, diet, and above all medicine, the numbers of Middlemas children born, declined. They lived longer, better, and their demography finally merged with the British average.

Obviously a migrant, wishing to become English and accepted, would soon acquire a north-east accent and conform to social norms south of the Border. But the Border Scots already spoke excellent English, if still accented. They had, as a whole in the 18th and 19th centuries, better schooling and perhaps more disciplined work-patterns. There was always the fear that they might have to move on, across the Atlantic, where Scotsmen often held a better reputation. It is likely that a core of Scottish identity persisted, up to a century after the actual migration.

But were they now British? With the kin-group divided, sub-divided, and spread across the British Empire as that stood in 1900, had they grown to be citizens of a United Kingdom that had become since the 1880s the greatest power in the world – albeit already rivalled by a united Germany and the United States? Or were those living south of the Border still in some indefinable sense Scottish?

Such a question could easily have been asked in 1900 of Bavarians, Sicilians, or peasants in the Auvergne and the Landes, and would not have received the answers: Germany, Italy, France. Of course, since the Act of Union, they had been legally British citizens. But in terms of identity and *mentalité*, they may not have felt so, especially if they lived in Scotland, Dunedin or Ontario. On the English side, however, the question is much more complex: assimilation may be a matter both of time and degree, and it was a very different question for 17th century settlers, from the fresh migrants of the 1830s. In the latter case, the 1841 census question "where born?" gives the entry *Scotland* not, as for those born in England, the parish or village or town. Prejudice takes many forms, even indirectly in official documents.

One way of answering may be to ask if prejudice still existed against which the former migrants had positively to react, reaction being a way to define identity. Samuel Johnson's well-known aphorism that the fairest sight a Scotchman ever sees is the high road to England, has enough wit to distance it from the sour residue of Elizabethan racism and tirades against James VI/I's retinue of carpet baggers.[262] Yet Boswell recorded in his diary of 1762 the protests of a London theatre audience "The mob in the gallery roared out, 'no Scots! no Scots! out with them,' hissed and pelted them with apples...my heart warmed to my countrymen...I hated the English: I wished from my soul that the Union was broke."

By the 1850s, the detritus amounted to no more than music hall and public house stereotypes. Berwick's anti-Scots statutes had been repealed in the 1600s. Jokes about Scots' meanness, lack of sense of humour, drunkenness, and hell-fire sermons barely counted, and derived partly from fear of their acknowledged competitiveness. Real xenophobia had disappeared, certainly if compared to vicious jokes about the Welsh or the contemptuous diatribes against Catholic Irish immigrants, who were seen as a class almost sub-human, but who nevertheless dug first England's canals and then constructed its railways.

It may be that, among the literate, the Scottish enlightenment helped, by stimulating London to meet the intellectual challenges from Edinburgh, then melding with the scientific, philosophical revolution which brought neoclassicism to Britain, particularly its architecture and design, and briefly turned the united country into the industrial/scientific powerhouse of Europe.

Perhaps for the farmer or labourer, soil was soil wherever, and whoever was the landlord or the man working next door. Nevertheless, it does seem, even in the mid-19th century, that *identifiable* Scots, like immigrants anywhere, had not only to be better in order to get jobs, but had to work that much harder to keep them. But at the top, among admirals, generals, empire builders, architects and engineers, bankers, or merchants across the entire Empire from England to India or Australia, Scots led in every field. Ferguson's dictum became a 19th century truism, that civilisation meant progress "from barbarism to being a Scotsman."

EMIGRATION TO CANADA.

**FOR QUEBEC AND MONTREAL,**

THE fine first-class British-built Barque JAMAICA, 550 tons burthen, Capt. THOMAS MARTIN, will be despatched on 4th June.

This fine Ship is well-known to be a very fast sailer, and, having a permanently laid lower deck, is admirably adapted for carrying passengers.

Apply to

M'SYMON & HUTTON,
87, Union Street.

Glasgow, 21st May, 1847.

*Emigration, 1847*

**In Memory of**
**Private J MIDDLEMISS**

**23/857, 20th (Tyneside Scottish) Bn., Northumberland Fusiliers**
**who died age 31**
**on 05 March 1917**
**Son of Thomas Middlemiss, of 6, Melrose Terrace, Bedlington Station, Northumberland, and the late Mary Middlemiss.**
**Remembered with honour**
**FAUBOURG D'AMIENS CEMETERY, ARRAS**

**Commemorated in perpetuity by**
**the Commonwealth War Graves Commission**

*Faubourg d'Amiens Cemetery, Arras. Private J. Middlemiss, killed 5 March 1917, Tyneside Scottish Fusiliers*

# 13.

# Conclusion

It started with a single horseman of Anglo-Norman origin, part of an already-established military elite in north Northumberland, riding over the then peaceful but ill-defined Border with Scotland, to take up the offer of a knight's fee just south of the river of Tweed from the Abbey of Kelso. It ends with a widely dispersed set of roughly 200 families recorded officially by the British state in 1841-51, together with up to a dozen more in North America and the Antipodes.

During the Middle Ages, as it grew into a kin-group, the family retained some Anglo-Norman characteristics: hereditary land ownership under the remnants of feudal tenure, held first from the Black Douglas earls, then from the King, and by purchase for themselves; it gave children Christian names, William, Walter, Robert which were not Scottish in origin and it displayed a symbol, the Cross of St Eustace (later St. Hubert) with its stag's head cabossed, of Continental rather than British significance. Like members of the Norman elite in Sicily, who settled comfortably among a mixture of part Christian, part Muslim inhabitants, these northern immigrants slowly merged, becoming definably Scottish by the late 15th century.[263]

They stayed, leaving descendents still in Kelso and the Border Shires. But the migrations that occurred from the 17th century onwards, mainly into north-eastern England, produced a growing diversity within what was, by then, a kin-group, made evident by the emergence of three definitive spellings of the name. This in turn led to the formation of sub-groups among the original group, and finally to the loss of its long-held generic sense of identity.

There had never been, as there was in Highland clans, a hereditary chief: that was alien to Border society. But in the troubled period from the mid-15th to the mid-17th centuries, the senior branch did style themselves Middlemas of Middlemas (otherwise "of that Ilk") and were accepted as such by the group. Since the Civil War, there has been no claimant to this title, and it would probably be impossible to revive it now – even though there is, somewhere but unidentifiable, a rightful claimant.

It is an old story, one of the oldest, the decline of a once-great family, especially in the transition from Middle Ages to early modern history. What is of interest here is not only to ask *how* and *why*, but what happened after decline set in. This is therefore a book about survival and limited recovery from the migrant depths, where men lacked the old advantages, in a world dominated by new families who had done well out of the monasteries, wars and their natural resources, rising to dominate the new capitalist order.

***

Middlemases now alive would, most likely, regard themselves as British or, as the fourth Earl of Aberdeen, British Prime Minister put it in 1852, as both Scottish and British, a dual identity "superior to the English on both fronts." By the 1850s of course, much of the old English antipathy to incoming Scots had been eroded by the surge of romantic interest in Scotland, and its romantisised past, seen through the novels of Sir Walter Scott and the long love affair of Queen Victoria and Prince Albert with the Highlands and Balmoral House.

In between, to add colour, came George IV's extravagant coronation in 1824 in Edinburgh, a somewhat grotesque spectacle with the corpulent monarch strapped into kilt and tartan hose; which indirectly recalled the inappropriate Holyrood coronation there of Charles I. A wholly new industry soon grew up, dedicated to weaving and marketing "clan" designs that owed less to real history than to "the invention of tradition."

How this complex overlay of Victorian patronage, bolstered by Landseer's paintings and the long 19th century popularity of historical fiction, coloured English visitors' perceptions, who saw the northern part of Britain mainly through tourist eyes, is hard to assess. But it does appear to have ameliorated ancient prejudices about the Scots when it came to migration and competition. Charles Dilke was to discover in the 1860s on a visit to India "for every Englishman who has worked himself up to wealth from small beginnings without external aid, you find two Scotsmen. It is strange indeed that Scotland has not become a popular name for the United Kingdom."

If there is any answer to the question about identity, set out in the previous chapter, it may be found in that early 20th century demonstration of British-ness, the line-up of volunteers in August 1914 and afterwards, to join the British Army in what became known as the Great War, 1914-18. When voluntary enlistment finally proved inadequate to feed the Western Front's catastrophic losses, it was overtaken of course by the state's necessary imposition of conscription 1916-17; but the first, volunteer stage, undoubtedly united motherland with colonies in an explosion of patriotism producing a higher percentage of recruits from Canada, Australia and New Zealand as well as India than in Britain itself.

How many Middlemases then chose to enlist in English, how many in Scottish regiments? There is no easy answer, since the vast majority picked their local regiment, wherever they lived; while those with particular skills naturally joined artillery or engineer equivalents, the Royal Horse Artillery, Ordnance Corps, or Royal Engineers. The majority of Middlemases were therefore to be found, before and after conscription, in the Black Watch, Scottish Borderers, Cameronians, Scots Guards and Fusiliers, Lothians, on one side,[264] the Northumberland Fusiliers, Durham Light Infantry, East and West Yorkshires, and Lancaster Fusiliers on the other, with a handful in northern Irish regiments such as the Inniskillin Fusiliers, and the London Regiment, the Rifle Brigade, the Household Cavalry and the West Kent.

Many of these regiments have ceased to exist as a result of successive reorganisations. But in one First World War instance, the combination of older identity and affiliation did show up clearly: the War Office, perhaps unusually, sanctioned the formation of six battalions within the Northumberland Fusiliers (who had already raised 48 battalions, more than any other regiment in British history, making 54 altogether) comprising the Tyneside Scottish (four battalions nos. 21 to 24) and the Tyneside Irish (two battalions). Subsequent recruitment along Tyneside proved highly effective, and all six were involved in some of the fiercest fighting on the Western Front. Three Middlemases served initially in the former, one in the latter, and Sergeant Walter Middlemiss was awarded the Military Medal; several more were conscripted into them in 1917.

In all, 51 Middlemases were killed in action in Army regiments in the four years of war, 24 Middlemas (s), 25 Middlemis (s), and one – possibly the last – Middlemist. There were fewer officers dead than might have been expected (3), fewer NCOs (9), the majority being privates, guardsmen or riflemen, above all in the Northumberland Fusiliers, Durham Light Infantry, and Scottish Borderers. Two were even killed after the war was over, fighting against the Bolsheviks in Russia, 1918-19, one in northern Russia (RHA) and one in the south (West Yorkshire). But those 51 were drawn from approximately 400 men of military age ... a greater proportionate slaughter of the kin-group than in any event since the Black Death.[265] One legacy for everyone in 1919 was a determination "never again," another, distorted marriage and birth rates across the British Isles for a generation to come.

Three conclusions might be drawn: that the Middlemases collectively rallied to the idea of British-ness (as they had not done in the war against Napoleon)[266]; second, that they did so in a predominantly local way, following the vast majority, apart from those with specialist skills; third, that by chance or aptitude they were placed in some of the worst battles of the Great War in France and Flanders. None can have had any idea that their remote ancestors had fought on similar fields in France, but for France and against England in the early 15th century.

Given the reorganisation of recruitment that the War Office introduced to obviate the calamitous effects of men's deaths or mutilation on a single town or locality, where after 1918 few women could ever hope for marriage, such an analysis would reveal little about the sense of identity during the Second World War, although rivalries and brawls between Scottish and English regiments still occurred in the 1950s, relations between the Fifth Fusiliers and the HLI or Black Watch being particularly volatile.

***

One persistent danger, inherent in writing family history over many centuries, is what might be called the D'Urberville syndrome: the yeoman farmer in Hardy's novel learns of his kinship with the ancient, aristocratic family and the airs he puts on, his frustrated longing for a mythical past, destroy both him and his daughter, Tess. It is a common enough pattern because older records, coming especially from the Middle Ages, contain the names and deeds only of notables and kings – unless they were criminals or perhaps heroes. Little or nothing in surviving documents reveals the stories of individual ordinary folk, so that much 19th century genealogy and contemporary internet blogs are filled up with tenuous or frankly bogus connections to remote royalty or ancient noblemen.

I have tried here to tell the history of a kin-group, unusual in possessing a unique name, from original sources in each generation, as the family grew up and broadened into a wider network, without aggrandisement, and acknowledging the gaps where records have been destroyed, or perhaps never existed. I have tried to give a factual answer to remedy their loss of a collective memory, oral tradition becoming especially vulnerable with the start of early modernity, and in the absence of any written memoir or family history.

Border kin-groups were not like Highland clans, whose contemporary members can still enjoy museums embodying a long-rehearsed collective memory, usually wrapped with a tartan armband. They did not often, except for noble families, centre on the aggregation of chiefly power as in Gaeldom to the north, being more support-groups aiming at land retention, status alliances and survival. Over 700 years, large gaps obviously exist, especially in the earlier period. But reasonable conjecture can be made on the basis of what remains, even before the Reformation.

The main thrust is clear enough. Beyond the narrative sequence, this story may be useful in other ways, to illuminate the history of small, very particular localities within the generally accepted national-historical scope of Scotland and north-eastern England; to add something to the heated debates among modern historians about the nature of identity and the development of what James VI/I called his "middle shires."

Where it cannot easily help is to answer the question, what part did women play? Given the nature of the sources, and of the male-dominated society of the times, that has to be answered in other ways than narrative history, and through other, related disciplines.

The old truism that all history can be read in a grain of sand could be reworded as "the view from Kelso." The Middlemases who appear here defined themselves in the Middle Ages by their land, social status and lineage; and after that, by their allegiance to the house of Douglas, the King or to God. Their Scottish-ness can be seen only through the glass of their regional context. It is necessary to reiterate that the Borders, like Yorkshire, East Anglia or Cornwall were for many centuries *sui generis*, regions with their own world-view, distinct from the whole; and this too can add to the long debate about the interplay between national and local history, how far each influenced the other, and how much of both it is necessary to understand before reaching judgement on what the overall historical canon may be.

Obvious problems of methodology and the limits of source materials make it unwise to tackle the history of Scotland from the standpoint of one small group. The most I can do is to set one in the *context* of the other, while acknowledging how problematic, in the light of modern research since the 1970s, the history of Scotland itself has become. Yet it has been surprising how often the Middlemas story coincides with or exemplifies the larger picture on one hand; on the other, how often divergences can be explained in terms of the controversies about what that larger picture may be.[267] Readers must decide whether this provides a useful exemplar or an illusion borne of too close a focus on a handful of individuals. In the crowded British Isles (leaving the "great" aside), however, the search has value. Within the United Kingdom (once misspelled by one of my students in a hurry as "Untied Kingdom") our identities are, in so far as we really address the question, a blend of family, locality, region, nationality, whether or not we aspire to the international dimensions – and who can be certain that within a century, the entity will be either united or a Kingdom?

***

Part of my agenda has been to chart the pattern of migration for economic rather than for reasons of religious persecution, despite the 17$^{th}$ century experience. What the Middlemases did was not a specifically Scottish phenomenon, because its various stages conformed to a universal early modern pattern, not essentially different from 19th century Indian or Chinese migrants going as indented labour to east and south Africa, Albanians to southern Italy, or Shangaan workers from Mozambique to the gold and diamond mines next door; the Irish navvies in Britain being only the most widely-studied, if not the largest.

With its searing consequences both for those who stayed behind and those who left to find work, betterment and a wider sort of life, that is a far wider, chronologically endless subject, for which tracing one kin-group can offer only a very partial insight. The fact that Middlemas migrants after 1603 shared a common if conflict-ridden geography, and aspects of Christianity, with the English, did not mean that, even after 1707, as legally-defined British citizens, they were not up against religious and racial prejudice, even hatred, masking fear of economic and social competition.

A migrant in today's world cannot hope, like the first Middlemas, for an invitation to land, title and social space in return for a well-defined military obligation. For much of the late medieval and early modern periods it was true, as a male South African once told me, that "the only things worth killing for are land, water and women." Those who entered England, like many who were left behind in hard times, could take nothing for granted. The migrants often carried so little with them that betterment chances for their children actually receded. Daughters might marry and stay, the old faced the poorhouse on either side; but most younger sons had to move on or take the toughest and most dangerous jobs available.

Some modern analysts argue that Scottish emigrants did very well out of the Union (and still do) because they gained access to the highest levels of the imperial, financial, industrial, and administrative powerhouse, and in particular its world-wide colonial footprint. So they did, if they were well-educated, able and fortunate in their starting point, to rise up an entirely new ladder. Conversely, Scotland lost permanently many of its best and brightest, who do not seem to have returned home in any great numbers between the Act of Union and the present day. But this whole argument rests more on saluting a new elite, than on studying the numerical majority who, like poor Irish, Welsh, southern Italians, or Sicilians landed in the Americas without much education, few opportunities and no money, seeking survival in an environment at best neutral, at worst actively hostile.

***

Being modern, even postmodern, we think we know what the past is and how little it determines what we do today. Hence our lack of attention to it in the state school curriculum. Equally, we hold an assumption that the past is something we can *know*, either via romanticised excerpts in televised dramas, or through academic research (with rather more reservations) – although few today would aspire, as Ranke did, to tell it *wie es eigentlich gewesen war*, as it *actually* was.

But this was not always so. A secular veneration of the past (as distinct from the religious view that it represented and exemplified divine providence) in the late medieval British Isles relied largely on myth and legend to validate statements about identity or origins: would-be conclusive vindications of essentially political outcomes such as a new line of kings, or defence against alien attackers. The Scottish assertion of national identity from Arbroath in 1320 onwards, like the rival claims to the throne after Alexander III's death, fall into these categories. For a family, the same was true, usually via the assertion of ancient lineage, bolstered by heraldry and courtly aspirations, vital to arranged marriages. Indeed, heraldry acquired significance in the 15th and 16th centuries for social reasons very different from its original aim of distinguishing fighting groups from each other.

If the first use of real scholarship about the past was Lorenzo Valli's mid-15th century demolition of papal claims to supremacy based on the forged "donation of Constantine," in England it can be dated from the incoming Tudors' search for legitimacy, first for their kingship and then their onslaught on Catholic church property, and finally to defend Henrician religious supremacy. In Scotland, the rewriting of history to justify what would now be called regime change was an integral part of Calvinist reformers' zeal to abolish an idolatrous past.

Early modern experience in the Borders, however, explored another theme, as John Leland noted in Britannia (1st edition 1586) with its use of reasonably accurate maps to describe the regions, and relics from the past, not as religious symbols but to present truths about a forgotten age. "The initial focus of this antiquarianism was monuments and muniments which revealed land rights, coats of arms, and all aspects of genealogy."[268] Such devices adorned the margins of John Speed's even better maps from the early 1600s.

This British renaissance mixture of purposes, scholarship vying with legitimation of the elite, may explain why the first manuscript of Scottish heraldry was put together by Seton in 1591, only ten years after the foundation in London of the first Society of Antiquaries. James VI/I in turn was obsessed by the attraction of secular symbols, notably royal regalia, in pursuit of his claim to divine right – hence his 1605 edict concerning what were to become the Crown Jewels; in turn, and for even weightier symbolic reasons, to be taken apart or melted down for coin under Cromwell's New Order.

Flower of the Scottish Enlightenment, David Hume's historical works seemed positively modern in comparison. Yet in spite of their European fame, and Scotland's long demonstrable links with the Continent, Scottish history is, perhaps inevitably, little known or studied in southern Britain. It may for that reason tend towards the parochial and is often seen through the distorting lens of opposition to the larger neighbour, absorbed ultimately as Scotland was, not by conquest but by assimilation into an imperial entity.

Scottish history is also riven by ideological disagreements, like the Kirk itself in the 19th century. Some are nationalist, some Marxist interpretations – this being the country where in 1917-21 John Maclean tried to establish a Scottish nationalist Communist party, in contradistinction to the Communist Party of Great Britain, and in defiance of the apparatchiks and Lenin himself. Yet Scotland's view of itself has also been conditioned by the wider context, not only in the late 18th century, but today, for example in the enduring controversy over whether or not it still benefits from the Union; and throughout by the need to accommodate in one frame, Highlands, fertile Lowlands, and the east/west divisions of the Borders.

To some extent, the Middlemas history is also that of a group outside the main trends, not resisting but set apart from the remorseless trend towards modern government with its formal institutions of centralised power. This is not to say that they – apart from a handful – lived beyond the law or religious discipline, rather that they remained even in the 19th century an independent-minded lot, rarely seeking to take part in Edinburgh politics, let alone those of London. Which raises, in a different form, the same questions about local in relation to national history. If there is a faint parallel after the 16th century between this kin-group and those in Sicily at the same time, so be it.

Three intrinsic themes run through this book: kinship and family continuity, strategies for survival, and migration when the latter failed. Migration is dangerous without the first two, because if voluntary, it requires transformations of attitude as a precondition for survival, and for adaptation to the homeland to come.

***

# Postscript

In writing this book I have been made aware of many people whom I had never even known existed, and whose inevitably fragmentary stories and identities I hope now better to understand. To any Middlemas who reads this and would like to link their branch to those described here, I offer a few rather obvious hints.

It would, of course, be easier if you have a family bible, with Victorian and later generations pencilled in. But in any case, the internet is full of information about how to begin, using the parish registers and the British censuses after 1841, the year when full details of name, residence and birthplace appear. Most libraries will offer advice, but remember that the Record Offices are overwhelmed these days with members of the public researching their own ancestries.

At a relatively small cost, and with luck, there should be no real difficulty in reaching back to the 18th century through the old parish register series (OPRS) now readily available, one generation at a time. It may be possible to reach even the 17th century because some parish registers start in the 1600s or earlier, though the first pages may well be stained, rat holed or illegible. But many do not begin until the 18th century and much depends on whether the connection between parents, children and grandchildren, often of the same forenames, can be sustained.

If land or houses are involved, wills and testaments are valuable. So are registers of tombstones in older churches, remembering that the Middlemases were Presbyterian as well as Anglican and sometimes switched between the two. So are early school registers and local archives or manorial records, and the Militia Lists and Hearth Tax archives.

By no means all Middlemases of the early modern period, i.e. post 1550, appear here. Many younger sons, destined to work on the family land or leave home altogether, made little impression or died without leaving children behind. Many do not appear on the tables of descent in Appendix A, because it gets harder to complete this going south, when there were no longer lands to be transferred and wills to prove. Nevertheless I have managed to prolong most of the main branches into the first half of the 18th century or later, some into the 19th, that is, up to twenty generations from the mid 13th century, and it should be possible for kin members to reach back that far, say, five or six generations, in order to make the links.

What I can say, with certainty, is that, however many families there were at any given time, there were no other kin-groups of this name. Whatever the spelling today, wherever Middlemases live, their origins are the same.

# Notes

[1] Many Jewish immigrants fleeing from Poland and Russia in the 1890s not only Anglicised their names but took Scottish ones, as if to deepen their commitment to British life – only to find themselves recruited into Scottish regiments after introduction of conscription in the Great War, 1916-1917.

[2] Notably in Scotland, women retained their family name on marriage, as was the early modern practice in Spain.

[3] Linda Colley, *The Ordeal of Elizabeth Marsh: A Woman in World History* (2007).

[4] Alice Munro, *The View from Castle Rock: Stories* (2006).

[5] To my readers I should apologise for giving modern English versions of the latter: colourless perhaps, but more easily assimilated without double exposition. A few examples I have left in the original.

[6] The most complete analysis (35 membranes out of 41) is in Bain, *Collection of Documents Related to Scotland (1880).* For the seals, many of which became detached over 700 years, see Vol. 2, Appendix III "The Chapter House Seals." But for a modern analysis, identifying almost twice as many as Bain, see Bruce McAndrew, "Sigillography of the Ragman Roll," *Proceedings of the Society of Antiquaries of Scotland*, 1994, pp. 667-773, with photographs of all of them (PRO reference E39/17/4).

[7] N 1227 in McAndrew's notation. The actual membrane is PRO E39/99/1.

[8] Quoted in GWS Barrow, *The Anglo Norman Era*, p. 84.

[9] N. Reid, *Scotland in the Reign of Alexander III*, p. 17.

[10] *Calendar of Documents Relating to Scotland*, Vol. 2, p. 736.

[11] *Anglo Norman Era*, p. 83.

[12] cf. V. Groebner, *Who Are You? Identification, Deception and Surveillance in Early Modern Europe* (2005).

[13] Middleton near Bamburgh belonged to the Mareschal (Marshall) family. But when David Le Mareschal joined the Scots against Edward III, he was known simply as "Le Scot" and his lands were forfeited to the Grays of Norham like those of Gilbert de Middleton.

[14] cf. "History of Northumberland" Vol. 7, pp. 53-55. Also JC Hodgson "Notes of the Three Middletons" *Archeologea Aelina*, 3rd series. (1911) Vol. 130.43.

[15] Northumberland Archeological and Building Sites Ancient Monuments Reports SMRID 1732, no. 29344.

[16] c.f. Sir Arthur Middleton: *Sir Gilbert de Middleton* (1894) pg. 95 et seq.

One of the family, John de Middleton also styled himself John de Thornborough, emphasising the point about the last name being a matter of choice (History of Northumberland, Vol. 10, p. 327).

[17] c.f. *Atlas of Scottish History*, pp. 363-65.

[18] G.W.S. Barrow, *The Anglo-Norman Era in Scottish History* (1974) pp. 7 – 10, 21-27, 39-49, etc. charted the subsequent internal migration of Anglo-Norman families, like the Haigs of Bemersyde (from La Hague) and Walter de Rydale (Yorkshire) who became Riddell of Lilliesleaf, to the upper valleys of Tweed and Teviot, before being forced to choose after 1296 between one side or the other – though since Edward I re-enacted the laws of David I in 1305, he did not actually force this. These middling sort first attached themselves as dependents to a noble house or monastery or to the king's court. Thus was population dispersed from northeast England (old Northumbria) across southeast Scotland (p. 107).

[19] William Kapelle, *The Norman Conquest of the North 1000-1135* (1998). See also on Wales, David Carpenter, *The Struggle for Mastery 1066-1284* (2004).

[20] Jean Froissart, *Chronicles*, Vol. 1, Chapter 17.

[21] This and the subsequent quotations are taken from the collection *Early Travels in Scotland.*

[22] N. Reid, *Scotland in the Reign of Alexander III*, p. 207.

[23] Alexander Grant, *Independence and Nationhood, Scotland 1306-1469* (passim).

[24] G.W.S. Barrow, "Lothian in the First War of Independence" SHR 1976. Sir Alexander Seton, for example, supported Robert I, reverted to Edward II, and then fought at Bannockburn, all within five years.

[25] The extent of this is clear, *Atlas of Scottish History*, p. 105.

[26] cf. John Barbour, *The Bruce (1375)* which propagated this version.

[27] A.A.M. Duncan, *Scotland: The Making of the Kingdom* (1976). Tenure of land was not the only reason for relationships, and was often sold or bought, so that lairds remained freer agents in the face of compelling adversity than the habitually-used feudal terminology allowed for.

[28] Notably in what was styled the Emerald Charter 1324, which gave the "good Sir James" tenure over the forests of Selkirk and Jedburgh, comprising most of Ettrick.

[29] Notably Sir Gilbert de Middleton, Captain of Mitford Castle whose family had originated, like the Middlemases, in one of the three Middletons. Gilbert revolted against Edward II ostensibly because of the King's appointment of the Bishop of Durham; between 1315 and 1318 he captured two papal legates returning from Edinburgh, joined

the Scottish army with his kinsmen, and held Horton Castle against Edward II until his capture and execution by the Sheriff of Roxburgh. He may have intended to revive the ancient Gospatric earldom in Northumbria, but became something of a pawn in Robert Bruce's game to secure papal recognition.

30 For this, see Ranald Nicholson, *Scotland in the Later Middle Ages*, 1974, and A. Tuck and A. Gordon, *War and Border Societies in the Middle Ages*, 1992 and C. Neville, *Violence, Custom and Law*, 1995.

31 Alan Young in M. Reid (ed) p. 18.

32 Michael Brown *The Black Douglas*, 1998 gives the most recent account of the family as a whole. But see also Sir William Fraser *The Douglas Book*, 4 volumes, 1885.

33 Michael Brown, p. 167. I am grateful to Dr Jenny Wormald for this reference.

34 Similar "new men" served the Percies on the other side: Ogles, Herons, Hetons, Greys, Strothers, and Widdringtons, many of whom also fought at Otterburn.

35 Colin McNamee, *Wars of the Bruces 1306-1328* (1997).

36 See p. 55. By 1400 in any case, the knightly heavy cavalry armed with lances had given way to much lighter mounts, ridden by hobbelars, or raiders who could dismount to fight as infantry with spears in the schilton formation developed much earlier by Wallace at Stirling Bridge.

37 The plague, second great pandemic since Byzantine times, reached Kelso and Selkirk with an English army. It was not, as commonly thought since, bubonic, but pneumonic, killing its victims in 48 hours and spreading by close contact, fastest in towns and villages. Of Scotland's total population in 1349, roughly one-third died, and only in the 16th century did numbers revive to their 1340 level. (Karen Jillings, *Scotland's Black Death*, pp. 16-20.) As in Italy, described in Boccaccio's *Decameron*, rural areas suffered less and the nobility and upper classes fled to their estates.

38 Bain, Vol. 2, p. 348 records a case in 1385 "in the King's hands by reason of the Scots war," and a group of lairds in 1399 petitioned Richard II for relief from distress and suffering caused by robberies, slaughters and non-enforcement of March Law (p. 523).

39 In this, Scottish kings preceded Henry VIII's debasement of the English coinage, as demonstrated in the 1366 land assessments.

40 *Chronyklle*, Vol. 1, p. 42.

41 Roxburgh Collection Historical mss., 1438.

42 Karen Jillings, *Scotland's Black Death*, pp. 78-79.

[43] Papal Petitions, Vol. 1, p. 624 "William de Meldiemast, for a benefice in the gift of the abbot and convent of Kelso, notwithstanding the right which he has to a perpetual vicarage of Durisdeer in the diocese of Glasgow."

[44] The fourth Earl had a chancellor and secretary to act as diplomats and messengers, a confessor-chaplain (John Fogo, former monk of Melrose, later secretary to King James I) a priest to serve him mass daily, a steward, responsible for his finances, a doctor and lesser officials, to say nothing of his 20 relatives and friends on his council, such as Alexander Hume.

[45] He and his brother James siphoned more than £7000 Scots from the royal customs in the 1410s which he used to ransom his hostage colleagues from the English after his own return.

[46] Michael Brown, *The Black Douglas*, p. 117. This account is based on his comprehensive and stimulating work.

[47] Brown, p. 167.

[48] Registry of the Great Seal, Vol. 2 (1426) pp. 10-11.

[49] Sir William Fraser, *The Douglas Book*, vol. 1, p. 404, note 2.

[50] In the Norman tradition of Bishop Odo of Bayeux, clerics could and did fight alongside their temporal Lords. The second Earl Douglas was defended to his death at Otterburn by his chaplain Richard Lundstre, later Archdeacon of Aberdeen.

[51] Brown, *Douglas*, pp. 247-50.

[52] Exchequer Rolls, vol. 3, p. 242.

[53] Brown, *Douglas*, p. 195. One example is his former chancellor, Alexander Cairns, Rector of Ettrick Forest, Provost of Lincluden Abbey, Canon of Dunbar, Vicar of Wigton. Such as he served twice over of course, at arms and at prayer.

[54] By this time, with incomes falling in all the 12 Scottish dioceses, with religious houses also suffering, as teinds (tithes) declined, a gulf had developed between the parish clergy, on £10-20 or more and the less-trained substitutes they employed. It had become harder to recruit monks too, even at £20 in the 1460s, and by the mid-15th century even Kelso, where Sir William's nephew John was a monk, held little more than half of its 13th century peak numbers.

[55] Register of the Great Seal, 1439, no. 209.

[56] Only the ruins remain, themselves mostly restoration of the original 12th century building, the nave and chancel walls to a height of six or eight feet. By Scottish standards, the original was probably quite fine, with painted walls, some stone carving, and early 15th century stained glass illustrating the Biblical stories.

[57] Kelso was a Tironensian foundation, similar to the Benedictine regime, which suffered repeatedly through the 14th century, so that in 1316 and again in 1420, its monks were reduced to begging. They had petitioned Edward I in 1305 to house their charters and muniments and as late as 1461 still lived in fear of the German mercenaries in Roxburgh Castle. The development of lay commendators during the Great Schism, usually scions of noble families, encouraged the selling off of monastic lands, cash for "feu-ferm" tenancies, which were in effect freeholds, and which in the long run diminished their revenues. Yet none of this had as bad effects as the Hertford Raids of 1544.

[58] The fourth Earl had played some part in helping to resolve the Great Schism when persuaded by the Burgundians in 1413 to switch from Avignon (Benedict XIII) to Rome (Martin V), against the advice of the Duke of Albany, which was of course the decision finally taken by James I. Four years later the Council of Constance adjudicated in Martin's favour and Douglas earned the support of St. Andrews dioceses as well. But the Scottish church remained a direct subject of the papacy, no archbishop being appointed till 1472.

[59] Brown, *Douglas*, p. 195.

[60] *Scottish Supplications to Rome*, Vol. 6, 1419-21; Vol. 7, 1424-32; Vol. 7, pp. 233-37 is the main source for what follows.

[61] The Little Schism 1433-49, tail end of the Great Schism, often involved Scotland and Piccolimini's mission in 1436 was also intended to restore Croyser in the King's favour (Brown, *Douglas*, pp. 294-98) one reason for suspecting that he must have met Sir William, then at the epicentre of the affair.

[62] *Papal Letters*, Lateran Register, Vol. 413, p. 452.

[63] Grant, *Independence and Nationhood*, pp. 94-95.

[64] Registry of the Great Seal, 1436, 24th August.

[65] Registry of the Great Seal, 1439, no. 209. The main indenture between "bailies and community" of Peebles burgh, is dated 4th February 1444-5 (Peebles Charters, pp. 9-12). St. Andrews was a Trinitarian church with a nave, choir and symmetric projecting chapels (outlined in the *Atlas of Scottish Historical Geography*, pp. 372-3). See also RCHAM Peebles: *Ecclesiastical Monuments*, no. 481, pp. 209-11, which shows that, after destruction by an English army in 1549, it was largely quarried for building materials, before being rebuilt in the 19th century. This records "a small chapel projecting from the centre of the north wall."

[66] Grant, *Independence and Nationhood*, pp. 98-99. It is possible that the collegiate church at Peebles, established by 1500, grew out of this

endowment. Such trusts were "intended to enhance the services offered by large burgh churches, often as an expression of civic pride. The founders were most often laymen, from the King down to wealthy burgesses, all seeking to provide for their own foundation..."

67 Brown, p. 279 "To many men in the south, from royal counsellors to freeholders, the efforts of Earl William...were unwelcome and resisted."

68 Brown, p. 330, The former Douglas lands now provided one-third of James II's revenues, but because of wars their value in Ettrick had fallen by three quarters since 1380.

69 S.I. Boardman, *Politics and the Feud in Late Medieval Scotland*, PhD, St. Andrews, 1990.

70 All of which inspired Lindsay's biting criticism *Ane Satyre of the Thrie Estatis* (1540).

71 *Liber de Calchou (Kelso)* Vol. 2, p. 534.

72 Acts of the Lord Auditors, 1494.

73 Acts of the Lords in Council, February, 1503.

74 This flagrant nepotism had been allowed by a papal indult of 1487 – a concession which perhaps only recognized the sad state into which once-great monasteries had fallen. One example of confusion and corruption is that the Selkirk revenue relinquished by Sir William only actually reached Kelso Abbey 25 years later in 1471.

75 Roxburgh ms. 1524.

76 Their son William of Lilliesleaf (born circa 1540) is dealt with in Chapter 7.

77 Exchequer Rolls, Vol. 6, p. 620.

78 These Scotts became Scott of Buccleugh and Branxholme: Scott of Rankillour had been a signatory to the Ragman Roll and the Scotts were by now hereditary masters of Ettrick, the most fertile of the three wards, as the family spread out between Teviot and Tweed. Scotts of Haining had died out by the time Sir William Fraser wrote *Scott of Buccleugh* (two volumes, 1878) but in the 15th and 16th centuries they were linked to Scotts of Harden and Cranston of that ilk, Murrays, Pringles and Rutherfords, all with lands in the Ettrick region (John M. Gilbert, *Hunting and Hunting Reserves in Medieval Scotland*, 1979).

79 Jenny Wormald, *Lords and Men in Scotland; Bonds of Man Rent, 1442-1603*, 1985, p. 87.

80 The first attempt, through a Scott-Kerr marriage, failed to avert Sir Walter Scott's murder in the streets of Edinburgh 20 years later (revenge always being, in the Spanish phrase "a meal best eaten cold"); and it broke out again in 1577.

[81] T. Craig-Brown, *History of Selkirk*, p. 97.

[82] Register of the Great Seal, 1476, no. 1273.

[83] Exchequer Roll 7, page 530, Vol. 9, page 473. The extra lands comprised Withop, Tynnis, Montberger, (Shepherd's Hill), Cathslake and Blakgrane.

[84] John Murray's son Patrick, now of Philiphaugh supplied carved stones for upgrading the castle as well.

[85] Acts of the Lords Auditors, 18 February 1492.

[86] Traquair Writs 21; Great Seal, Vol. 2, p. 259 confirmed by James III, no. 1762, 21 December 1476. What the actual cash price was is not recorded.

[87] The building was substantially larger than Grieston, the tower being 32' x 22' with walls 4'3" thick; the great hall 54' x 20' and the servants quarters 40' x 20'. Farm buildings occupied one side of the middle terrace, and there were three others further away to the northeast (RCAM Peebles, p. 263-4).

[88] Acts of the Lords Auditors, 1466-94, p. 193.

[89] Acts of the Lords of Council, Vol. 2, 1478-95, page 228, March 1491. The actual trial 2 March 1494, took place at Jedworth Assizes (Pitcairn, *Ancient Criminal Trials*, pp. 20-1. See also T. Craig-Brown, *History of Selkirkshire*, Vol. 1, pp. 414-5).

[90] The total value is comparable with the inventory of Sir Walter Scott of Branxholme nearly a century later in 1574.

[91] Lords in Council, Civil Causes 15 February 1493, nos. 285 and 314, Exchequer Rolls 1492-3.

[92] Acts of the Lords Auditors, Vol. 1466-94, page 96.

[93] Robert Pitcairn, *Ancient Criminal Trials* (1833, page 31). That Pitcairn printed this case is an indication of its contemporary notoriety.

[94] Pitcairn, Vol. 1, p. 133.

[95] Ibid., p. 147.

[96] Jenny Brown, *Bonds of Manrent before 1603* (Glasgow, D. Phil thesis 1974).

[97] Early 16$^{th}$ century instances: Rutherfords to Lord Hume 1516, Cockburn to Lord Hay of Yester 1511, or Murray of Falahill to Walter Kerr of Cessford 1531 (cf. Brown, note 32).

[98] Following an armed fight at Melrose in which Andrew Kerr of Cessford and John Scott of Erskine died, a bond was signed committing each side to complete a pilgrimage to the four most holy sites in Scotland, to pay for many masses, and to marry Branxholme's son to Cessford's sister. This was personal and did not require any Middlemas contribution, as did the formal bond of 1591 (below, Chapter 7).

[99] Jenny Wormald: "a reflection of the social status of Middlemas lairds... in a world of obligation to their kin, their lords and to their own dependants and followers.." letter to the author 8 December 2006.

[100] A. Ribera, *Fashion and Fiction, Dress in Art and Literature in Stuart England* (2005).

[101] Meikle. *Op. cit.* Of these, in the years 1540-1603, 29 died out altogether, another 4 sold their land or lost it – a far slower rate of extinction than that of the century before 1540.

[102] Fuller, p. 600-01.

[103] Scotland's total population, perhaps 1 million at the peak in 1300, was still only 1.1 million in the 1690s and by then only one-sixth of England's total (SHR, Vol. 75[2] pp. 143-89).

[104] Grant, p. 82.

[105] *Ane Satyre of the Thrie Estatis.*

[106] R. P. Hanson, *Forests, the Shadow of Civilisation* (1992) describes well this traditional forest culture whose origins go back to the 11th century and the Legend of the Green Man.

[107] Dogshon, p. 216, note 28 gives an average for Roxburgh of 400 acres, rising to 1,000 in Eildon; and in Kale Water 25 farmers – probably one-eighth of whom were Middlemases – held on average between 400-1,000 acres.

[108] By 1550 three of the four county sheriffdoms had become hereditary, under Douglas of Cavers, Murray of Falahill (later Philliphaugh), Hay of Yester; whose sheriffs depute, including Middlemas of Lilliesleaf did much of the court work.

[109] The relevant burgh markets Peebles, Selkirk, Melrose, Kelso, each of about 1.500 inhabitants, in effect circumscribe their families' geography.

[110] P. Dixon, *Towerhouses, Peelhouses and Border Society*, Archeological Journal, 1979, Vol. 5 (136) pp. 240-52.

[111] RCAM Peebleshire, no. 281. Fragments of the house were still visible in the mid-19th century.

[112] RCAM Roxburghshire, Vol. 1, pp. 538-39.

[113] RCAM Peebleshire, no. 525, pp. 263-65.

[114] RCAM Roxburghshire, Vol. 1, pp. 538-39.

[115] Craig-Brown, *History of Selkirkshire*, Vol. 1, p. 137.

[116] Craig-Brown, *History of Selkirkshire*, Vol. 1, p. 230.

[117] For this subject, generally see L. Stone, *Family and Fortune: Studies in Aristocratic Finance in the 16th and 17th Century*; for tower houses, Nigel Tranter, op cit.

[118] Quoted in E. Williamson "Horse Racing in Scotland in the 16th

Century." See also J. Burnett, *Riot, Revelry and Rout, Sport in Lowland Scotland Before 1860* (2000).

[119] Houston and Whyte, *Scottish Society, 1500-1800* (1989).

[120] J. Wormald, *Bonds of Manrent*, p. 91, suggests that the 15 lairds who presented 1128 men at a 1541 wapenschaw were typical. Taylor, the Water Poet, in his 1618 *Tour of Scotland* rated a plain laird's house at 30-50 servants, but since he had in mind a banquet for an earl, this can hardly be called typical.

[121] On this debate see J. Wormald, *Court, Kirk and Community, 1470-1625* (1981) and Cynthia Neville, *Violence, Custom, and Law: The Anglo-Scottish Borders in the Later Middle Ages.*

[122] T. Rae, *Administration of the Scottish Borders 1513-1603* (1966).

[123] *Border Laws* (1705) p. 340

[124] William Bishop of Carlisle, *Border Laws (1705)* gives a compendium, up to the time of Queen Elizabeth, preparatory to the Act of Union in 1707, which naturally enough glorified the latter by deprecating what had gone before.

[125] Border Papers, Vol. 2, p. 57 suggests that there might have been at any one time in the 16th century as many as 10,000 Scottish sheep grazing on English soil, taken there via the well-worn "dry marches."

[126] Angered by a village herdsman driving out his single cow, Scott of Harden cried "Is it come to that pass? By my faith, they shall soon say Harden's kye." On his way back with many English cows, he rode past a newly cut haystack and said again "By my soul, had ye but feet, ye should not stand long there."

[127] T. Rae, *Administration of the Scottish Borders 1513-1603* (1966).

[128] K. MacFarlane, *The Nobility of Later Medieval England*, pp. 84-5.

[129] Ian Green and David Easen, *Medieval Religious Houses in Scotland* (1976).

[130] Only two were executed in the Borders and no others until George Wishart in 1545.

[131] Andrew Pettigree, *Reformation and the Culture of Persuasion* (2005).

[132] But out of roughly 1000 names of collaborators, there is no mention of a Middlemas or a Scott of Buccleugh.

[133] Gordon Donaldson, *All the Queen's Men: Power and Politics in Mary Stewart's Scotland*, 1983, pp. 71-85. The sixth Lord Hume's ill-timed defence of Mary led to forfeiture and Regent Morton's attempt to ruin him.

[134] Accounts of the Lord High Treasurer, November 1576. Regent Morton's third justice ayre for Roxburgh and Selkirk.

[135] The Scots exchange rate against the pound Sterling fell by 50% 1565 to

1601; prices, but not necessarily rents, rose accordingly.

[136] Robert Bowes to Burghley, June 1592, *Calendar of State Papers Scotland.* See also *Acts of the Parliaments of Scotland* Vol. 3, p. 528.

[137] Register of the Privy Council, Vol. 21, November 1592, and Vols. 26-27. There is no evidence as to whether this was ever paid either for the dead William or the live George.

[138] Acts of the Parliaments of Scotland, Vol. 3, 1567-92, p. 528.

[139] Pitcairn, *Ancient Criminal Trials*, Vol. 1, p. 133.

[140] Register of the Privy Council, Vol. 2, pp. 622 and 639-40.

[141] T. Rae, *Administration of the Scottish Frontier* (1966) and K.M. Brown, *Blood Feud in Scotland 1573-1625* (1986). Meikle (op cit.) sees Cessford as a sort of juvenile delinquent; he and Scott of Buccleugh did well out of Bothwell's forfeited lands.

[142] Register of the Great Seal, Vol. 4, no. 1749. Thomas was not then 20 years old and the father may have been terminally ill.

[143] Register of the Privy Council, Vol. 1, p. 168.

[144] Sasine 29 June 1618 (GRS Peebles) in Latin, sealed (i.e. with his crested seal) "thus wrote Thomas Grierson [sic]." According to the original contract of 17 June 1615, John Murray paid 6000 merks for this infeftment.

[145] John Hume had been appointed first as a lay cleric of Kelso when young in 1512. Becoming a Lord of Council, he remained a public figure into the 1550s, and was the only thoroughly un-celibate Abbot among the four great houses. Though he ceded the abbey eventually to his nephew, he retained the revenues. All five of his children, including Mariota, were subsequently legitimated by Mary or James VI. As Mark Dilworth puts it: "Abbey superiors were appointed for reasons of state or selfish gain...indeed the Border abbeys were regarded not as spiritual power houses but as sources of revenue and positions for royal servants or predatory individuals." (*The Border Abbeys in the 16th Century*, p. 247.)

[146] Register of the Great Seal, Vol. 4, nos. 422 and 1402; see also Book of the Assumption of Thirds of Benefices.

[147] Lewis: *Dictionary of Scotland* (1851), page 181. See also RCAM Roxburgh, nos. 538 and 539. The Riddell family's motte and bailey tower is farther out from the town (534).

[148] Roxburgh Retours Vol. 3, p. 137, nos. 1811-16, largely repeated in 1678.

[149] *Melrose Regality Records*, (ed. C.S. Romanes) pp. 357-9.

[150] Thomas, John's father, subinfeudated parts of his land in Eildon to various tenants.

151 Thomas, of Eildon and Newstead, married Agnes Mein, having inherited a fair-sized farm (the teinds being set at £46 per annum) in 1635.

152 According to a 1576 contract between John Stewart of Eildon and Thomas Middlemas and others, Thomas bought out his feu holding of 2 husband lands (originally from Kelso Abbey, 52 acres in the field plus perhaps 100 outfield). Both Grubet and Corbet were burned by Robert Collingwood's force during the "rough wooing" of 1544-5 when they stole from Kale Valley 280 nolts, 200 sheep, 40 horses, and took many prisoners.

153 Secret Seal Register, 1576, Great Seal, 1577. The Rutherfords sued him and his brother George again in 1588 (Privy Council Records, Vol. 5, pp. 69-70), and he was also involved with Kerr of Ferniehurst in the 1571 raid on Jedburgh.

154 Of 60 parishes in the southeast, only 17 had ministers in 1574. This had risen to 40 in 1590, several of which were held in plurality.

155 Meikle, p. 265 and J.A. Galloway and Ian Murray: *Scottish Migration to England 1400-1600* [Scottish Geographical Magazine 1996, Vol. 112.1, pp. 29-38].

156 Calendar of Border Papers, Vol. 1, p. 160.

157 Berwick Borough Statutes: Bailiff Court Proceedings 1570-1599. *Guild History*, pp. 302-9. It seems clear that part of the "prohibition harboring of Scottish persons, especially Scottish women as well as for nurses as for spinning, without special licence" (13 May 1598) was to inhibit their competition with English women in the garrison sex trade. The penalty for being found at night in 1602 was first "have their hair polled off their heads and afterwards be carted out of the town."

158 THES 1.3.1985 "The thistle and the rose" p. 17. For James I generally, see M. Lee, *Government by Pen: Scotland under James VI and I* (1996) and B. Galloway, *The Union of England and Scotland* (1985).

159 Register of the Privy Council, 1599-1602, p. 825.

160 These had been part of the 15th century Middlemas lands and after James Scott's death went to Andrew Hay, a relation of Hay of Yester. Meanwhile Margaret sold her portion of Ettrick to the Earl of Buccleugh in 1626 (Minute Book of Sasines Peebles 16, 1626).

161 Register of Sasines 29-6, 1618.

162 RPC, 1611, p. 9.

163 RPC, 1614, appendices Earl of Orkney, pp. 132-34.

164 Ibid. p. 262.

165 RPC, Vol. 7, pp. 200-01 and 208-09.

166 Earl of Mar and Kellie. Correspondence RHMSC 28 July 1622, p. 114.

167 He had served in the trial of Johnnie Maxwell and his son for a murder

committed in 1618. Such a trial of a laird demanded a distinguished tribunal, which duly sentenced both to be beheaded.

168 RPC, 1627, pp. 64-5.

169 RPC, Vol. 3, 1649-60, p. 720.

170 Registry of Sasines Peebles, 1711-01.

171 Register of the Privy Council, no. 7, 1607. By 1615, this taxation had fallen to £11 for the Belses barony.

172 *Pitcairn Trials*, pp. 379-80 and p. 445.

173 Retours Roxburgh, 1619 and 1622. Further land was held of Sir Walter Riddell of that ilk (his feudal superior).

174 Hay of Yester Papers, March 1617.

175 RPC, 1616, p. 180. James was "declared rebel" for this.

176 RPC, 1618, p. 382. Both William and Walter were committed to the Tolbooth for a short time (RPC, p. 382) until George Kerr of Cavers stood surety for them, at 300 merks each, not to repeat the offence.

177 They were Janet Minto and Bessie Main of Selkirk, Isobel Wright of Melrose, Bessie Cumming of Bowden, Janet Henderson of Lilliesleaf. The rate in Scotland of execution was much higher than in England or most Continental countries.

178 In *Witch Craze: Terror and Fantasy in Baroque Germany* (2004) Lynden Roper points out the relevance of this to fears about fertility, which witches were believed to attack – human and crop fertility alike – and argues that this put elderly women living alone first in line of peasant suspicion.

179 Registry of Sasines, Roxburgh, 10 May 1632 [in Latin].

180 Retours Roxburgh, Vol. 2, 1678. Repeating a Latin original of 1629.

181 Cessford's Roll of Wrongs 1596.

182 According to *The Calendar of Border Papers*, Vol. 6, p. 364, John Middlemas of Hownam Grange was accused as a "horse stealer" along with two Kerrs, sons of the Lord of Corbet, two Douglases of Hownam and Dandie of the Brae (*History of Northumberland*, Vol. 2, p. 64).

183 General Register of Sasines, 1608.

184 Court of Sessions documents, Roxburgh, Middlemas vs. Kerr 1672. From this, it seems that George Middlemas son of John, also in Grubet, made a similar sale to the parson of Ancrum of 1¾ husband lands in 1633, as did Andrew/Dand – both for over £300 and John Middlemas to the same parson.

185 Lawrence Stone, *Crisis of the Aristocracy*, p. 362 and E. Hughes, *North Country Life in the 18th Century* (Vol. 1, 1952).

186 David Levine and Keith Wrighton, *The Making of an Industrial Society: Whickham 1560 to 1765* (1991) p. 110.

187 Members were elected in the southeast Border Shires from Teviot, Chirnside, Duns, Earlston, Kelso, Jedburgh, Selkirk, and Peebles.

188 In general, see David Stevenson, *Scottish Revolution 1637-1644*, (1998), pp. 133–53. For the particular growth of an English aristocratic-clerical opposition in Parliament, 1640-42, see *The Noble Revolt: The Overthrow of Charles I*, by John Adamson (2007).

189 18,000 foot soldiers, 20,000 horses, 1,000 dragoons and artillery, a formidable force costing £30,000 a month.

190 C.S. Terry, *The Army of the Covenant 1643-1647* (1917), pp. 100-02.

191 Their names are in the Hawick Covenant preserved at Cavers House. The involvement of the Covenanting army in Ireland 1641-48 is extremely complicated (cf. David Stevens, *Scottish Covenanters and Irish Confederates* (1980) with allegiances frequently changing in response to the balance in England.

192 Ironically in two ways, first because his appointment had caused much jealousy among noble and laird families because of his humble birth, second because his assumption of a shield of arms identical to that of Grieston, appears to have been a tangible set-back for the family's senior branch (see Appendix B).

193 D. Stephens, *The Scottish Covenanters*, p. 12.

194 Register of the Privy Council, 1676, pp. 79-80.

195 *The Scottish Covenanters*, p. 122.

196 CS137/388. One tombstone in Yetholm churchyard, dated 1743, starts with James Middlemest and gives two other variants underneath.

197 Roxburgh Retours 18 July 1662, RD2/5 pp. 770-2.

198 The Sasines always speak of Raperlaw as having the 11½ husbandlands as originally described in the Hume dowry of 1576. In one case the feudal superior was Lord Hume, in the other Lord Kerr, Earl of Lothian.

199 Lately possessed by Robert Scott, tenant, in the lordship of Kelso, free of all debts save one wadset (mortgage) given by James Scott to the late James Middlemas portioner of Raperlaw.

200 Cf. Sir William Fraser, *The Scotts of Buccleugh* (2 vols.) 1878.

201 James and his wife Janet Turnbull inherited 1662. John and his wife Margaret Scott inherited 1662. Anna and her husband Walter Scott inherited 1670.

202 How closely interwoven Middlemases and Meins were can be seen from records of witnesses at baptisms in the 1680s (Melrose Regality Records).

203 Ian Whyte, *Agriculture and Society in 17th Century Scotland*, p. 148, Table 9.

[204] Roxburgh Retours 1699.

[205] *Inquisitions*, Vol. 2, XXI p. 50.

[206] Kerr versus Middlemas, CS 138/3042.

[207] Melrose Regality Records, vol. 3, pp. 107-8.

[208] James Middlemas' testament in Hownam 1685 was similar: agricultural inventory £364, debts £163.

[209] RPC vol. 13, 1663.

[210] Large-scale raiding ended after 1611. Feud virtually disappeared by the 1630s (see M.F. Ferguson, *Law and Order on the Scottish Border 1603-1707*, St Andrews PhD, 1981).

[211] For the case, see CS226/6027 (NAS Archives).

[212] There had already been spasms of increasing mortality, e.g. during and after the disastrous harvest of 1621-22, which brought starvation and disease to the Border counties. Border agriculture was adequate in most years for local populations' needs but depended on costly imports in bad years such as 1643-4, when the Scot's Covenanting army crossed the Tweed in mid-January over the ice. Scotland's total population, 800,000 in 1600 and only 1 million in 1700 (comparable to Switzerland rather than England's 5.5million) disguised the sparseness of Border population, with its high infant death rate obviating a high birth rate, and life expectancy stuck in the early 40s till the end of the 18th century.

[213] Hearth tax figures for 1691 give it a population of nearly 6000, more than the whole county of Berwickshire around it (5470). John was already in practice by 1693 with clients as far away as Dunbar. As an instance of the time the legal process could take, one case on behalf of a Dunbar merchant and Baillie for a debt of £26 took ten years from 1693-1704.

[214] Kelso had by then recovered from the appalling experience of bubonic plague in 1645-6, when much of the town had been burned down in an over-zealous attempt to disinfect the largely wooden houses. Seven-hundred or more inhabitants died and many others from starvation, as soldiers imposed a cordon, following orders to shoot anyone trying to escape. (M. Lynch, *The Early Modern Town in Scotland*, 1987) This may have been worse proportionately than the combined plague and Great Fire in London in 1665-6.

[215] According to J.A. Galloway and I. Murray-Smith "Scottish Migration" *Scottish Geographical Magazine*, 1996, pp. 29-38, in Edinburgh at least, 70% of apprentices before 1700 can be classified as migrants.

[216] *Scottish Geographical* magazine, op.cit.

[217] *History of Northumberland*, Vol. 14, p. 154.

[218] Quoted in J.U. Nef, *Rise of the British Coal Industry* (1932) p. 135.

[219] Without this, even inside Scotland, the job market might be closed. Ian Whyte (Agriculture and Society in 17th Century Scotland) quotes a case in Peebles in 1683 where lack of it led to the order, "leave or be branded..."

[220] Well described by E. Cockayne, *Hubbub: Filth, Noise and Stench in England 1600-1770* (2006).

[221] Earlier, in 1678-1685, over 800 Scots had been transported to North American plantations, mainly prisoners taken after Bothwell Brig. According to the shipping registers, no Middlemas went voluntarily to the United States or Canada before the 1820s.

[222] M. Flinn, *Scottish Population History from the 17th Century* (1977).

[223] Douglas of Cavers' two brothers lost £500 each; Hume of Polwarth £200; Walter Riddell £400; various Scotts, including Mangerton, between £200 and £500.

[224] Alexander Jeffrey, *History of Roxburghshire*, 4 Vols. (1856) notes that "at one time it was the property of the clan Middlemas who, at the end of the 16th century, were guilty of the greatest atrocities (unspecified). The tower, taken down c. 1790, was the chief of the clan's."

[225] Tom Lubbock, writing in *The Independent*, Britain's Art Treasures No. 3.

[226] C.f. George Lockhart, *Memoirs, 1715* gives an account of how £20,000 was dispensed in bribes.

[227] C.A. Whatly and D.J. Patrick, *The Scots and the Union* (2006).

[228] G. Whittington and I. Whyte, *An Historical Geography of Scotland* (1983) p. 135.

[229] Sasine, 11 September 1727 RS3/130 et seq.

[230] *Baron Court of Stichel*, p. 199 (SHS October 1905).

[231] NAS, CS 175/491 and CS 175/465.

[232] John Fuller's History of Berwickshire (1799) pp. 600-02 noted bad roads and the run-rig system of tenure, "a miserable picture...when for mutual defence and scarcity, every man's lands were so interwoven with those of others as to resemble the teeth of a comb – the greatest obstacle to any improvement of agriculture." By the time he published his book, "the exertions of public spirited farmers have made it the Norfolk of Scotland."

[233] He earned £78 per acre until the Treasury intervened, compelling him to sell for only 4 pence a pound, one-third of that, to force growers out of a business which threatened Glasgow and Bristol tobacco importers. "It was raised in hotbeds, planted like cabbages, and was acknowledged to be equal to a grass crop for clearing the land." Craig

Brown, *History of Roxburghshire*, Vol. 4, pp. 349-50.

[234] "An English visitor was amazed to discover that the 'shrine of festivities' for Edinburgh's best families was a local oyster house with huge tables piled high with oysters." Arthur Herman, *The Scottish Enlightenment* (2003), p. 182. The Club (one of the principal ones) also met at an oyster tavern in the 1750s. See David McElroy, *Scotland's Age of Improvement* (1969), pp. 163 and 177.

[235] OSA, Vol. 4, pp. 467-8.

[236] Ibid. p. 365.

[237] R. Timperly (ed.) SHS 1976.

[238] 1873 Land Returns.

[239] Typical size for tenant farmers of the 1840s, East Lothian 200 acres, Berwick 197, Roxburgh 146 (Whittington and Whyte, *Historical Geography of Scotland*).

[240] C.f. Bailey and Colley, *A General View of Agriculture of Northumberland*, etc. (1805).

[241] *A General View of Agriculture of the County of Peebles* (1799) p. 100. This had already been true of the Merse twenty-five years earlier.

[242] New Statistical Account of Scotland, 1823.

[243] As Table 4 of the clusters shows, it was still very much a minority choice to migrate beyond the Merse up to 1750. By 1841 an actual majority of Middlemases, parents and children, 462 over 334 lived in England. By 1900 this had become Scotland 651, England 516.

[244] In the 1730s the northeast remained almost as cut off by land as it had been in the Middle Ages. By 1790, Flying Coaches moving at 5 miles an hour began to match the 1771 Flying Post (Edinburgh to Newcastle in one and a half days); the same, by return for £1 /11 shillings, even on routes such as Langholm–Hawick (22 miles, 8 hours post chaise and 2 horses).

[245] Some improvement came, with the introduction of Sir Humphrey Davy's safety lamp, replacing the caged canary as a test for gas; more, after the 1833 Committee of Enquiry report revealed some of the worst practices and child labour exploitation.

[246] Sunderland produced a lustreware, now a field for collectors, as well as goblets engraved with the town's new bridge, famous in the 1830s and 40s. Generally see Norman McCord, *Northeast England: The Region's Development, 1760-1960.*

[247] Alice Munro, *The View from Castle Hill* (2007) p. 165. "Peasant proprietorship was unknown and, by the 1840s, most Lowland (and Border) rural Scots were non-inheriting children of farmers, farm servants, country tradesmen, textile weavers or day labourers." T.M.

Devine, *Scottish Emigration and Scottish Society* (1992) p. 6.

248 Not, significantly, by the disappearance of major disease: like England, Scotland continued to be plagued by cholera (and for the same water-borne causes), the epidemics coming in 1832, 1848-9, 1853-4, and as late as 1866-7, while dysentery, tuberculosis and typhoid remained endemic until the early 20th century.

249 The shift away from the pits of Whickham and continuing migration patterns can be detected in the lack of alignment between marriages and children baptised in the same place: 1700-1750, 6 marriages compared to 16 baptisms; 1750-1800, 40 to 64; 1800-1850 26 to 61; 1850-1900 13 to 29.

250 The last of all seems to have been a soldier killed in World War I in 1917 serving in the Northumberland Fusiliers.

251 Ian White, *Pre-Industrial Society of Scotland* (Edinburgh PhD, 1989).

252 For example, Middlemases working over four generations before 1830 spanned the area Alnwick, Lowick and Spittal.

253 See in particular Gregory Clark, *A Farewell to Alms* (2006).

254 Shortly after the 1660 Restoration "Mercurius Caledoniensis" announced the return to hunting, hawking and coursing (No. 21, p. 1-2). Competitiveness at whatever cost reigned in archery, racing or golf in late 17th and early 18th century, as skill and gambling ran together. (c.f. John Barnet, *Riot Revelry and Rout*, 2000).

255 Edinburgh golfers laid down a set of rules in 1775. John Leech's well-known cartoon of a hunt meet with a finely mounted duke in the centre, surrounded by a very mixed group on assorted nags, has the local tailor declare, "the beauty of 'untin, your Grace, is what it brings all classes of people together" – which was indeed true in 1853 when he drew it.

256 A possible exception may be George Middlemane, which may be a misreading of Middlemas, who settled in Virginia in 1679 and became a plantation owner.

257 2006, p. 130.

258 T.M. Devine, op cit. p.34. Devine quotes many letters from Ontario, mostly written by Scots coming from Bewlie, Lilliesleaf, Eildon, Minto, and Kale Water (p. 72-4, also SRO GD1, 1813: 1-15); the very areas from which Middlemases had been migrating for over a century. See also S.H. Moore, *Pilgrims: New World Settlers and the Call of Home* (2008).

259 This branch probably came from Langton during the Civil War, when John Middlemass farmer died leaving a small inventory of £63.

260 He was not the only one: Christian Middlemass did the same with

house, barns and stables in Kelso in 1835 and John Middlemass, overseer, in Galasheils in the 1820s.

261 Both the diary and the letter book are held in the Ayrshire Archive Centre, for whose help I am most grateful.

262 Prejudice was rife in the 18th century West Indies, and not just against black slaves. Thomas Thistlewood's diaries (edited in D. Hamilton's *Scotland, the Caribbean and the Atlantic World*), date from 1750-1820 and display much animus directed at the Scots there, despite their self-evident role in fostering and financing links between the sugar and tobacco planters and Britain.

263 It is worth noting that, in Palermo's Palazzo Normanni's inner hall, there is a mosaic of the same hunter and his stag, c. 1180.

264 Others were even more local. Thus the Kelso County Border Rifles, who shot for the "Middlemas prize" in 1907, A. Campbell and R. Robeson, "Kelso History in Focus" (Rotary Club of Kelso).

265 Overall, Scotland like Wales, lost one-tenth of its population of military age, higher than England alone.

266 Only one Middlemas signed up as a militia volunteer for the Defence against France in 1800. Joseph Middlemiss of Dryburgh agreed "to be trained in the use of arms for the purpose of being called into actual service in the event of invasion" in the Merton Volunteers (Scott of Harden Papers, GD 157/1535).

267 A richer but chronologically much narrower example of this is the social history of the Verney family in 17th century Buckinghamshire, facing the dilemmas created by the Civil War (Adrian Tinniswood, *The Verneys*, 2006).

268 Roy Strong, *Lost Treasures of Britain* (1990) p. 4.

269 The contemporary Hague's Armorial 1592 does not contain it at all.

# Note on Sources

The majority of original sources are held in the National Archives of Scotland, while the printed books and articles can nearly always be found in the National Library of Scotland; to these should be added the Public Record Office in London, the Ayrshire Archives, the Berwick on Tweed Archives, and the Scottish Border Archives at Selkirk; together with various estate collections such as Hay of Yester and Scott of Buccleugh.

Acts of the Lords Auditors
Acts of the Lord Treasurer
Acts of the Lords in Council
Acts of the Parliament
Ancient Criminal Trials in Scotland (Pitcairn, 3 vols. 1833)
Calendar of Border Papers (ed. T. Bain, vols. 1894-96)
Calendar of Documents Relating to Scotland (5 vols. 1881-88)
Calendar of Papal Registers and Petitions (1893-96)
Exchequer Rolls
General Register of Sasines
Liber de St. Marie de Mailrose (2 vols. 1846)
Liber de St.Maria de Calchou
Melrose Regality Records (ed. Romanes, from 1917)
Register of the Great Seal
Register of the Privy Council of Scotland
Register of the Privy Seal
Regesta Regum Scottorum (ed. Duncan, 1983)
Rotuli Scotiae (2 vols. Ed Macpherson 1814-19)
Retours (service of heirs of land, etc. Decreets, Sasines, Warrants, etc.)
RCAMS for Berwickshire (1915) Roxburghshire (1955) Selkirkshire (1957

# Selected Bibliography

Below is a list of some of the more obvious printed works: a full list of those consulted, together with scholarly articles, theses, etc., can be found in the Notes.


Barrow, G.W.S. (1980) *The Anglo-Norman Era in Scottish History.*
Brown, M. (1998) *The Black Douglases.*
Burnett, J. (2000) *Riot, Revelry and Rout.*
Cowan, I.B. (1976) *Medieval Religious Houses in Scotland.*
Cullan, Karen (1977) *Scottish Population History.*
Devine, T.M. (1999) *The Scottish Nation, 1700-2000*
Dodgshon, R.A. (1981) *Land and Society in Scotland.*
Donaldson, G. (1988) *History of Scotland in the Reigns of James V to James VII.*
Donalson, G. (1981) *All the Queen's Men, Power and Politics in Mary's Scotland.*
Dow, F.D. (1979) *Cromwellian Scotland.*
*Edinburgh History of Scotland,* vols. 1-3.
Flinn, M. et al. (1990) *Scottish Population History, 17th Century to the 1930s.*
Galloway, B. (1983) *The Union of England and Scotland.*
Grant, A. (1984) *Independence and Nationhood in Scotland,* 1306-1469.
Grant, I. and D. Witherington, eds. *Statistical Account of Scotland 1791-99.*
Houston, R.A. and I. Whyte (1990) *Scottish Society 1500-1800.*
Kidd, C. (1993) *Subverting Scotland's Past.*
Lerman, B. (1981) *Integration, Enlightenment and Industrialisation 1746-1832.*
Lynch, M. (1987) *The Early Modern Town in Scotland.*
Mason, R.A. (1987) *Scotland and England 1286-1815.*
McNeill, P.G.B. (1996) *Atlas of Scottish History to 1707.*
Meikle, M.M. (2004) *A British Frontier, Lairds and Gentlemen in the Eastern Borders 1540-1603.*
Nicholson, R. (1978) *Scotland in the Later Middle Ages.*
Pryde, G.S. (1993) *Scotland from 1603 to the Present Day.*
Rae, T. (1966) *Administration of the Scottish Frontier 1513-1603.*
Sanderson, M.H.B. (1982) *Scottish Rural Society in the 16th Century.*
Stevenson, D. (1973) *The Scottish Revolution 1637-44: Triumph of the Covenanters*

Tough, D.L. (1928) *The Last Years of a Frontier.*
Watson, G. (1974) *The Border Reivers.*
Whittington, G. and I. Whyte (1983) *Historical Geography of Scotland.*
Wormald, J. (1985) *Lords and Men in Scottish Manrent.*
Wormald, J (1990) *Court, Kirk and Community 1470-1625.*
Wormald, J., G., Donaldson, and C. Smout (eds.) *New History of Scotland* (8 vols. 1981-83).
Whyte, D. (1979) *Agriculture and Society in 17th Century Scotland.*

## Local Histories

Buchan, J. and H. Paton eds. (1927) *Peebleshire.*
Craig-Brown, T. (1886) *Selkirkshire.*
Jeffrey, A. (1864) *Roxburghshire.*

# Appendices

# A1: Origins

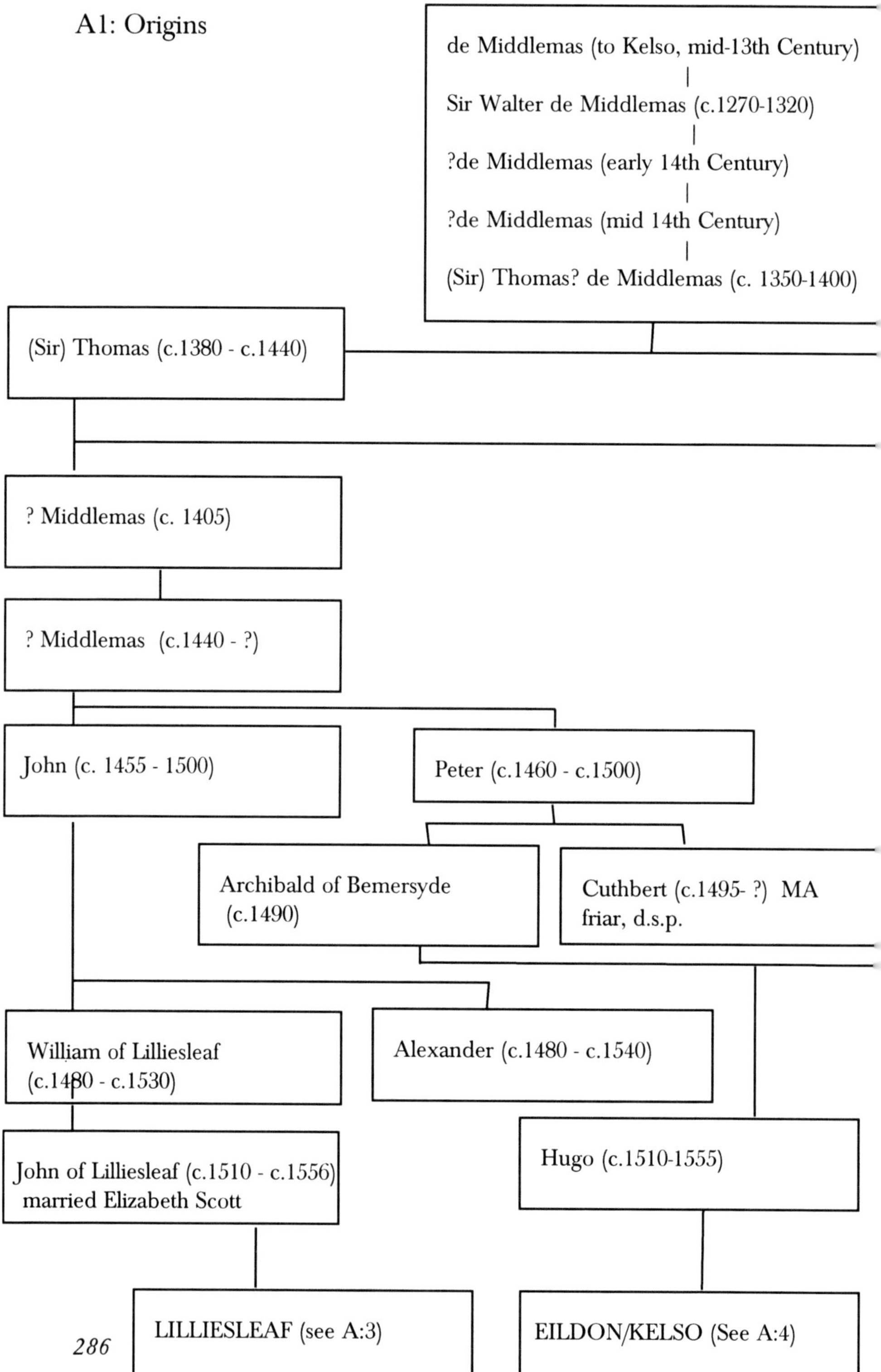
de Middlemas (to Kelso, mid-13th Century)
Sir Walter de Middlemas (c.1270-1320)
?de Middlemas (early 14th Century)
?de Middlemas (mid 14th Century)
(Sir) Thomas? de Middlemas (c. 1350-1400)
(Sir) Thomas (c.1380 - c.1440)
? Middlemas (c. 1405)
? Middlemas (c.1440 - ?)
John (c. 1455 - 1500)
Peter (c.1460 - c.1500)
Archibald of Bemersyde (c.1490)
Cuthbert (c.1495- ?) MA friar, d.s.p.
William of Lilliesleaf (c.1480 - c.1530)
Alexander (c.1480 - c.1540)
Hugo (c.1510-1555)
John of Lilliesleaf (c.1510 - c.1556) married Elizabeth Scott
LILLIESLEAF (see A:3)
EILDON/KELSO (See A:4)

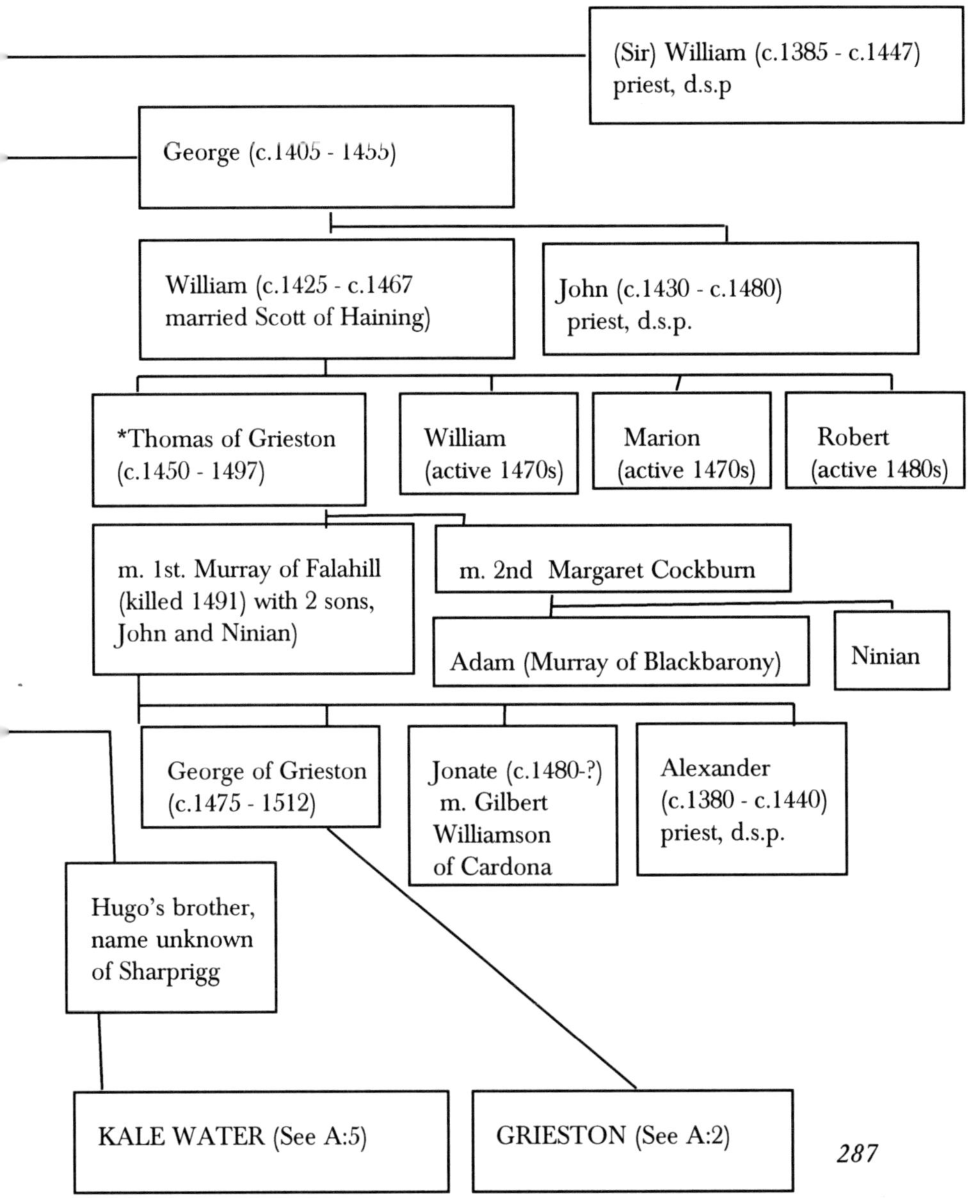
(Sir) William (c.1385 - c.1447) priest, d.s.p
George (c.1405 - 1455)
William (c.1425 - c.1467 married Scott of Haining)
John (c.1430 - c.1480) priest, d.s.p.
*Thomas of Grieston (c.1450 - 1497)
William (active 1470s)
Marion (active 1470s)
Robert (active 1480s)
m. 1st. Murray of Falahill (killed 1491) with 2 sons, John and Ninian)
m. 2nd Margaret Cockburn
Adam (Murray of Blackbarony)
Ninian
George of Grieston (c.1475 - 1512)
Jonate (c.1480-?) m. Gilbert Williamson of Cardona
Alexander (c.1380 - c.1440) priest, d.s.p.
Hugo's brother, name unknown of Sharprigg
KALE WATER (See A:5)
GRIESTON (See A:2)

## A: 2 GRIESTON

Thomas c. 1450-1497 of Grieston and Plora m. – Murray of Falahill (killed 1491)

His son: George (c. 1475-1512) of Grieston

Daughter: Jonata (c. 1480—) married Gilbert Williamson of Cardrona

Thomas (c. 1505-1565) of Grieston, married Maria.

2nd son, John (early 16th century) English captive, 1535)

Sons of Thomas: (1) Thomas (c. 1540-1603) of Grieston, married 1st Katherine Stewart of Traquair; married 2nd Marion Sinclair, 1599.

(2) William (1550-1592) Killed at Falkland Palace

(1) Thomas (c. 1565-1630s) of Grieston, married Janet Kerr, 1590

(2) Margaret (c. 1565-1615) married 1st, Patrick Murray of Falahill, m. 2nd Robert Scott of Huntley

Thomas of Grieston's only child: Marion (1592-?) married John Murray of Syndhope

Margaret's child, James Scott (1590-1629) of Huntley

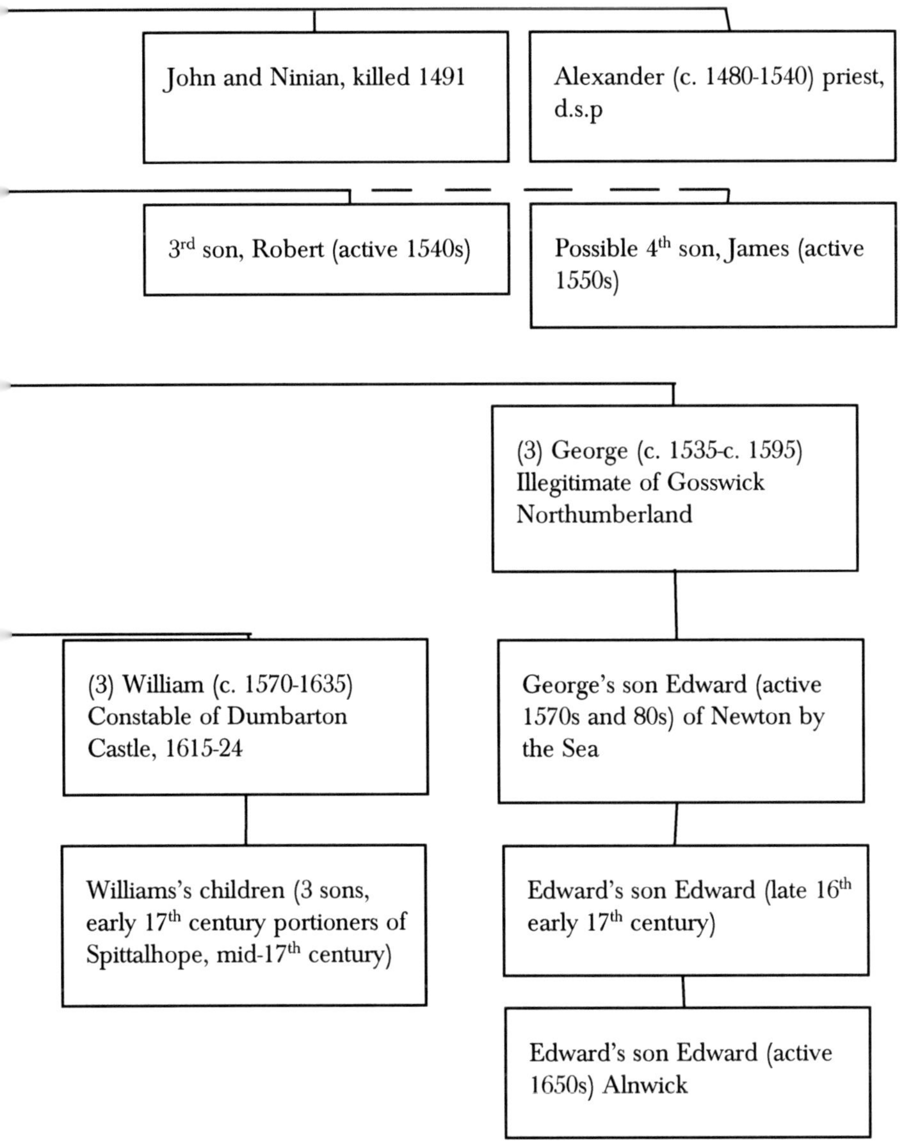
John and Ninian, killed 1491
Alexander (c. 1480-1540) priest, d.s.p
3rd son, Robert (active 1540s)
Possible 4th son, James (active 1550s)
(3) George (c. 1535-c. 1595) Illegitimate of Gosswick Northumberland
(3) William (c. 1570-1635) Constable of Dumbarton Castle, 1615-24
George's son Edward (active 1570s and 80s) of Newton by the Sea
Williams's children (3 sons, early 17th century portioners of Spittalhope, mid-17th century)
Edward's son Edward (late 16th early 17th century)
Edward's son Edward (active 1650s) Alnwick

A : 3 LILLIESLEAF

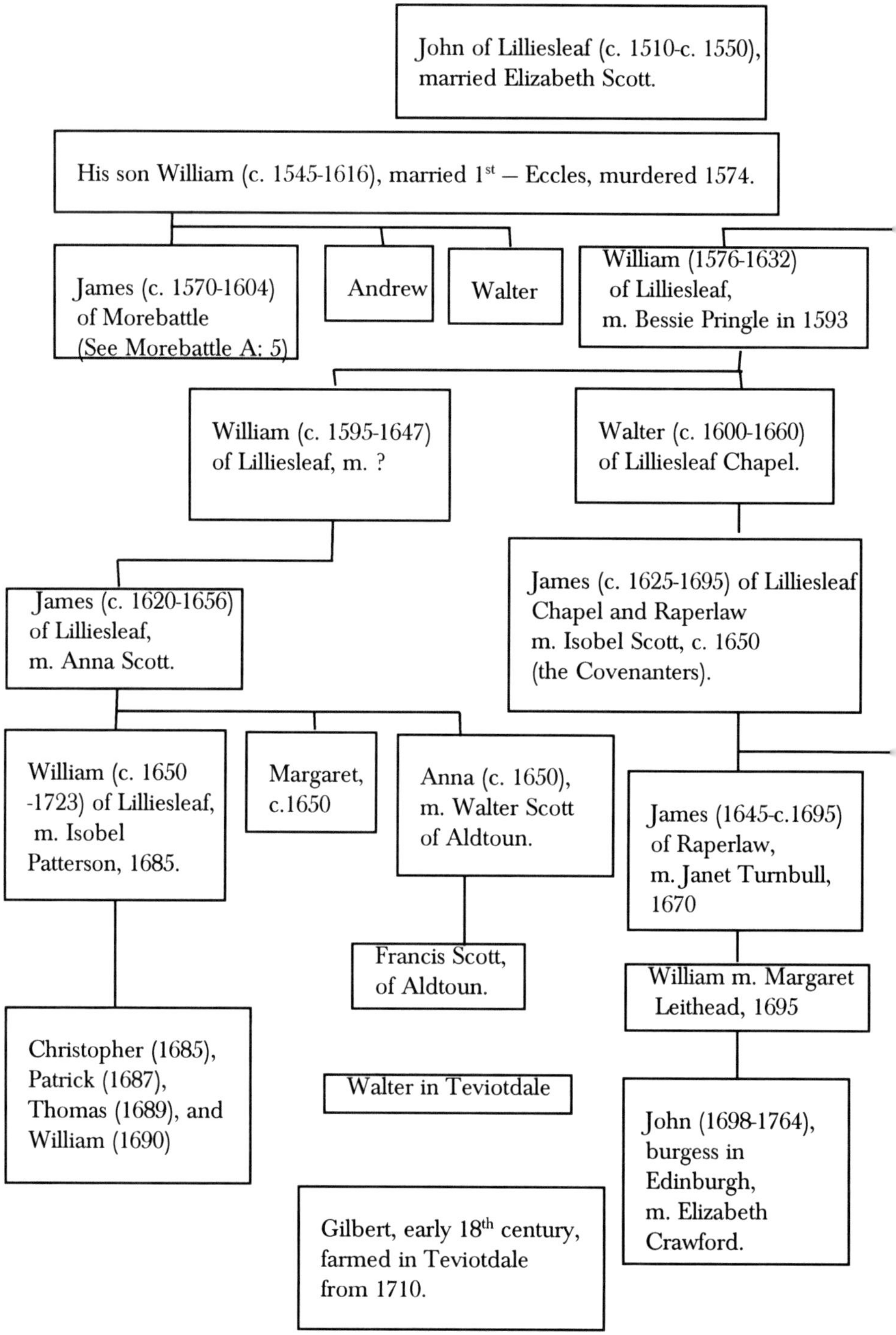

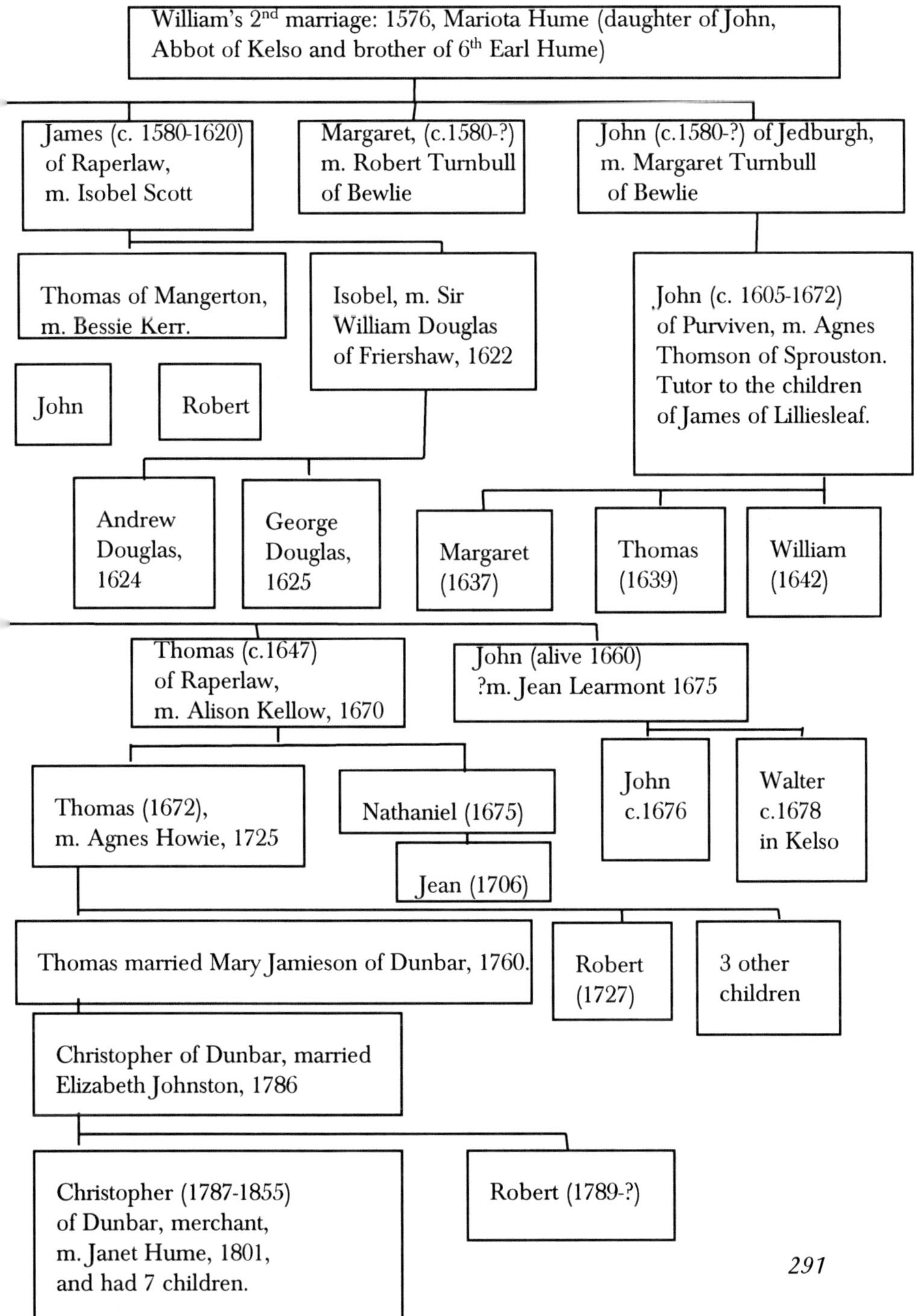
William's 2nd marriage: 1576, Mariota Hume (daughter of John, Abbot of Kelso and brother of 6th Earl Hume)
James (c. 1580-1620) of Raperlaw, m. Isobel Scott
Margaret, (c.1580-?) m. Robert Turnbull of Bewlie
John (c.1580-?) of Jedburgh, m. Margaret Turnbull of Bewlie
Thomas of Mangerton, m. Bessie Kerr.
Isobel, m. Sir William Douglas of Friershaw, 1622
John (c. 1605-1672) of Purviven, m. Agnes Thomson of Sprouston. Tutor to the children of James of Lilliesleaf.
John
Robert
Andrew Douglas, 1624
George Douglas, 1625
Margaret (1637)
Thomas (1639)
William (1642)
Thomas (c.1647) of Raperlaw, m. Alison Kellow, 1670
John (alive 1660) ?m. Jean Learmont 1675
Thomas (1672), m. Agnes Howie, 1725
Nathaniel (1675)
Jean (1706)
John c.1676
Walter c.1678 in Kelso
Thomas married Mary Jamieson of Dunbar, 1760.
Robert (1727)
3 other children
Christopher of Dunbar, married Elizabeth Johnston, 1786
Christopher (1787-1855) of Dunbar, merchant, m. Janet Hume, 1801, and had 7 children.
Robert (1789-?)

## A: 4 EILDON/KELSO

Hugo (c. 1510-1555) of Midlem,

John (c. 1540-1606) of Newstead and Kelso

Malie of Kelso

Thomas (1575-1638) of Newstead and Eildon, married Agnes Mein, c. 1600.

John (c. 1575-mid 17th) of Melrose, who married Janet Marshall, 1609.

William (c. 1580-1650) of Minto.

Thomas (1601-1647) of Eildon.

Margaret (b.1610).

John (1611-1675) of Myneholme, m. Margaret Scott of Kelso, 1632.

Robert (1625-1675), who married, successively, Alison Chisholm, 1651, Alison Riddell, 1657, and Margaret Sprotts, 1668.

Peter (c. 1630-1699) of Eildon, MA Edinburgh, 1670.

Patrick (c. 1670-1742) of Eildon, MA Edinburgh, 1693.

m. 1st Agnes Chirnside of Semprin, 1698.

Robert (1674-?), m. Janet Renwick, 1708.

Thomas (1708), Lancelot (1711), Jennet (1713).

Christian (c. 1675)

John (1699-mid 18th) of Semprin, who married Mary Cockburn of Yetholm.

Jane (1722), David (1728) and Jean (1730).

Thomas (1701-mid 18th century) of Eildon.

Thomas (1721.

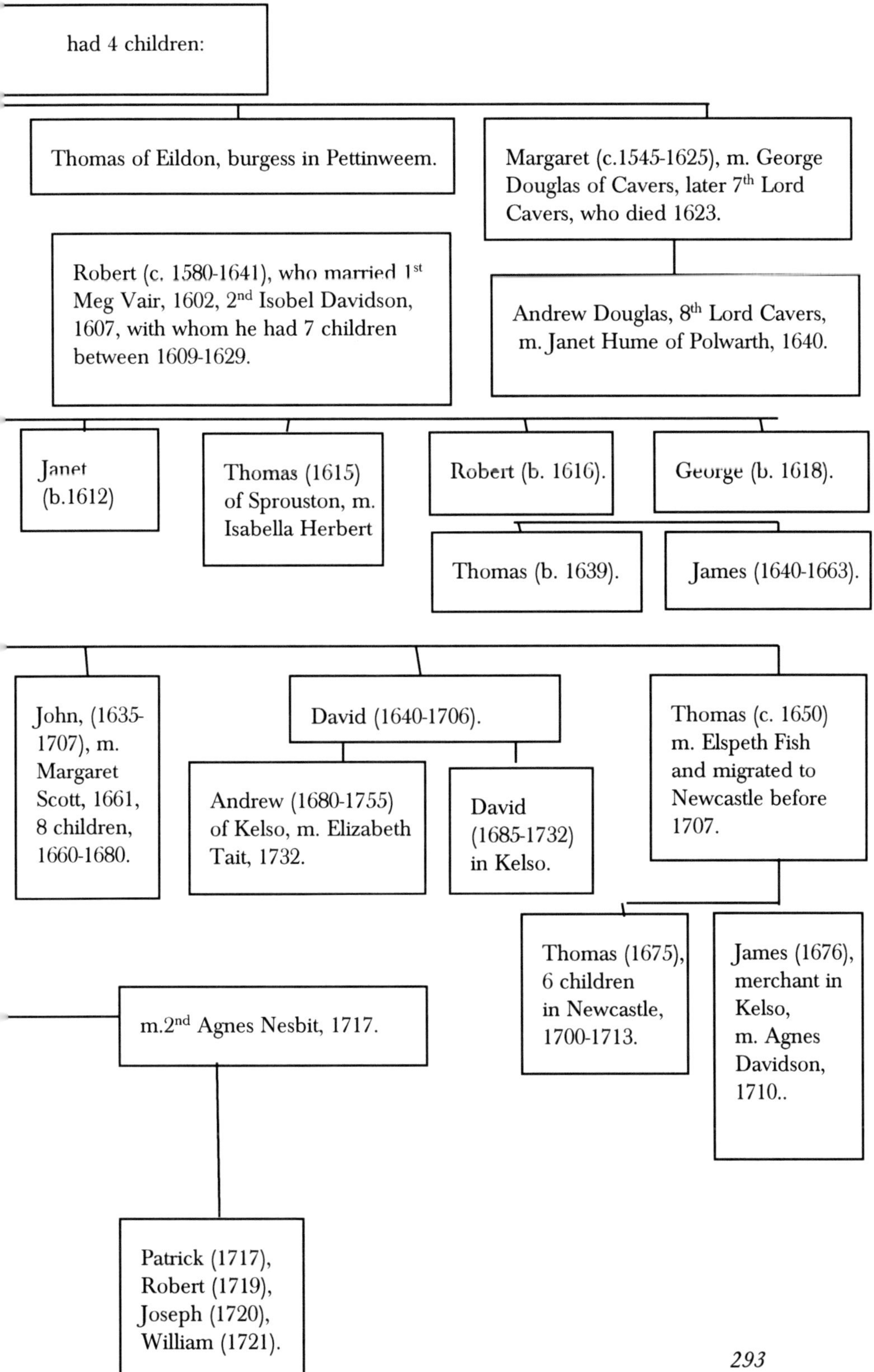
had 4 children:
Thomas of Eildon, burgess in Pettinweem.
Margaret (c.1545-1625), m. George Douglas of Cavers, later 7th Lord Cavers, who died 1623.
Robert (c. 1580-1641), who married 1st Meg Vair, 1602, 2nd Isobel Davidson, 1607, with whom he had 7 children between 1609-1629.
Andrew Douglas, 8th Lord Cavers, m. Janet Hume of Polwarth, 1640.
Janet (b.1612)
Thomas (1615) of Sprouston, m. Isabella Herbert
Robert (b. 1616).
George (b. 1618).
Thomas (b. 1639).
James (1640-1663).
John, (1635-1707), m. Margaret Scott, 1661, 8 children, 1660-1680.
David (1640-1706).
Thomas (c. 1650) m. Elspeth Fish and migrated to Newcastle before 1707.
Andrew (1680-1755) of Kelso, m. Elizabeth Tait, 1732.
David (1685-1732) in Kelso.
Thomas (1675), 6 children in Newcastle, 1700-1713.
James (1676), merchant in Kelso, m. Agnes Davidson, 1710..
m.2nd Agnes Nesbit, 1717.
Patrick (1717), Robert (1719), Joseph (1720), William (1721).

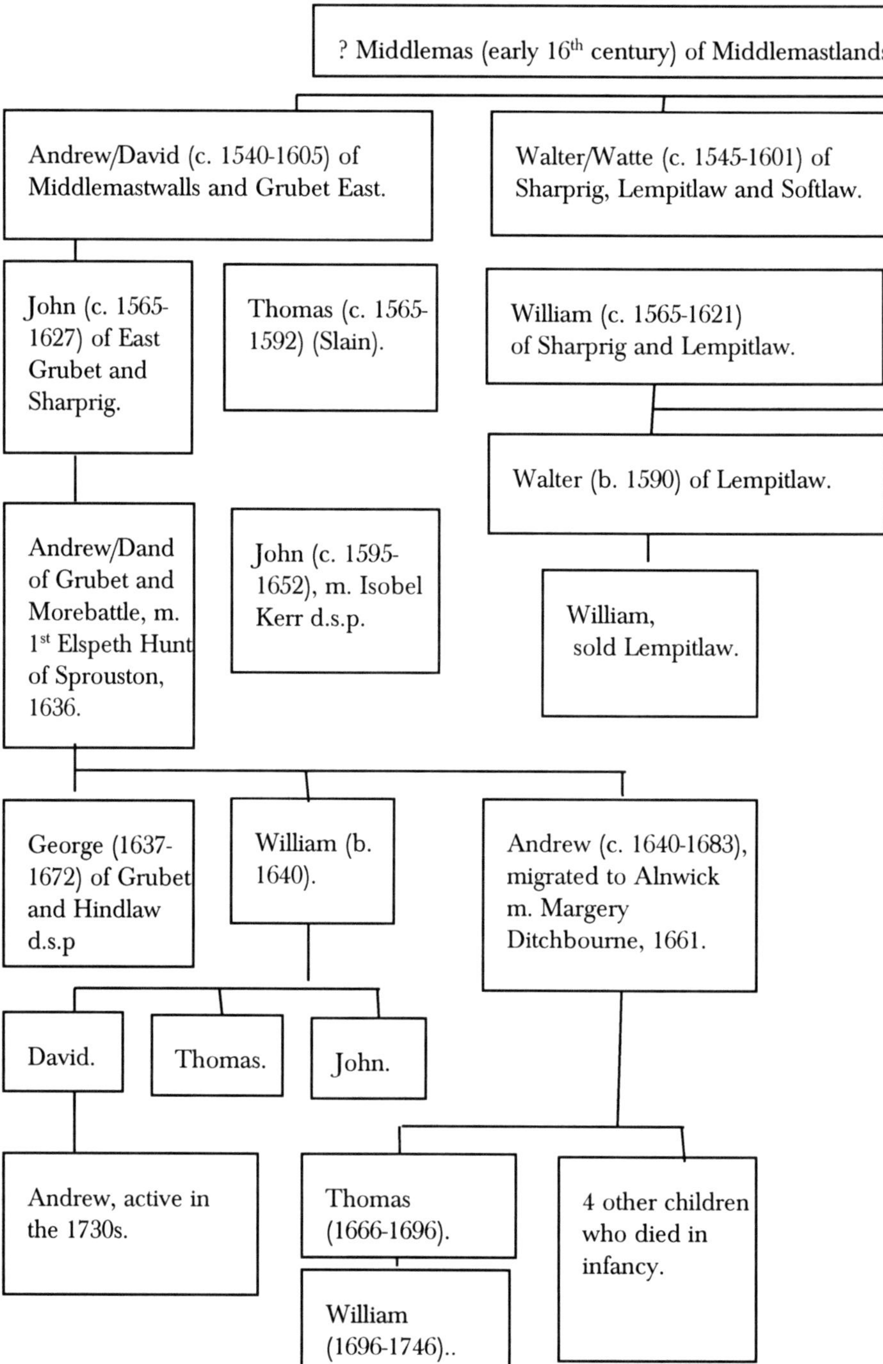
? Middlemas (early 16th century) of Middlemastlands
Andrew/David (c. 1540-1605) of Middlemastwalls and Grubet East.
Walter/Watte (c. 1545-1601) of Sharprig, Lempitlaw and Softlaw.
John (c. 1565-1627) of East Grubet and Sharprig.
Thomas (c. 1565-1592) (Slain).
William (c. 1565-1621) of Sharprig and Lempitlaw.
Walter (b. 1590) of Lempitlaw.
Andrew/Dand of Grubet and Morebattle, m. 1st Elspeth Hunt of Sprouston, 1636.
John (c. 1595-1652), m. Isobel Kerr d.s.p.
William, sold Lempitlaw.
George (1637-1672) of Grubet and Hindlaw d.s.p
William (b. 1640).
Andrew (c. 1640-1683), migrated to Alnwick m. Margery Ditchbourne, 1661.
David.
Thomas.
John.
Andrew, active in the 1730s.
Thomas (1666-1696).
William (1696-1746)..
4 other children who died in infancy.

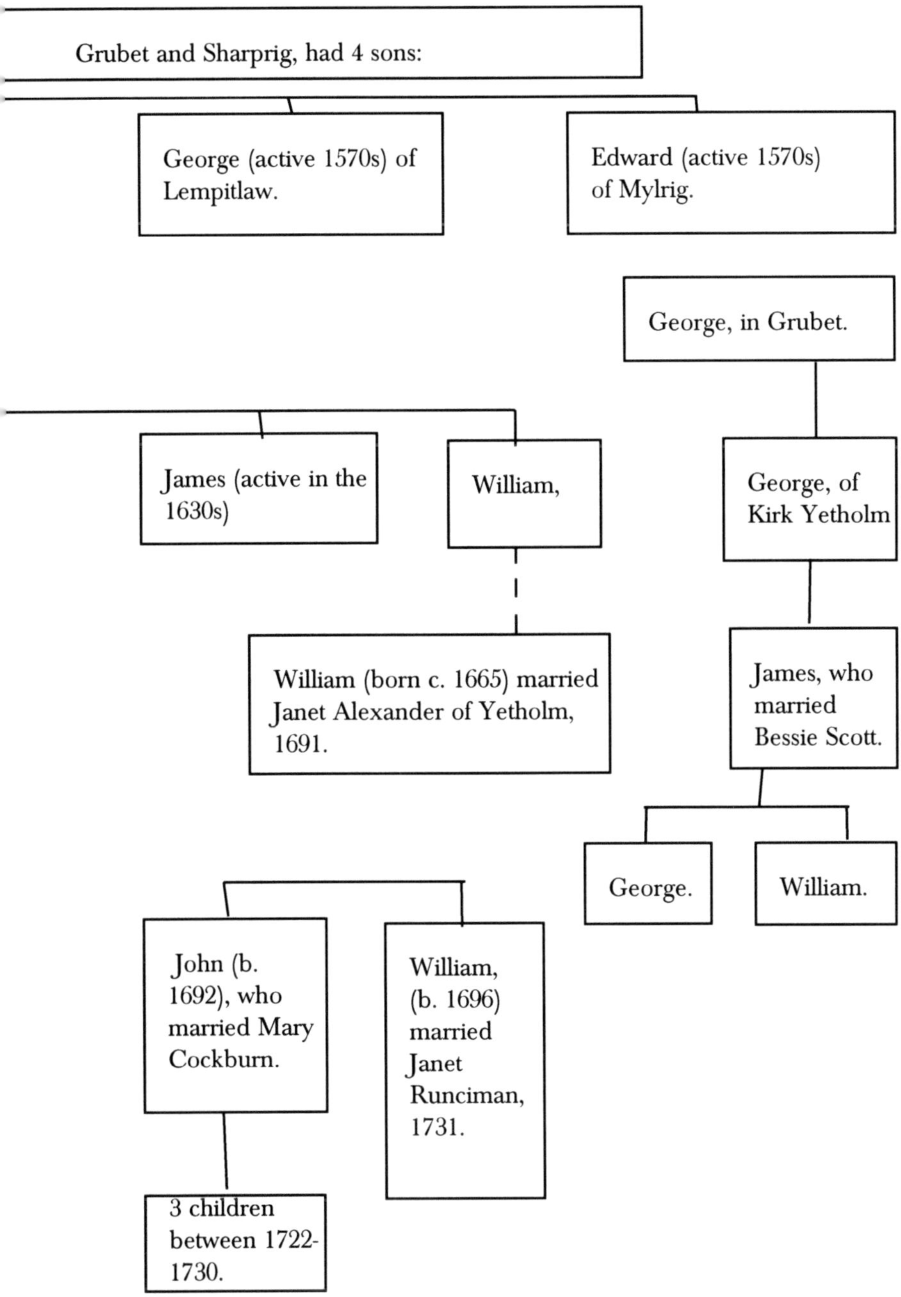
Grubet and Sharprig, had 4 sons:
George (active 1570s) of Lempitlaw.
Edward (active 1570s) of Mylrig.
George, in Grubet.
James (active in the 1630s)
William,
George, of Kirk Yetholm
William (born c. 1665) married Janet Alexander of Yetholm, 1691.
James, who married Bessie Scott.
George.
William.
John (b. 1692), who married Mary Cockburn.
William, (b. 1696) married Janet Runciman, 1731.
3 children between 1722-1730.

# A : 5b MOREBATTLE

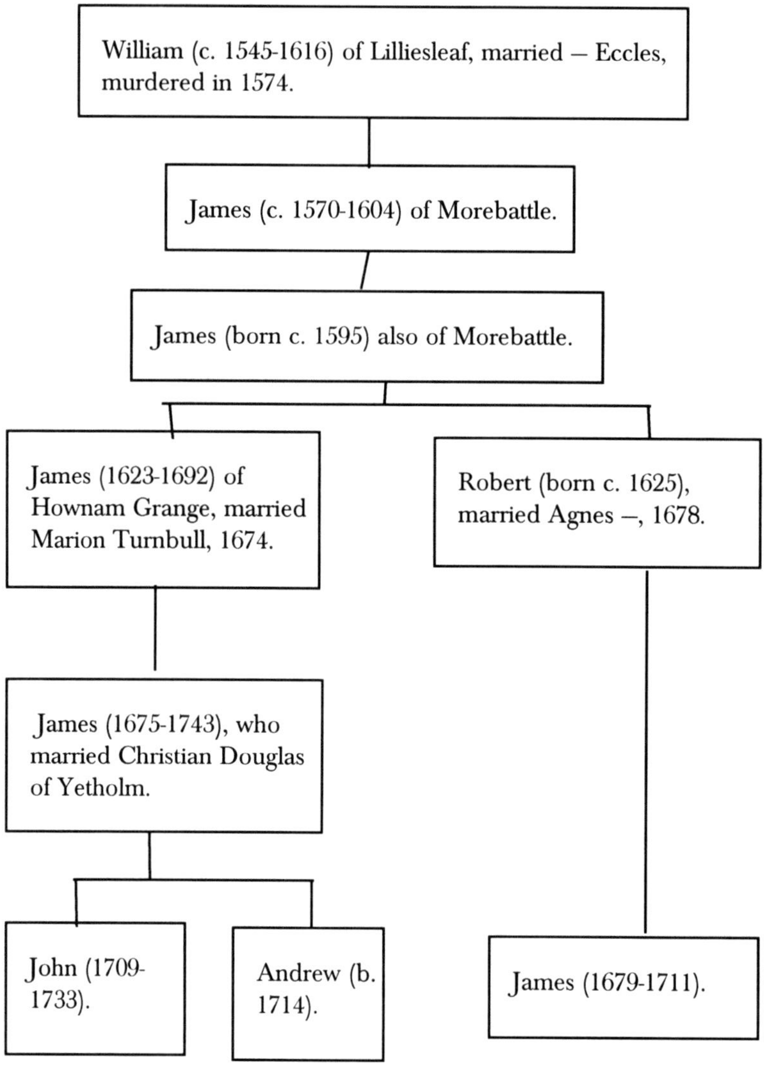

# Appendix B.

Although there can be no question about the Middlemas crest, the stag's head cabossed with a cross between the antlers, unique in Britain apart from the Irish Earls of Waterford, displayed on at least two surviving seals to documents in Scottish or English archives, the accompanying shield of arms offers a confused, perhaps insoluble problem.

Put simply, two of the early manuscript collections of Scottish arms,[269] Seton's ms of 1591, and following that, James Pont's ms of 1624 (nearly forty years before the formal registration of arms by the Lord Lyon King at Arms Court in 1672), displays a rampant lion on a gold and scarlet ground – in heraldic terms, "parti per fess or and gules, a lion rampant of the ane and other," as being the arms of Middleton of Killhill and Grieston. This was in due course incorporated into the arms of John Earl of Middleton (1619-1674) Charles II's High Commissioner to Parliament after the Restoration – until he fell into royal disfavour.

One later 19th century herald, Robert Stodart in the classic text *Scottish Arms, 1370-1678* (1881) vol. 2, pp. 387-9, points out that this attribution was dubious if not impossible. There had never been a Middleton of Grieston only a Middlemas, from the 15th to the mid-17th centuries after which Grieston itself disappeared. Killhill is in the parish of Ceres, mid-Fife, five miles east of Falkland Palace and there were Middlemases settled there in the 16th century and later. Stodart added that there was a profusion of arms granted to John Earl of Middleton at a time when his brother-in-law, Sir Alexander Denham held the post of Lord Lyon King at Arms.

All this seems to have occurred at least ten years before the 1672 Registration made the whole subject a matter of formal record. Although Porteus Herald c. 1660 repeated the Seton and Pont ascriptions, he omitted the "and Grieston" which was itself oddly suspicious. Stodart plainly charged that the Earl had stolen a far more ancient armorial, with his brother-in-law's connivance, and built the later heraldry around it (cf. the Middleton window in St. Mungo's Cathedral in Glasgow). To set this right might be easy, if it were not for the fact that both Seton and Pont predate Middleton's earldom.

True, he was often mocked at the time for his obscure and humble origins, having first appeared as a pikeman in Hepburn's regiment in France in the 1630s before rising to Lieutenant-General at the time of Philiphaugh (1645); and there is no proof of where he was born. Neither did he have estates, only a soldier of fortune's career behind him before the Civil War. His pedigree may not have been improved during his lifetime, but he does appear to have come from Killhill. It was not the only time that the two names had overlapped. But if not him, who among his forebears was Middleton of Killhill?

Killhill was a small village or toun with a mill, at the end of the 16th century. The Registry of the Great Seal, 1595, records a curious confusion: the index, compiled in the 19th century, refers to "Middlemas of Killhill see Middleton of Killhill." The actual *text*, however, refers on one hand to John Middleton, son of John Middleton of Kincardine (on the Firth of Forth nowhere near Killhill), but on the other to John Middlemast of Killhill (entry no. 1940). The Great Seal for 1607 records that James Livingstone received from King James VI the mains and mill of Killhill "which were to John Middlemass/Middleton formerly of Killhill in the parish of Forfar.") Various other entries in the state papers late 16th century do nothing to clear up the difficulty, though they do add that two Middletons were burgesses of Aberdeen 1570 and 1592.

It was, as Laurence Stone has pointed out, a time of "lush profusion of improbable quarterings (which) supplemented the simple coats of arms of a less sophisticated and pretentious age." But to misappropriate the late-medieval arms of another family, albeit in another part of Scotland and in decline, was unusual. Neither Seton nor Pont's manuscripts were published, the former being made for Sir James Balfour, and only became property of the Lord Lyon in 1793; and were available then only to select enquiry – so there is no reason to think that such fraud would have been detected at the time. By 1672, in any case, there was no Middlemas of Grieston left to register the arms.

Yet some doubt must remain, given the Great Seal evidence of apparent interchange between the two names as early as 1607, for which there are several possible explanations, apart from outright fraud:

- Simple confusion in transcription, either between an original document and the Great Seal register, or in setting the latter manuscript in print – this might explain the erroneous 19th century index entry.
- A change of name in Killhill at the time (improbable) or a marriage connection between the two (possible), if a Middlemas who had settled in Killhill and acquired the farm and mill had married the daughter of one of the Aberdeen burgesses.
- Confusion between a seal and a shield of arms: the *seal* of John Middleton is recorded in 1588 as a lion rampant and a motto "heir lord" (now lost); which appears on a seal of Patrick Middleton, chaplain of the collegiate church of St Salvator, on a document of 1528. These are both entirely different from the Middlemas seal 1296 and 1436 extant and in use till the 17th century when it was last described but has not since been used.
- Decline of Middlemas of Grieston so that by 1607 Middleton appeared a more obvious choice to the transcriber when reading a badly written document. This is unlikely since John Middleton who became the Earl was not even born until 1619 and did not rise to celebrity until the Civil War.
- Straightforward error by Seton in 1591, repeated or compounded by Pont 30 years later, and justified by Porteus' omission of Grieston in 1660.

Whatever the answer, by the mid-17th century, the Middlemas of Grieston branch had died out, Lilliesleaf was under siege as Covenanters and impoverished, and the senior branch, Middlemas of Middlemas originally from Kelso, had been dispersed to smaller farms around Morebattle and Kale Water. None had the power or perhaps inclination to challenge Middleton and the Lord Lyon, even if they had known of it.

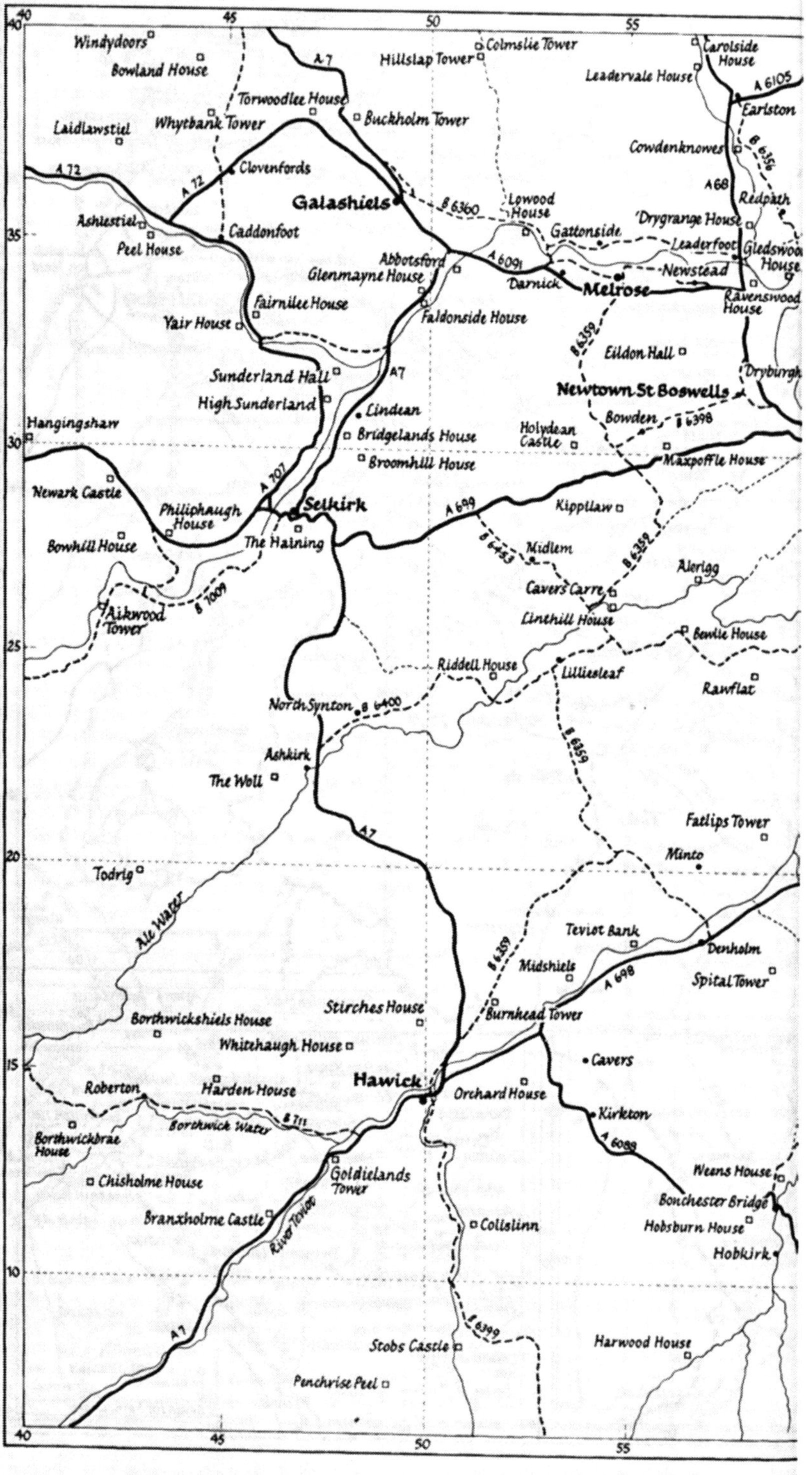


Map of Central Borders Region

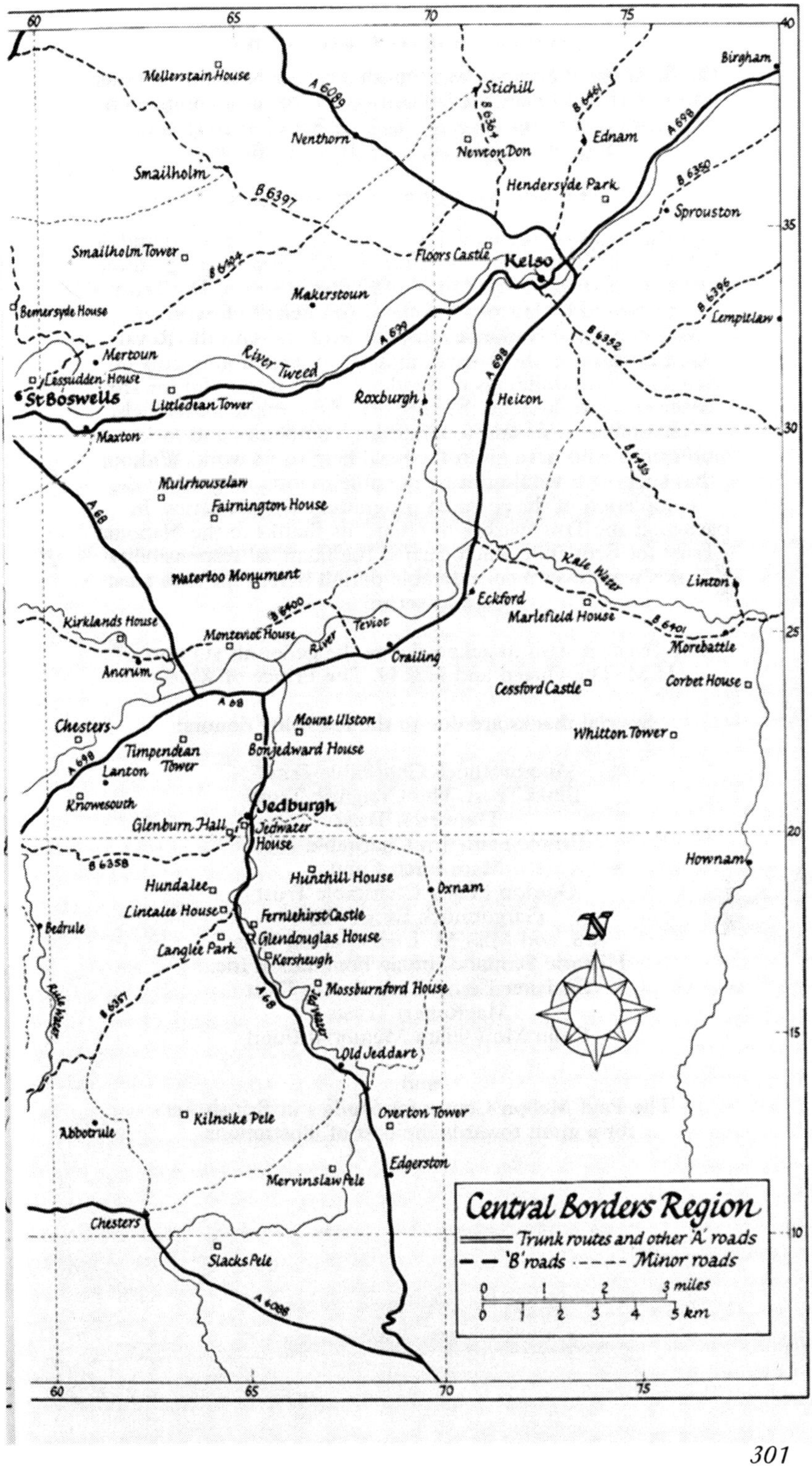
Central Borders Region
Trunk routes and other 'A' roads
'B' roads
Minor roads
3 miles
5 km
Mellerstain House
Stichill
Birgham
Nenthorn
Newton Don
Ednam
Smailholm
Hendersyde Park
Sprouston
Smailholm Tower
Floors Castle
Kelso
Makerstoun
Bemersyde House
Lempitlaw
Mertoun
River Tweed
Lessudden House
St Boswells
Littledean Tower
Roxburgh
Heiton
Maxton
Muirhouselaw
Fairnington House
Kale Water
Waterloo Monument
Linton
Eckford
Marlefield House
Kirklands House
Teviot
Monteviot House
River
Crailing
Morebattle
Ancrum
Corbet House
Cessford Castle
Chesters
Mount Ulston
Whitton Tower
Timpendean Tower
Bonjedward House
Lanton
Knowesouth
Jedburgh
Glenburn Hall
Jedwater House
Hownam
Hundalee
Hunthill House
Oxnam
Lintalee House
Fernlehirst Castle
Bedrule
Glendouglas House
Langlee Park
Kersheugh
Mossburnford House
Old Jeddart
Kilnsike Pele
Overton Tower
Abbotrule
Edgerston
Mervinslaw Pele
Chesters
Slacks Pele

*Map of Ettrick Forest: (Timothy Pont/ Blaeu) late 16th century*

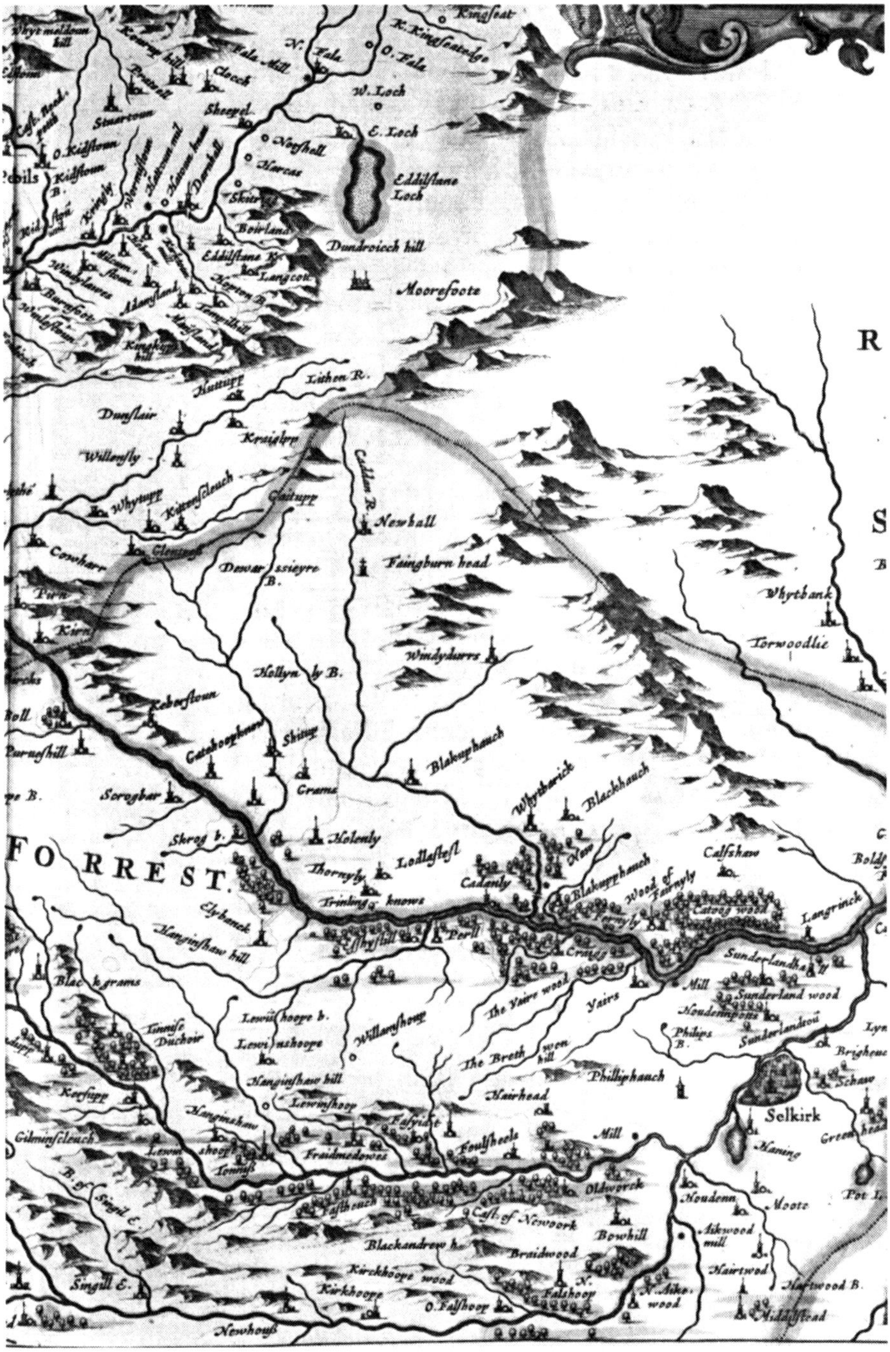
Kingseat
N. Fala
O. Fala
W. Loch
E. Loch
Eddilstane Loch
Sheepel
Dundroiech hill
Moorefoote
Lithen R.
Kraiglop
Willensly
Whytupp
Cowharr
Newhall
Faingburn head
Windydurrs
Hollyn ly B.
Shitup
Grams
Blakuphauch
Whytbarick
Blackhauch
Scrogbar
Molenly
Lodlasteel
Thornyly
Caddonly
Trinling knows
Hangingshaw hill
Peril
Calfshaw
Langrinck
Whytbank
Torwoodlie
FO RREST.
Sunderland wood
Philips B.
Philiphauch
Selkirk
Mill
Yairs
The Yairs wood
The Broth won hill
Hairhead
Foulsheels
Oldworck
Bowhill
Blackandrew h.
Braidwood
Kirckhoope wood
Kirkhoope
Falshoop
O. Falshoop
Newhous
Singill E.
Haining
Moote
Houdenn
Aikwood mill
Hairtwod
Hartwood B.
Middlestead
Tinnis Duchoir
Lewinshoope
Willamshoop
Fraidmedowes
Cast. of Newoork
N. Aike wood
R
S

*Map of part of the County of Roxburgh (Matthew Stobie 1765)*

COUNTY
NORTHUMBERLAND
COUNTY
EDNAM
PARISH
TWEED RIVER
WARK COMMONS
Redden
Hadden
Sproustoun
SPROUSTOUN
PARISH
Lempitlaw
LINTON
PARISH
YETHOLM
Kirkyetholm
PARISH
Whitelaw
Blackhag
Chillhill
MORBATTLE
PARISH
HOWNAM
PARISH
Cocklaw
Windygate Hill

Map of Lilliesleaf Parish (John Ainslie 1772)

*Plan of Plora Tower (RCHMS)*

# Index

Printed in the United Kingdom by
Lightning Source UK Ltd., Milton Keynes
139641UK00001B/61/P

9 781845 300647